Japan's Minoriti es

D0780954

Based on original research, *Japan's Minorities* provides a clear historical introduction to the formation of individual minorities, followed by an analysis of the contemporary situation.

This second edition identifies and explores the six principal minority groups in Japan: the Ainu, the Burakumin, the Chinese, the Koreans, the Nikkeijin and the Okinawans. Examining the ways in which the Japanese have manipulated historical memory, such as the destruction of Hiroshima and Nagasaki, the contributors reveal the presence of an underlying concept of 'Japaneseness' that excludes members of these minorities. The key themes addressed in this book include:

- the role of the ideology of 'race' in the construction of the Japanese identity
- historical memory and its suppression
- contemporary labour migration to Japan
- the three-hundred-year existence of Chinese communities in Japan
- 'mixed-race' children in Japan
- the construction of Black otherness in modern and contemporary Japan.

Still the only scholarly examination of issues of race, ethnicity and marginality in Japan from both a historical and comparative perspective, this new edition will be essential reading for scholars and students of Japanese studies, ethnic and racial studies, culture and society, anthropology and politics.

Michael Weiner is Professor of Modern Japanese History and Director of International Studies at Soka University of America.

Sheffield Centre for Japanese Studies/Routledge series

Series Editor: Glenn D. Hook
Professor of Japanese Studies, University of Sheffield

This series, published by Routledge in association with the Centre for Japanese Studies at the University of Sheffield, makes available original research on a wide range of subjects dealing with Japan and provides introductory overviews of key topics in Japanese studies.

Japan's Minorities

The illusion of homogeneity

Second edition

Edited by Michael Weiner

Routledge
Taylor & Francis Group

LONDON AND NEW YORK

This book is dedicated to my wife, Pam, and to my daughters, Jessica and Leah.

First edition published 1997 by Routledge
Second edition published 2009 by Routledge
2 Park Square, Milton Park, Abingdon, Oxon, OX14 4RN

Simultaneously published in the USA and Canada
by Routledge
270 Madison Ave, New York NY 10016

Routledge is an imprint of the Taylor & Francis Group, an informa business

Transferred to Digital Printing 2010

© 1997, 2009 Editorial selection and matter, Michael Weiner. Individual chapters, the contributors.

Typeset in Times New Roman by Pindar NZ, Auckland, New Zealand

British Library Cataloguing in Publication Data
A catalogue record for this book is available from the British Library

Library of Congress Cataloging-in-Publication Data
Japan's minorities : the illusion of homogeneity / edited by
Michael Weiner. — 2nd ed.
  p. cm.
  1. Minorities—Japan. 2. Japan—Ethnic relations. 3. Japan—
Social conditions—1945- I. Weiner, Michael.
  DS830.J356 2008
  305.800952—dc22   2008027757

ISBN10: 0-415-77263-X (hbk)
ISBN10: 0-415-77264-8 (pbk)
ISBN10: 0-203-88499-X (ebk)

ISBN13: 978-0-415-77263-1(hbk)
ISBN13: 978-0-415-77264-8(pbk)
ISBN13: 978-0-203-88499-7(ebk)

Contents

Figures and tables

Figures

Tables

Contributors

Matthew Allen is Associate Professor of Japanese History at the University of Auckland, New Zealand. His major publications include *Undermining the Japanese Miracle* (Cambridge University Press, 1994), and *Identity and Resistance in Okinawa* (Rowman and Littlefield, 2002). In 2006 he edited *Popular Culture, Globalization and Japan* (Routledge) with Rumi Sakamoto. He has also published numerous chapters in collected editions, and articles in anthropology, psychiatry and history journals. Currently he spends the other half of his working life on his vanilla farm in Far North Queensland.

David Chapman is Convenor of Japanese Studies at the University of South Australia. His recent publications include *Zainichi Korean Identity and Ethnicity* (Routledge, 2008) and a special issue ('Korea in Japan') of the journal *Japanese Studies* (2006). His current research focuses on the history of Japan's population registration systems and their role in the construction of identity in Japan.

Robert A. Fish is Director of Education and Lecture Programs at Japan Society of New York. Prior to joining Japan Society, he was Assistant Professor of History at Indiana State University and a social studies teacher at Tenafly High School in New Jersey. His research focuses on the history of childhood and education in modern Japan, and includes a book manuscript about the history of 'mixed-blood' orphans in post-war Japan, as well as work about the 'textbook controversy' in post-war Japan. Fish earned his Ph.D. in modern Japanese history at the University of Hawaii at Manoa.

Gracia Liu-Farrer holds concurrent lectureships at Sophia University and Keio University, both of which are in Japan. She will take up the position of Visiting Associate Professor at Hitotsubashi University, Japan from October 1, 2008. Her dissertation, titled *Educationally Channeled International Labor Migration: Post-1978 student mobility from China to Japan* (University of Chicago, 2007), examines the diverse labour-market outcomes of contemporary Chinese student migrants in Japan. She is the author of articles and book chapters about the economic, social and emotional lives of the Chinese in Japan, written in both English and Japanese. She is currently investigating Chinese migrants' transnational labour-market practices and career mobility and the issues of racial and gender stratifications emerging in the transnational labour market between Japan and China.

Ian J. Neary is Director of the Nissan Institute of Japanese Studies, University of Oxford, a Fellow of St Antony's College and University Lecturer in the Politics of Japan. He is the author of numerous articles and books, including *Political Protest and Social Control in Pre-war Japan: Origins of buraku liberation* (1989), *Intervention and Technological Innovation: Government and the pharmaceutical industry in the UK and Japan* (with J. Howells, 1995), *Human Rights in Japan, South Korea and Taiwan* (2002) and *The State and Politics in Japan* (2002). He is currently working on a biography of the buraku leader Matsumoto Jiichiro.

John G. Russell is Professor of Anthropology at the Faculty of Regional Studies, Gifu University, Japan. His books include: *Nihonjin no kokujin-kan (Japanese Perceptions of Blacks*, Tokyo: Shinhyoron, 1991), *Henken to Sabetsu wa dono yo ni tsukurareru ka (How are Prejudice and Discrimination Produced?*, Tokyo, Akashi Shoten, 1995). Other publications include, 'Consuming Passions: Spectacle, self-transformation, and the commodification of blackness in Japan', *Positions: east asia cultures critique*, 6:1 (1998) and 'Race and Reflexivity: The black other in contemporary Japanese mass culture', *Cultural Anthropology* 6:1 (1991). His research interests focus on constructions of otherness in scholarly and popular discourse, advertising, and the media in Japan and the United States. Currently he is researching constructions of race in contemporary American and Japanese science fiction.

Richard M. Siddle is Lecturer in Japanese Studies at the University of Sheffield. He researches and teaches in the areas of modern Japanese history and minority issues with particular emphasis on race, ethnicity, nationalism and identity politics. His publications include *Race, Resistance and the Ainu of Japan* (Routledge, 1996) and *Japan and Okinawa: Structure and subjectivity* (co-editor, Routledge, 2003) as well as numerous journal articles and book chapters on Ainu and Okinawan issues. His current research interests include identity and tourism, and he is presently involved in research on the outer islands of Okinawa.

Eika Tai is Professor of Japanese at North Carolina State University. She has also taught at San Francisco State University. Since receiving a Ph.D. in anthropology from the University of California at Berkeley, she has written on colonial education, ethnicity, diaspora and multiculturalism as played out in the context of multiethnic Japan. Her publications include 'Korean Ethnic Education in Japanese Public Schools' (*Asian Ethnicity*, 8.1), 'Korean Activism and Ethnicity in the Changing Ethnic Landscape of Urban Japan' (*Asian Studies Review*, 30) and ' "Korean Japanese": A New Identity Option for Resident Koreans in Japan' (*Critical Asian Studies*, 36.3). She has also published extensively in Japanese and is the author of *Tabunkashugi to Diasupora* (*Multiculturalism and Diaspora*, Tokyo: Akashi Shoten). She is the recipient of an Osaka City University Fellowship for Foreign Researchers and has co-authored a book on diaspora studies in the context of Japan with faculty of that university.

Takeyuki (Gaku) Tsuda is Associate Professor of Anthropology in the School of Human Evolution and Social Change at Arizona State University. After receiving his Ph.D. in anthropology in 1997 from the University of California at Berkeley, he was a Collegiate Assistant Professor at the University of Chicago and then served as Associate Director of the Center for Comparative Immigration Studies at the University of California at San Diego. His primary academic interests include international migration, diasporas, ethnic minorities, ethnic and national identity, transnationalism and globalization, ethnic return migrants, the Japanese diaspora in the Americas and contemporary Japanese society. His publications include numerous articles in anthropological and interdisciplinary journals, as well as a book entitled *Strangers in the Ethnic Homeland: Japanese Brazilian return migration in transnational perspective* (Columbia University Press, 2003). He is the editor of *Local Citizenship in Recent Countries of Immigration: Japan in comparative perspective* (Lexington Books, 2006) and co-editor of *Controlling Immigration: A global perspective* (second edition, Stanford University Press, 2004) and *Ethnic Identity: Problems and prospects for the twenty-first century* (Alta Mira Press, 2006). He has received research grants and fellowships from the University of California (Berkeley and San Diego), Fulbright-Hays, the Wenner-Gren Foundation, the Social Science Research Council, the Japan Foundation and the Hewlett Foundation, among others.

Michael Weiner is Professor of Modern Japanese History and Director of International Studies at Soka University of America. He has previously held positions at San Diego State University and at the School of East Asian Studies, University of Sheffield, where he served as Director of the Centre for Japanese Studies. He has formerly been the Managing Editor of *Japan Forum*, and he serves on the advisory board of a number of international journals. His books include *The Origins of the Korean Community in Japan: 1910–1923* (Manchester University Press [UK] and Humanities Press [USA], 1989), *The Internationalization of Japan* (with G.D. Hook, Routledge, 1992), *Race and Migration in Imperial Japan* (Routledge, 1994), *Japan's Minorities: The illusion of homogeneity* (first edition, Routledge, 1997), and *Race, Ethnicity and Migration in Modern Japan* (three vols, Routledge, 2004). His current research focuses on the history of medicine in Japan. He has received grants from the Japan Foundation, the Nippon Foundation, the British Academy and the Economic and Social Research Council (UK). Through funding provided by the American Association of State Colleges and Universities, he served from 2000 to 2005 as Director of the Japan Studies Institute at San Diego State University, where he holds the title of Emeritus Professor of Asian Studies.

Editor's introduction

Early in the twentieth century, in his book *The Souls of Black Folk*, W.E.B. Du Bois predicted that issues of 'race', or, in his terms, the 'Colour Line', would be the defining problem of that century (Du Bois 1961: 23). Given both the historical context within which the prediction was made and the evidence that marches across our television screens on a daily basis, there can be little doubt that 'race' remains a primary determinant of social relations. Nevertheless, while the invidious imagery of biological superiority and inferiority certainly informs some contemporary forms of racism, the colonial-inspired paradigm of race offers little in the way of explanatory power. In the first place, emphasis on the 'Colour Line', as conceptualized by Du Bois, runs the risk of reifying skin colour – of ignoring the fact that the visibility of somatic difference is itself a social construct. Of course, the existence of physical differences between human populations is not disputed here. But of far greater relevance are the processes of signification that attribute meaning to these differences. Historically, a wide range of both physiological and cultural characteristics, either real or imagined, have been employed as natural or 'racial' signifiers. The assumption that one historically specific instance of signification can provide an adequate explanation for all forms of racial or ethnic exclusion ignores evidence which illustrates that other populations (Jews in central Europe, Irish in Britain, and Koreans, Chinese, burakumin, Okinawan and Ainu in Japan) have been defined as distinct and inferior races without reference to the colour stigmata. Once constructed, moreover, a racialized 'otherness' can be projected onto either real or imagined populations. The recrudescence of anti-Semitism in parts of post-Soviet central Europe, where the Jewish presence was eliminated some sixty years ago, and in Japan, a nation where the historical presence of Jews has been minimal, are but two recent manifestations of this phenomenon.

Although there is a temptation to offer a global definition of race, there are compelling reasons not to do so. First, race is a social construct, fluid in content, whose meanings are determined by historical and national context.

Of far greater value as a subject of inquiry are the processes that have led to groups that were not previously defined in racial terms being defined as races. These are processes within which the state has functioned as both a primary site of racial articulation and contestation, and as an arena where minority voices have been constrained and suppressed. Second, while racialized notions of citizenship, inclusion and exclusion undoubtedly exist in, for example, the United States, Britain, France and Japan, the historical experience of the excluded and racialized 'others' in each of these countries reveals both continuities and discontinuities. Unlike the United States, where racial identities were initially produced within the institutions of slavery, and were reproduced during the course of several centuries of territorial expansion and immigration, the racialization of identities in Japan is of far more recent origin; it lacks the pedigree of plantation slavery. Racialized minority populations are also distinguished by their relative size, settlement pattern, length and status of residence, degree of social, economic and political integration, or by a combination of these factors. Finally, any attempt to generate a global definition of race contains the potential for either distorting the historical/national context, or of imbuing races, as naturally occurring phenomena, with even greater explanatory power.

Thus, while there exists an extensive literature on race and race relations, it tends to be country specific. This is not, however, to suggest the complete absence of continuities or similarities. The minority experience in each of the societies referred to here has been characterized by the existence of multi-layered racisms, systematic exclusions, and relative disadvantage – economic, political and social. Rather than addressing issues of race, as such, the point of departure for this book is an analysis of the historically specific factors involved in the appearance and maintenance of racialized relations in Japan. By this, I refer to processes of attribution, inclusion and exclusion, all of which have been shaped and reshaped by historical context.

Although there have been divergences in the representation of 'self', expressed variously in terms of a Japanese race, ethnicity, or culture, all have been grounded in notions of an essentialized identity that distinguishes the Japanese from other populations (Masuda 1967; Ishida 1974; Ueyama 1990; Kawakatsu 1991). To a certain extent, more recent conceptualizations of Japanese uniqueness also reflect a political agenda designed to: (a) suppress or reconfigure specific memories of the Pacific War and (b) assist in the production, or, in this case, the re-production, of a more muscular form of nationalism. Historically, moreover, cultural determinants (religious values, language, patterns of social and economic organization), rather than genetic or physiological markers, have been deployed to signify the existence of an immutable and homogeneous Japanese identity. Within this literature, the Japanese present is transformed by an idealized past, heterogeneity is ignored, and historical memory is suppressed. Over time, the resilience of this narrative has been succinctly expressed not only in the numerous 'off-the-record' comments made by senior Japanese politicians, but in Japan's initial submission to the Human Rights Committee of the United Nations in 1980, which denied the existence of minority populations.

The dominant paradigm of homogeneity has, however, been challenged by a number of recent studies that have sought to locate the construction of this identity within the appropriate historical context/s (Yoshino 1992; Befu 1993; Amino 1994; Weiner 1995, 1997, 2004; Morris-Suzuki 1995). Similarly, in its 1998 United Nations submission, the Committee on Elimination of Racial Discrimination (CERD) noted that, while, for example, the state had introduced programmes to preserve and promote Ainu culture, legislative reforms did not include any positive measures to improve the livelihood of the Ainu people. Two years later, in its own submission to CERD, the Japanese government highlighted the invisibility of minorities within state institutions by providing no information on Okinawa or its people. Most recently, in a report commissioned by the Economic and Social Council of the United Nations in 2006, the Special Rapporteur (Doudou Diène) concluded that racial discrimination and xenophobia remain widespread in Japan, and that minority populations continue to suffer from political, social, economic and cultural marginalization. While recognizing that the situation of certain minorities had been partly ameliorated by specific legislative action, the Special Rapporteur proposed the following recommendations:

- the recognition of the existence of racial discrimination in Japan, and the expression of political will to combat it;
- the adoption of a national law against discrimination;
- the establishment of a national commission for equality and human rights, whose mandate should bring together the most important fields of contemporary discrimination: race, colour, gender, descent, nationality, ethnic origin, disability, age, religion, and sexual orientation;
- a focus on the process of rewriting and teaching of history.

Despite the lengths to which ideologues have gone in denying the existence of minorities, the social construction of 'self' in Japan has always presumed the existence of its opposite, the excluded 'other', against whom notions of Japanese homogeneity and purity could be measured. Publications that focus upon the historical formation of minority populations have tended to address the situation of a particular population in isolation from other groups that have been subjected to comparable exclusions (DeVos and Wagatsuma 1972; Pak 1978; Lee and DeVos 1981; Pak 1988; Neary 1989;

Weiner 1989, 1994). In contrast to these studies, the intention here is to provide a historically contextualized analysis of 'otherness' in Japan, with particular, but by no means exclusive, reference to its principal minority populations: Ainu, Koreans, burakumin, Chinese, Okinawans and, of most recent origin, nikkeijin.

Despite a master narrative of racial and cultural homogeneity that precludes the existence of minorities, Japan is home to diverse populations. Of these, only the burakumin, descendants of the *eta* and *hinin* outcasts of the Tokugawa period, could be described as indigenous. Both Ainu and Okinawan populations were incorporated as subaltern peoples within the borders of modern Japan only during the late nineteenth century. While the historical evidence of earlier migrations from the Asian mainland is not in doubt, the so-called 'oldtimer' Korean and Chinese communities are largely a consequence of Japanese imperialism during the late nineteenth and twentieth centuries. In contrast to these well-established though by no means fully integrated populations, this volume also includes for discussion the nikkeijin, primarily Latin Americans of Japanese descent, whose emergence as a distinct minority population coincided with the demand for inexpensive, low-level labour in Japan during the 1980s. In light of the above, state encouragement for the recruitment of nikkeijin is an especially significant phenomenon, since it also provides an opportunity to reconsider the claim that the Japanese nation state has evolved as an expression of the enduring purity of a homogeneous people.

The objectives of this volume are multiple. First, to critically evaluate both the historical construction and contemporary manifestations of a racialized Japanese identity, the corollary of which has been the exclusion of other populations, including children of mixed parentage, on the basis of characteristics assumed to be inherent. Second, to provide an historical analysis of the formation of Japan's principal minority populations. Third, to consider aspects of minority life within the contemporary context of the early twenty-first century. Fourth, to evaluate recent attempts within minority communities to challenge the perpetuation of discriminatory images and practices. Finally, and in a marked departure from the first edition, John Russell offers a carefully nuanced analysis of how the construction of 'black otherness' within the Japanese context has reflected indigenous attempts to negotiate a privileged and racialized space within the conventional binary of 'black–white' race relations.

In the case of the burakumin, the Koreans and, to a somewhat lesser extent, the Ainu, about whom there already exists a substantial literature, the emphasis throughout has been placed on contemporary issues of integration, exclusion and identity. Although comparatively smaller, there is a growing body of literature regarding the Okinawan and Chinese populations in Japan.

Matthew Allen addresses the former, and focuses on both the historical processes that led to the incorporation of the Ryūkyū Kingdom and the emergence of contested identities in the contemporary milieu. Similarly, Gracia Liu-Farrer provides both a historical summary of the Chinese presence in Japan and a more focused analysis of the 'newcomer' Chinese population in contemporary Japan. Since the nikkeijin, the subject of Chapter 10, are a phenomenon of the past two decades, Takeyuki Tsuda considers the status of this community within a contemporary and comparative framework.

The point of departure for the chapters that comprise this volume is the period 1868–1945. Although there is a substantial literature that covers the economic, political and institutional aspects of Japan's transformation from an isolated semi-feudal state on the Asian periphery to a modern imperial power, relatively less attention has been given to the ideological contours of this process. In Chapter 1, the construction of a Japanese identity, incorporating both the naturalization of selected cultural characteristics and the grafting of pseudo-scientific notions of biological determinism borrowed from the West, is considered. The binary coding – the division of people into the categories of 'self' and 'other' – was not only reflected in relations between, for example, *naichijin* (the population of Japan proper) and *gaichijin* (lit. peoples of the outer territories, e.g. Taiwanese and Koreans), but was similarly deployed to categorize particular populations within Japan as unfit or, in the pseudo-scientific terminology of the day, dysgenic. As a direct consequence of government policies, sufferers of certain chronic diseases, such as leprosy, constituted a particular type of internal 'other', whose existence was regarded as a literal and metaphorical threat to a presumed organic polity. Although the categories of race and nation are often regarded as analytically distinct, the argument advanced is that in the pre-1945 context there was a high degree of overlap between them, and that this was a critical element in the racialization of the national community.

The appearance of Ainu representatives at the United Nations and other international fora in recent years contrasts sharply with mainstream Japanese perceptions of the Ainu as assimilated and culturally extinct. Following on from an overview of the incorporation and subsequent marginalization of the Ainu, the focus of Chapter 2, by Richard Siddle, shifts to contemporary issues of Ainu identity and nationalism. Rather than a revival of vestigial tribal identities, Siddle argues that the resurgence of ethnicity, expressed as Ainu nationalism, represents a reconstruction of ethnic identity in response to deprivation and structural inequalities.

In Chapter 3, Robert Fish addresses the topic of children of mixed parentage, which has only rarely been the subject of academic inquiry. Variously referred to as *konketsuji* (lit. mixed-blood children), *haafu* or *daburu*, the liminality of mixed-blood children is contextualized within the tides of internationalisation – a process in which their differentness has been simultaneously extolled and subordinated.

In Chapter 4, Ian Neary's discussion of the burakumin focuses upon the activities of the Buraku Liberation League (BLL) and on the extent to which the introduction of post-war legislation has facilitated an improvement in the social, political and economic position of buraku communities. Given that the material circumstances of many burakumin have undoubtedly been improved by the introduction of the Special Measures Law and subsequent Dōwa projects, Neary addresses the question of how the BLL is seeking to redefine itself in the 1990s. As in the case of the Ainu, the burakumin struggle to end inequality has also developed an international dimension in recent years. Finally, Neary asks what else can be done to eliminate discrimination and what role buraku organizations can play in that process.

Chapter 5, by contrast, is concerned with both the production and incorporation of contrasting images of 'blackness' in Japan over the past 500 years. While noting how images of black people in Japan have conventionally been deployed to denote alien and inferior qualities, John Russell challenges the conventional view that these owe their resilience to deeply embedded indigenous sources. On the contrary, Russell finds that it was the nineteenth-century encounter with racialized global power relations that impelled the codification of blacks as inferior. Drawing upon a wealth of literary, artistic and historical sources, Russell contends that images of black people in the modern era have been fluid and contingent, incorporating both positive and negative aspects.

There are a number of factors that, at least on the surface, distinguish 'oldtimer' Chinese residents from other minority communities. From a comparative perspective, far less is known about the history of this community, a fact that served to perpetuate an image of the Chinese as highly assimilated, economically successful and largely disinterested in the political activism associated with their Korean or burakumin counterparts. From this perspective, Chinese residents filled a role structurally analogous to certain 'model' minority populations in North America throughout most of the post-war period. Although often mistakenly perceived as a single homogeneous grouping, Chinese residents have historically been distinguished, and have defined themselves, on the basis of lineage, province of origin or political affiliation. In Chapter 6, Gracia Liu-Farrer traces the development of this community from its origins during the Edo period, when a Chinese commercial community was established in Nagasaki, through to the present day. Her focus, however, is contemporary, and in particular falls on the lives of Chinese students and entrepreneurs in present-day Japan. Farrer's findings point to the emergence of a transnational community of expatriates, who, irrespective of citizenship or residency rights, inhabit an important economic niche between Japan and China and increasingly regard themselves as part of a globalized overseas Chinese community.

In Chapter 7, Eika Tai provides a detailed analysis of the creation of two recent museum exhibitions in Osaka that have re-examined Japan's multiethnic past and present. Tai offers a careful account of the various actors involved in mounting these exhibitions, and delineates their success in challenging conventional stereotypes of 'otherness' and images of a homogeneous Japanese identity. A second strand of analysis, supported by interviews with a range of actors, considers both majority and minority responses to these same representations. In contrast to internationalization (*kokusaika*), which reiterated assimilationist formulations, Tai also examines local-level efforts to foster the development of a *tabunka kyōsei shakai* (multicultural coexisting society) through education. It remains to be seen, however, whether *kyōsei* (coexistence) in the contemporary context reflects equality and inclusion in the broadest sense, or whether it reinforces the essential 'differences' of foreign and other marginal populations.

Chapter 8, by Michael Weiner and David Chapman, offers a threefold analysis of the Korean community in Japan. The first section provides a summary analysis of the colonial migration and settlement of Koreans in Japan between 1910 and 1945. The section that follows is primarily concerned with the politics of historical memory in post-war Japan. It represents an attempt to map a particular terrain in which conflicting representations of the past and present coexist. For many Japanese, the atomic bombings were the defining moments in their nation's modern history. At a discursive level, however, the atomic bombings have been situated within a post-war master narrative that not only enhances a well-constructed image of Japan as a (if not *the*) victim of the Pacific War, but has also relegated other dissonant histories to the periphery of public consciousness. It is against this background that third and fourth generation zainichi, in particular, have struggled to construct an identity that is congruent with both a neglected past and a fractured present. Thus, the third and final section addresses the issue of identity politics within zainichi communities and the decades-long search for a 'third way'.

In 1879, the Japanese state forcibly absorbed the Ryūkyū Kingdom. Until that time, the status of the Ryūkyūs had been defined both by its traditional tributary relationship with Qing China and by its increasing political and economic subservience to the daimiate of Satsuma. These ambiguities were ultimately resolved by Japan's victory in the Sino-Japanese War of 1894–5 and by the subsequent Japanization of Ryūkyūans as imperial subjects within Okinawa Prefecture. For more than quarter of a century after the Pacific War, Okinawa remained under American occupation, with reversion to Japan not taking place until 1972. Chapter 9, by Matthew Allen, provides an historical analysis of the evolution of Ryūkyūan society, its responses to modern Japan, the Japanization of Ryūkyū as an internal colony, the post-war responses to American occupation, and more recent efforts to reassert an Okinawan identity distinct from that of Japan proper.

Chapter 10, by Takeyuki Tsuda, considers the phenomenon of 'return migration' and the establishment of Nikkeijin communities within the framework of current labour flows to Japan. As noted at the outset, current immigration laws have been designed to prevent the entry of unskilled labour. An exception to these laws is made in the case of the nikkeijin, foreign workers, primarily of Latin American origin, who are of Japanese descent. Following on from a discussion of both current patterns of migration and the response of the state to the entry of migrant labour, Tsuda provides a detailed analysis of nikkeijin settlement, nikkeijin areas of employment and relations between the newcomers and the host communities. Although regarded by others as Japanese in terms of lineage, the majority of nikkkeijin, whose links with Japan prior to migration were tenuous at best, do not share this view. Tsuda questions the viability of policies that have encouraged nikkeijin settlement, assesses the social costs involved and examines the emergence of a 'new' minority. In the concluding section, the ideological significance of nikkeijin migration is addressed.

Though not relevant in the case of the nikkeijin, a critical aspect of the minority experience in modern Japan has been resistance to racialized exclusion, exploitation and oppression. Although often cast in the roles of victims, Japan's minorities, at both the individual and organizational levels, have contested the imposition of structural inequalities. Over time, these oppositional strategies have assumed a variety of forms, involving both domestic and international actors. Yet, in a society that remains wedded to the myth of racial and cultural homogeneity, where the state denies the existence of minority populations and where minority access to economic, political and social opportunities remains limited, it is difficult to offer generalizations about future developments. To be sure, as the chapters in this volume suggest, positive changes have taken place, particularly at the local level and with regard to specific minority populations. There is little doubt that nikkeijin occupy a privileged space in particular sectors of the marketplace, as do highly skilled newcomers from China, but this has not necessarily translated into social acceptance. It remains the hope of the contributors that this volume will in some way assist in the struggle for human rights and dignity in Japan.

As is customary, there are a number of individuals whose support I would like to acknowledge. First, a special note of thanks to the contributors to this volume, without whom it would not have been possible. I would also like to extend my appreciation to the editorial board at Routledge for their patience and continued support.

Michael Weiner,
San Diego,
April 2008

References

Amino, Y. (1994) 'Nihon Minzoku to Iwareru Mono no Seitai', *Chūō Kōron*: February.

Befu, H. (ed.) (1993) *Cultural Nationalism in East Asia*, Berkeley: University of California Press.

DeVos, G. and Wagatsuma, H. (1972) *Japan's Invisible Race: Caste in culture and personality*, Berkeley: University of California Press.

Du Bois, W.E.B (1961) *The Souls of Black Folk*, New York: Fawcett World Library.

Ishida, E. (1974) *Japanese Culture: A study of origins and characterisics*, Tokyo: University of Tokyo Press.

Kawakatsu, H. (1991) *Nihon Bunmei to Kindai Seiyō*, Tokyo: NHK Books.

Lee, C. and DeVos, G. (1981) *Koreans in Japan: Ethnic conflict and accommodation*, Berkeley: University of California Press.

Masuda, Y. (1967) *Junsui Bunka no Jōken, Nihon Bunka wa Shōgeki ni dō Taetaka*, Tokyo: Kōdansha.

Morris-Suzuki, T. (1995) 'The Invention and Reinvention of "Japanese Culture"', *The Journal of Asian Studies*, 54, 3: 759–80.

Neary, I. (1989) *Political Protest and Social Control in Pre-War Japan: The origins of buraku liberation*, Atlantic Highlands: Humanities Press.

Pak, K. (1978) *Zainichi Chōsenjin Undōshi Kaihō mae*, Tokyo: San'ichi Shobo.

—— (1988) *Zainichi Chōsenjin Undōshi Kaihō go*, Tokyo: San'ichi Shobo.

Ueyama, S. (1990) *Nihon Bunmeishi no Kōsō: Juyō to sōzō no kiseki*, Tokyo: Kadokawa Shoten.

Weiner, M. (1989) *The Origins of the Korean Community in Japan 1910–1923*, Atlantic Highlands: Humanities Press.

—— (1994) *Race and Migration in Imperial Japan*, London: Routledge.

—— (1995) 'Discourses of Race, Nation and Empire in Pre-1945 Japan', *Ethnic and Racial Studies*, 18, 3: 433–56.

—— (1997) *Japan's Minorities: the illusion of homogeneity* (first edition), London: Routledge.

—— (2004) *Race, Ethnicity and Migration in Modern Japan* [3 vols.], London: Routledge.

Yoshino, K. (1992) *Cultural Nationalism in Contemporary Japan*, London: Routledge.

1 'Self' and 'other' in imperial Japan

Michael Weiner

Nationalisms are rarely consistent in content; what remains permanent are their bases in national consciousness. Depending upon the specific historical context, nationalism has most often been expressed in terms of economic or territorial expansion, the establishment of political sovereignty, or social and cultural norms of behaviour. In contrast, national consciousness, which serves as a pre-condition to the development of nationalism, implies the existence of historically embedded and culturally transmitted assumptions concerning the imagined community of the nation and its citizens. The modality of nationalism that emerged in the context of post-Restoration Japan was one that idealized cultural and racial homogeneity as the foundation of the nation state.

What had been a political, economic and social rupture was redefined to connote linkages with an ancient past, thus locating the events of 1868 within a continuous and unbroken chain of events culminating in the restoration of imperial rule. Paralleling this were the increasingly organized efforts by the new Meiji state to infuse a heterogeneous population with a sense of homogeneity and community (Fujitani 1993: 77–106). Along the way, powerful but selective cultural empathies were mobilized, while regional identities were either suppressed or subjected to a process of cultural redefinition, the objective of which was to bring reality into line with ideology. Within this framework, the *kazoku kokka* (family state) was projected as an enduring essence, which provided the state with an elevated iconography of consanguineous unity, enhanced the legitimacy of new economic, social and political relations, and provided the Japanese people with a new sense of national purpose and identity. It was a national identity forged from both indigenous and imported elements, and it rested upon the assumed unique qualities and capacities of the Japanese *minzoku* (Weiner 1995: 433–42). The argument pursued here is that rather than existing as independent categories of inclusion and exclusion, race and nation inhabited the same ideological space, with each functioning to define the parameters of the other. Set within the dominant paradigm of *minzoku*, both race and nation were regarded as naturally occurring phenomena, further reinforcing their credibility as explanatory factors in social, political and economic relationships (Yoshino 1992: 25).

In erecting a set of new symbolic boundaries around Japan, the language, imagery and iconography of nationalism suggested that the nation was the modern manifestation of a primordial community of which the citizenry had always been a part (Yasuda 1992: 63). Set against the background of a radically transformed environment, the efforts of state propagandists, the selective revival of ancient institutions, as in the case of Jingikan (Department of Shinto Affairs), the transformation of local or folk shrines, as in the case of Ise, into sites of national memory and pilgrimage, and the invention of commemorative structures, linking an imagined imperial past with present accomplishments, were designed to connote, diffuse and sustain a particular landscape. The naturalization of culture, of which these processes formed an integral part, recast the meaning of 'Japaneseness' in powerful images of the enduring purity and homogeneity of the nation, the family and the Japanese way of life. The nation was projected as an extended family, and the emperor was established as both head of state and semi-divine father to the national community. Ultimate sanctification of the imagined community was thus located at the sacred level, in Shinto, while reverence for the emperor as *minzoku no ōsa* (head of the people) and loyalty and obedience to the state were rendered equivalent (Gluck 1985: 91–3).

The conflation of cultural and racial criteria by which membership within the imagined community of the nation could be identified has assumed various guises. Anticipating the later genre of literature associated with the Nihonjinron and Nihon Bunka-ron, Takakusu Junjiro, in a 1938 publication, argued in favour of the existence of a dominant *Yamato*, or stem race, which had assimilated various prehistoric racial groupings. The consanguineous unity, or 'culture of the Japanese blood', to which Takakusu referred had subsequently been preserved through the 'virtuous rule of succeeding emperors'. The putative relationship between blood and culture is made more explicit in Kada Tetsuji's *Jinshu Minzoku Senso* (Jinshu, Minzoku and War), published in 1940. While the title implies a conceptual distinction between *jinshu* (race) and *minzoku* (ethnicity; people; nation), Kada consistently reaffirms the biological basis of *minzoku*. Indeed, for Kada, the origins of *minzoku* can only be found in the distinctive *jinshuteki* (racial) and *seishinteki* (spiritual) qualities of people. 'We cannot consider *minzoku*', he concludes, 'without taking into account its relation to blood' (Kada 1940: 70–1). In arguing a biological or genetic basis for the distinctiveness and superiority of the Japanese people, Kada was also reinforcing what one writer has termed *ketsuzokushugi* (the ideology of the blood family) (Hayashida 1976: 82).

Parallels can also be drawn between the racial literature of the inter-war years and, for example, Hozumi Nobushige's 1901 publication, *Ancestor Worship and Japanese Law* (Kikuchi 1972: 24–5). Here, the imagined community of the nation was conceived as a consanguineous community comprised of three primary constituent elements (the imperial family, the regional clan and the family unit) (Ito 1982: 31–3).

The argument advanced in this present work is that social structures and attitudes in Japan have historically been imbued with racial meaning, and that these meanings are themselves dynamic and contingent. That is to say, both racial meanings and racialized identities are historically specific, and can only be understood in relation to other factors – economic and political – and in relation to the international environment within which they emerged and have since been reproduced (Gilroy 1990: 264–5). In developing this argument, I also suggest that the construction of a Japanese national identity has entailed the transformation of culture, through an overarching discourse of race, into a 'pseudobiological property of communal life' (Gilroy 1990: 267). An objective here is to identify the various strands of racialized discourse that were developed during the period 1868–1945, and the channels through which European imperialist perspectives on race and native populations were domesticated within the Japanese context. In tracing the relationship between ideologies of race and nation in the construction of the modern Japanese identity, I seek also to identify the discursive elements that have informed perceptions of the excluded 'other' (both external and internal) against whom this identity has been produced and reproduced at particular historical junctures.

New ideologies and configurations of social power do not emerge unchallenged within an empty space (Greenfeld 1992: 399–403). As in Europe and North America, ideas of 'self' and 'other' in Japan were moulded both by the broader international context in which they evolved and through the appropriation of indigenous themes in Japanese history. The 'experts in legitimation' who contributed to the diffusion of racial knowledge and the dissemination of scientific racism in Japan were themselves aware of and deeply influenced by European scholarship in particular (Shimao 1981: 93–8). The scientification of knowledge, of which these processes were an integral part, also provided the means by which the civilized 'self' could be distinguished from the uncivilized 'other'. Just as Meiji industrialization was dependent upon the prior existence of well-established market relations and the importation of Western capital and technology, in their construction of a national identity, Japanese ideologues drew inspiration from both the West and through the appropriation and manipulation of indigenous myths. The search for a usable past engaged the resources of academics, educators, journalists, politicians and government officials alike. Their interests and concerns often overlapped; politicians were frequent contributors to news-papers, while academics were often called upon to advise on matters of public policy and education. Although there was no master narrative to which they all subscribed, nor a smoothly orchestrated discourse imposed upon a passive audience, their efforts would assist in the dissemination of racial knowledge and the necessary production of 'otherness'.

The intention thus far has been to suggest a high degree of functional equivalence between cultural and racial categories within pre-war racial discourse. If, as is argued here, culture is conceptualized as the manifestation of a primordial or innate essence, reliance on cultural or ethnic criteria in distinguishing between peoples functions in the same way as biological determinism (Miles 1993: 101). The essential distinction to be drawn is not between assumed cultural or physiological characteristics, but how these criteria are signified and subsequently acted upon. Rather than making the marginalized the focus of analysis, the subject of our inquiry should become the historical processes through which groups or nations have been constructed on the basis of these assumed innate qualities and subsequently located within specific material and power relations. In this sense, the dichotomy between the *Yamato jinshu* (race) and *Yamato minzoku* (ethnicity/people/nation) is more apparent then real. Barshay's observation that, in the pre-1945 context, the ideological terrain defined by *minzoku* 'overcame universality' and itself became 'absolute' is particularly salient (Barshay 1988: 230).

Throughout the final decades of the nineteenth century, in particular, attempts to establish the criteria for what constituted 'Japaneseness' occupied the energy and resources of statesmen, bureaucrats and unofficial publicists alike. It was a preoccupation which reflected a recognition that the muscular nationalism of the Western powers would have to be met by an equally assertive Japanese national identity if sovereignty were to be preserved (Pyle 1969: 75). The contours of this Japanese identity, which invoked powerful images of communal solidarity and exclusivity, were further refined through the lens of scientific racism as embodied in the writings of Galton, Haeckel, Lamarck and Spencer (Shimao 1981: 93–102; Nolte 1987: 44). A Japanese translation of Spencer's evolutionary theory first appeared in 1884, and, in total, some thirty translations of his works had appeared by the turn of the century. The provision of a classificatory grid that located the Japanese within a clearly defined hierarchy of race while offering a scientifically reasoned yet easily accessible explanation for both the complexities of a modern society and national survival found a receptive audience among academics, journalists and politicians alike. Set within the colonial context, to which we shall return later in this chapter, the diffusion of social Darwinism also made it possible to demonstrate 'scientifically' that some cultures were advanced and civilized while others remained backward and uncivilized (Weiner 1989: 14–22).

For the young intellectuals associated with the newspaper *Nihon* and the journal *Nihonjin*, the nation was increasingly identified with *minzoku* – a term first popularized by Shiga Shigetaka in the 1880s. In common with other terms such as *kokusui* (national essence) and *kokuminshugi* (civil nationalism), *minzoku* was a critical element in the development of a popular nationalism, which arose partly in response to what was regarded as the over-Westernization of the previous decades. As articulated by Shiga and his contemporaries, *minzoku* reflected what were assumed to be the unique characteristics (historical, geographical and cultural) of the Japanese nation (Gluck 1985: 110–15). This sense of nation, as expressed by *minzoku*, was subsequently appropriated by constitutional scholars like Hozumi Yatsuka, for whom the *kokutai* (national polity) was identified with the imperial line and the network of beliefs that sustained it, principally ancestor worship. In common with Inoue Tetsujiro, Kato Hiroyuki and other family state theoreticians, Hozumi conceived of the Japanese *minzoku* as a manifestation of common ancestry rather than shared culture. Ueda Katsutoshi pursued a parallel line of argument in *Kokugo to Kokka to*, published in 1894. In this seminal piece, Ueda emphasized that the Japanese polity had been, and would continue to be, sustained by the Japanese race, and argued that the Japanese language itself was a manifestation of the inherited qualities of its people (Yun 1993: 16). Although he originally challenged the legitimacy of a *kokutai* that located sovereignty in the person of the emperor, Kato Hiroyuki's early enthusiasm for and advocacy of the 'natural rights' of man and representative government was replaced by a firm commitment to Darwinian theories of social evolution (Kato 1955: 111–12; Irokawa 1986: 253). With the publication of *Shinkagaku Yori Kansatsu shitaru Nichiro no Unmei*, in 1905, Kato applied Darwinian inspired notions of *seizon kyōsō* (struggle for survival) and *yūshō reppai* (survival or the fittest) to an analysis of the current struggle between Japan and Russia. He concluded that a Japanese victory was inevitable due to the superiority of a homogeneous polity that had been thoroughly integrated within the emperor system (Kawamura 1990: 67).

The dissemination of social Darwinism was also encouraged by early Japanese encounters with the various racisms prevalent in the United States and in the European colonies. These date from an 1860 mission to the United States and extend through to the Iwakura mission of 1871–73. In addition to the official reports, which were unavailable to the public, individual envoys and their attendants published personal accounts, often in diary form. Yanagawa Kenzaburo, a member of the 1860 mission, seems to have uncritically imbibed the prejudices of his American hosts. Yanagawa's reference to the inherent stupidity and inferiority of black people is paralleled by comparisons between black people and the *eta* outcasts drawn by Kimura Tetsuya. Morita Kiyoyuki, too, commented on the ugliness and uncivilized behaviour of the Hawaiian 'natives' (Leupp 1995: 7). Far more expansive was Kume Kunitake, later professor of history at Tokyo University, one of two official secretaries who accompanied the Iwakura mission to Europe and the United States. Kume's two-volume account of the mission, first published in 1878, contains lengthy references to the origins and distinctive characteristics of the various peoples encountered by the mission. In contrast to the British, for example, whose inherent industriousness Kume regarded as the basis of their country's wealth and power, he opined that Spain's decline as a world power had come about as a result of the equally inherent indolence of its people (Kume 1985: Vol. 2, 39).

The conflation of physiological and cultural characteristics is also apparent in an earlier passage where Kume assesses the inevitable decline of the 'Indian' population of North America. Like Kimura a decade earlier, Kume draws a direct physiological comparison between certain North American 'Indians' and the *senmin* (lit. lowly people) of Japan, a category which had incorporated the *eta* and *hinin* outcast groups during the Tokugawa period (Kume 1985: Vol. 1, 132–5).

The Galtonian imprint is equally evident in Takahashi Yoshio's *Nihon Jinshu Kairyōron* (Improvement of the Japanese Race), published in 1883, which argued in favour of miscegenation with Westerners (Ishii 1937: 38–9). Takahashi was by no means alone in advocating intermarriage with Westerners as the preferred means of enhancing the inferior physical and intellectual capacities of the Japanese. Four years later, Katō Hiroyuki proposed an identical course of action in a short piece entitled *Nihon Jinshu Kairyō no Ben* (A Justification for the Improvement of the Japanese Race) (Yun 1993: 15). The then prime minister, Itō Hirobumi, sought a second opinion from Herbert Spencer, who subsequently advised against interbreeding with Europeans on the grounds that hybridization between disparate races would, as it had in Latin America, produce disastrous consequences for both (Stepan 1982: 105). What concerned Japanese admirers of Galton was a fundamental, if methodological, question: how could improved offspring be produced? During the 1880s, Japanese eugenics debated the value of the miscegenation of Japanese and Europeans, but, with the rediscovery of Mendelian genetics in 1900, the debate had moved on, separating the nation into genetically superior and inferior Japanese. Driven by the power of science, Japan could now seek ways to improve the capacities of future generations without recourse to foreign intervention.

The impact of racial, as well as related theories of geographical or climatic determinism, was evident in contemporary textbooks (Tanaka 1993: 39–40).

Along with history, geography formed an integral part of the national curriculum in Meiji schools, as well as providing a conduit for knowledge of the outside world generally. Early texts like Fukuzawa Yukichi's *Sekai Kunizukushi* (World Geography [1869]), of which more than a million copies were sold, ranked countries within an evolutionary hierarchy of barbarian, semi-civilized states. While all civilized states were European in character, not all European nations were civilized. Echoing the views of Kume Kunitake, Fukuzawa wrote of Spain as a nation whose decline as a world power had come about as a result of inherent deficiencies in the character of its people. Japan, by comparison, was depicted as a country in transition from semi-civilized to civilized status.

Scholarly enthusiasm for deterministic theories of social evolution also ensured that the assumed relationship between geography and *kokka ishiki* (national consciousness) featured prominently in secondary-school textbooks. Increased ministerial control over textbook content in the years following the Imperial Rescript on Education (1890) did little to dampen enthusiasm for deterministic theories of social evolution. On the contrary, racial differences between and within individual nations featured even more prominently. In that part of the 1893 edition of *Bankoku Chiri Shoho* (Geography For Beginners) that charts relations between the Native American and Caucasian populations of the United States, the destitution of the former is portrayed as a consequence of their 'primitive and simple nature' (Takeuchi 1987: 9).

Although intellectuals and journalists performed an important role as channels of legitimation, institutions of the state were the primary sites of ideological articulation. By the end of the first decade of the twentieth century, state-inspired nationalism had penetrated all strata of society, and it offered the Japanese people an easily accessible explanation for their social, political and economic position, both domestically and in terms of the wider international context. It was a nationalist ideology with a central motif of the *kazoku kokka* (family state), itself the product of a reworking of the concepts of citizen and nation in accordance with myths of common ancestry. The existence of a *Yamato minzoku* sharing a common ancestry, history and culture had become as canonical and natural to the Japanese as it was to their European counterparts. While the physical and historical evidence of migrations to the Japanese islands could not be ignored, these were deemed to be of such antiquity that a single 'race' and culture had long since formed (Yun 1993: 27). Cultural indebtedness to China was acknowledged, but this too was relegated to the distant past. As represented in school textbooks after 1910, it had become axiomatic that responsibility for the regeneration of Asia had fallen to the Japanese by virtue of their innately superior qualities (Tanaka 1993: 201).

In defining the Japanese nation as a collective personality, characterized by uniformity and homogeneity, the family state was itself conceived as a reflection of the inherited qualities and capacities of its people. The immutable characteristics that distinguished the *Yamato minzoku* provided what Balibar has termed 'a historical backbone'; 'a concentration of qualities that belong "exclusively" to the nationals: it is in the race of "its children" that the nation can contemplate its true identity at its purest' (Balibar 1990: 284). As enshrined in the national school curriculum, and projected through a variety of channels, both formal and informal, the criteria for membership in this uniquely powerful national collectivity were construed as both racial and cultural. A corollary of this construction of a Japanese race would be the simultaneous categorization of other populations as members of equally distinct but subordinate races.

The articulation of an ideology in which the categories of race and nation so clearly overlapped was not unique to Japan. The reification of the nation as an organic entity had clear parallels in contemporary Europe, where the conceptualization of nations as 'naturally occurring groups identified by cultural *differentiae*' implied that the 'symbols of "nation" were themselves grounded in race' (Miles 1993: 62; Lauren 1988: 40). This was certainly the case in Czarist Russia, where 'the nation was (1) defined as a collective individual, and (2) formed by ethnic primordial factors, and (3) characterized by the enigmatic soul or spirit' (Greenfeld 1992: 261). Given that Japan was consciously modelling its behaviour in other spheres of activity on that of its European and North American contemporaries, it is hardly surprising that Japanese racial discourse was inspired by, and developed in response to, that of the most advanced western nations.

THE 'OTHER' WITHIN

The notion of a civilized Japan presumed its opposite, the existence of which provided both a measure by which Japanese accomplishments could be judged and a reminder of the fate that awaited those who failed to become civilized. But modern narratives of inclusion and exclusion, like those of the Tokugawa period, were not limited to those 'others' who lived beyond the spatial confines of Japan. New social and economic relations within Japan were also commonly viewed through a parallel and equally deterministic framework of the survival of the fittest. These racisms of the interior affected not only traditional outsider populations, such as the former outcasts and the Ainu, but the urban and rural poor in general, and those who suffered from congenital or chronic illness. In each case, particular groups were identified not only by their material deprivation, but also by certain assumed physical or cultural characteristics. In late nineteenth and early twentieth century Japan, members of *kasō shakai* (lower-class society) were excluded from main-stream society by virtue of both the material conditions of their existence and what were perceived as inherent moral deficiencies. Although such groups were also referred to as *tennō no sekishi* (children of the emperor), evoking images of a seamless family state, they existed for the most part beyond the pale of civilized society. Early accounts of the urban poor often read like adventure stories in faraway lands. That such reports were often compiled by officials engaged in the task of civilizing the savage interior was itself significant, since it was dependent upon the prior identification and exclusion of certain groups within the boundaries of the state. The urban slum was represented in contemporary newspapers and journals as the symbolic opposite of *bunmei* (civilization); its inhabitants were depicted as the descendants of 'remote foreign races' upon whom were projected images of savagery and barbarism. In a 1897 account of Osaka slum dwellers, for example, the area is described as otherworldly, inhabited by 'countless deaf, crippled, limbless, and pygmies, all wrapped up in worse rags, wriggling like worms with griefs filling the air' (Chubachi and Taira 1976: 404).

Such contemporary accounts of the urban poor are broadly comparable to those applied to the peasantry, whose 'physiognomy', like the odour peculiar to animals, made them readily identifiable (Hane 1982: 35). In Mayama Seika's *Minami Koizumi-mura*, published several years after the Russo-Japanese War, peasant life was depicted as one of unspeakable misery, and the peasantry likened to 'insects that crawl on the ground'. The author found it inconceivable that 'the blood flowing in those miserable peasants also flows in my body' (Irokawa 1986: 223, 244). In each case, parallels can be drawn across time to the negative images of commoner and peasant held by the samurai elites of the Tokugawa period, and across space to the imagery employed against the 'lower orders' in the industrializing nation states of late nineteenth and early twentieth century Europe and North America.

These preoccupations were also reflected in the creation of elaborate and powerful bureaucratic instruments for the compilation of data that subsequently formed the basis for social policy in the areas of public hygiene and sanitation, gender relations, reproduction and sexuality. During the empire-building decades (1880–1945), notions of 'blood' purity were invoked not only as a metaphor for shared heredity or ancestry, but also as the essential 'stuff' of race and national identity. Within a public discourse of modernization, the *yūsei* (eugenics) project was premised upon the construction of a racially defined nation state, whose people could be physically and intellectually moulded through conformance with new scientific regimes. As a morally acceptable and verifiable means of transforming the Japanese polity, race science was transmitted through networks of modern institutions and industries. Eugenics was appropriated to portray society as an organic entity governed by scientific laws. But awareness of assumed difference and a determination to preserve an imagined homogeneous core population also fuelled a determination to police deviance. The imperial melting pot melted its ore selectively, and for that reason alone served as a useful metaphor for national identity.

This was readily apparent in the treatment of *raija* (lepers) as established in the *Rai Yobō ni kansuru Ken* (Leprosy Prevention Law – hereafter LPL) of 1907. The earliest references to *rai* as a family of skin diseases can, in fact, be found in the *Nihon Shoki* (720 CE). Under the influence of Buddhism, *rai* came to be understood as a form of *gōbyō* (karmic disease), or as punishment for crimes committed in a previous lifetime (Kanai 2003: 10). There is evidence that during the late medieval and early modern eras special facilities attached to Buddhist temples, like those at Kitayama Jūhachi Kendo in Nara and Monoyoshimura in Kyoto, provided housing and care for lepers. Lepers who were attached to these facilities possessed the right to beg for alms, and the sites themselves were open to the public. (Kanai 2003: 53, 56, 63–4, 70; Niunoya 2001: 80–2). Where a sufferer lived and for how long, however, varied by region, class, gender and family circumstances. Many lepers, perhaps the majority, remained with their families and continued to make some contribution to the household income. The medical literature (both lay and specialist) of the Tokugawa period suggests that during the seventeenth and eighteenth centuries leprosy increasingly came to be understood as a disease of the *iesuji* (family line) or *ketsumyaku* (blood line). In certain feudal domains, lepers were assigned the status of *rai mibun* and placed under the control of local *eta* headmen, later giving rise to the belief that *eta* were more likely to contract leprosy. Others spent their lives at home, generated income through begging, or made pilgrimages in search of hot springs curatives. That many remained with their families is also borne out by the numerous pamphlets advertising *fūraimaru* (medicinal cures for leprosy) dating from the early part of the nineteenth century (Kenshōkaigi 2005: 10–11, 18–25).

The first modern specialist leprosy facility, the Kihai Byōin (Kihai Hospital), was founded in 1875. During the years that followed, its founder and manager, Gotō Masafumi, published regularly on the causes and treatment of leprosy. His findings, perhaps influenced by the discoveries of Hansen, were published in the *Kihai Byōin Iji Zasshi* (Kihai Hospital Medical Journal), and they provided empirical evidence of the infectiousness of leprosy. As knowledge of Hansen's discovery of the leprosy bacteria became widespread in Japan, it accelerated interest in, and publications on, leprosy. These ranged from serious medical treatises like *Lessons on Leprosy Treatment* (1886), by Matsuda Gentoku, to the *Autobiography of a Leper* (1895), by Oki Kōtarō. However, commonsense understandings of leprosy as a hereditary disease remained widespread. These were evident in the

Takahashi Oden Monogatari (Tales of Takahasi Oden), which first appeared in 1879. Based upon an actual murder case and the subsequent execution of the murderess, Takahashi Den, whose husband suffered from leprosy, these often-exaggerated stories reinforced popular belief in the hereditary nature of leprosy. A 1921 version of the story written by Suzuki Seizaburō highlighted the presumed association of leprosy with the burakumin (former outcasts) (Kenshōkaigi 2005: 44–9).

During the first decades of the Meiji Period, the care and treatment of lepers was undertaken either by individuals, such as Gotō, or by Christian missionaries, such as Hannah Ridell, who founded the Kaishun Hospital in Kumamoto Prefecture in 1895. Until that time, public health administration, under the aegis of the Ministry of Home Affairs, was primarily concerned either with raising general levels of hygiene or with the prevention of acute infectious diseases such as cholera and smallpox. Stimulated by two events that were separated by space and time, however, by 1907 national legislation that led to the compulsory segregation of all leprosy sufferers was in place. The first World Leprosy Conference, held in Berlin in 1897, not only confirmed that Hansen's disease was infectious but also equated partial isolation of sufferers with prevention. This was followed in 1899 by revision of the Unequal Treaties, under which European and American residence had been restricted to a limited number of the treaty ports. Treaty revision brought with it *naichizakkyo* (the right of foreigners to travel and reside freely within Japan). For a nation that had emerged victorious from the Sino-Japanese War (1894–5) and had successfully negotiated an end to the humiliation of the Unequal Treaties, the visibility of tens of thousands of lepers was regarded as a national disgrace (Fujino 2001: 39; Kenshōkaigi 2005: 53).

The Imperial Diet first took up the issue of leprosy control and prevention during the thirteenth session of the House of Representatives in March 1899, immediately before *naichizakkyo* came into effect. Demands for stricter controls emanated from various quarters. One Diet member, Nemoto Tadashi, argued that for a civilized society to disregard the existence of 50,000 wandering lepers undermined *kokka no taimen* (national prestige), and he urged the government to pursue a policy of segregation (Kenshōkaigi 2005: 54). In March 1902, the debate was renewed, with Representative Saitō Masuo, a medical doctor who also served as Director of the Gunma Medical Association, commenting that:

> Now that leprosy, like cholera or black plague, has been internationally confirmed as an infectious disease caused by a type of bacteria, we cannot leave the disease unattended … What foreigners fear most when they visit Japan is the high visibility of lepers along the roadsides.
>
> (Fujino 2001: 40)

A further five years would pass before comprehensive anti-leprosy legislation would be introduced and subsequently adopted by the Diet. In 1905, Representative Yamane Masatsugu, a former chief police surgeon, submitted an amendment to the Infectious Disease Prevention Law (IDPL) of 1897. The IDPL had targeted eight acute infectious diseases (cholera, dysentery, typhoid, smallpox, typhus, scarlet fever, diphtheria and black plague) for government action. Under the IDPL, sufferers of these diseases were segregated from the healthy population, while entry to and exit from epidemic areas was prohibited. Yamane's proposal called for the inclusion of leprosy among these diseases. In response, the Director of the Hygiene Bureau of the Ministry of Home Affairs, Kubota Shizutarō, cautioned that a distinction had to be made between acute infectious diseases (smallpox, for example) that required isolation, and chronic infectious diseases that did not. In other words, the government was not only aware of this important distinction, but knew that there was no medical justification for the complete segregation of leprosy sufferers (Kenshōkaigi 2005: 54–5; Fujino 2006: 4).

As reported by the *Tokyo Nichinichi Shinbun* (November 7, 1905), soon after victory in the Russo-Japanese War had been achieved, Baron Eiichi Shibusawa hosted a meeting of leprosy specialists (November 6, 1905), including Ridell, Kubota, and a rising star in the field, Dr Mitsuda Kensuke. In its commentary on the meeting, the *Nichinichi* noted that

> 'Our nation has a great number of leprosy sufferers. This is second only to India, and the proportion of sufferers to the total population [here] is the greatest in the world. This is a national disgrace.'
>
> (Kenshōkaigi 2005: 56)

Thus, while the government and people of Japan might regard themselves as members of an *ittō koku* (first-class nation), Japan was no better than a colony when it came to leprosy control.

Years later, as Director of the Zensei Byōin (Zensei Hospital), renamed Zenshō in 1941, Mitsuda would be regarded as Japan's leading specialist in the treatment of leprosy, and in 1951 he was awarded the Order of Culture in recognition of his achievements. On his death in 1964, Mitsuda was hailed as the Albert Schweitzer of Japan (Kenshōkaigi 2005: 56; Fujino 2001: 48; Sawano 1994: 92). Indeed, at the November 1905 meeting Mitsuda outlined a program of leprosy prevention that would become the basis of national policies for nearly a century – policies that would result in enforced isolation, compulsory abortion and sterilization, and the loss of all human dignity for leprosy sufferers. Although almost certainly aware of the distinction between acute and chronic infectious diseases, Mitsuda argued that leprosy presented a threat of the same magnitude as the black plague, and should be treated accordingly. Reflecting the conceptualization of society as an organic entity, he concluded that the existence of tens of thousands of *furō rai kanja* (homeless lepers) presented a national health threat, and that failure to introduce a policy of complete segregation would be tantamount to committing a sin. Moreover, Mitsuda not only recommended prohibitions on sufferers entering professions that involved interaction with the public (such as laundry work, hairdressing, the practice of law), but he also recommended prohibitions on access to public spaces, including schools, libraries, hot springs, theatres and inns (Kenshōkaigi 2005: 57; Fujino 2001: 46–8).

By enacting the LPL in 1907 (effective in April 1909), the government and Diet, while distinguishing leprosy from acute contagious diseases, adopted virtually all of Mitsuda's earlier recommendations. Japan was divided into five regions, with a sanatorium located in each. Due to budgetary constraints, however, the capacity of this national network was only 1,100 people, which represented less than four percent of the estimated 30,000 leprosy sufferers in Japan at that time. The financial burden of staffing and maintaining the sanatoria was delegated to the prefectures. The fact that itinerant lepers were the initial targets of the policy of absolute segregation had enormous implications for future care. Since they were regarded as possessing the requisite skills (control) the first sanatoria directors and virtually all staff were recruited from among the pool of former police officers, (Fujino 2005: 49–51; Sawano 1994: 46; Kenshōkaigi 2005: 59–60). In fact, soon after he assumed the position of director of the Zensei Byōin in 1915, and without legal authorization, Mitsuda introduced the compulsory sterilization of male patients. Due to the unavailability of staff (skilled or otherwise), inmates were required to perform a wide range of services, including providing care for the most infirm, the washing of bandages, maintainence of facilities, waste removal, and general construction.

Further recommendations from Mitsuda Kensuke resulted in the first amendment to the LPL in 1916. Under the revised law, leprosauria directors were empowered to: (a) imprison recalcitrant inmates for up to sixty days, (b) reduce the daily food allowance for disobedient patients by 50 per cent for a period of seven days and (c) confine inmates to their rooms for up to thirty days (Kenshōkaigi 2005: 61).

In the same year, a Health and Hygiene Study Committee was established within the Ministry of Home Affairs. Its report, *Konponteki Rai Yobōsaku Yōkō* (Outline of Fundamental Measures for the Prevention of Leprosy), submitted in 1921, called for the expansion of existing facilities and the creation of national sanatoria based upon the principle of absolute segregation. This was enacted during the fifty-sixth session of the Imperial Diet, and in the following year, the Health Bureau proposed a 'Twenty-Year Programme' designed to eradicate leprosy. This master plan was predicated on the assumption that all remaining lepers (10,000 people) would be incarcerated within ten years, and that they could be expected to die off within a further decade (Kenshōkaigi 2005: 73; Fujino 2001: 126–129). To garner public support and encourage acceptance of segregation, the Ministry of Home Affairs, supported by Baron Shibusawa, established the Leprosy Prevention Association (LPA) in 1930. In recognition of generous support provided by the imperial family, June 25 (the birthday of the then empress) was selected as 'Leprosy Prevention Day'. In subsequent years, the weeks before and after June 25 were marked by film screenings, public lectures and the distribution of pamphlets – all of which were designed to encourage support for official policies (Kenshōkaigi 2005: 171; Fujino 2001: 132–4). In 1934, a satisfied Mitsuda wrote:

> In the same way that men in the military are prepared to die for the sake of the nation on the battlefields of Manchuria, leprosy sufferers should also be willing to enter leprosaria. Day and night, Her Imperial Majesty graciously worries about these sufferers. Knowing this, lepers should leave their villages and go to leprosaria as soon as possible.
>
> (Kenshōkaigi 2005: 173)

Compulsory sterilization of leprosy sufferers was neither condoned nor prohibited under contemporary legal codes. Even the National Eugenic Law of 1940, which provided for the sterilization of individuals suffering from hereditary diseases, specifically excluded leprosy patients from this procedure. Nonetheless, compulsory sterilization of leprosy patients at state-operated leprosaria not only continued throughout the Pacific War, but was finally legalized under the Eugenic Protection Law (EPL) of 1948. The explicit purpose of the law was 'to prevent the birth of eugenically inferior offspring and to protect the health and life of the mother'. Between 1948 and 1996, when compulsory sterilization was written out of the EPL and the enabling LPL was finally repealed, an estimated 1,500 sterilizations and nearly 8,000 involuntary abortions were carried out (Kenshōkaigi 2005: 203–8; Fujino 2001: 480–2). Under the terms of a 2001 compensation agreement stemming from a series of civil actions taken by former inmates, the Koizumi Government reluctantly agreed, in 2002, to pay between US$40,000 and US$100,000 to each of 2,000 plaintiffs, including both leprosaria inmates and their families. In October 2005, a three-judge panel of the Tokyo District Court upheld a lawsuit filed by twenty-five Taiwanese leprosy sufferers who had endured compulsory segregation during the colonial period. Yet, on the same day, a second panel of the Tokyo District Court denied claims for compensation from a further 117 Koreans who had been similarly incarcerated in colonial Korea, on the grounds that the 2001 law did not specifically include inmates of leprosaria located outside of Japan. This was despite the fact that, as colonial subjects, both Taiwanese and Koreans had been guaranteed the right to take up residence anywhere within the former Japanese Empire, and had been subject to both labour and military conscription during the Pacific War.

THE COLONIAL 'OTHER'

The Meiji period also witnessed the establishment of a colonial order in Hokkaido. Employing institutional and administrative mechanisms very similar to those that would later be deployed in Korea and Taiwan, the Meiji state moved to exploit the island's strategic and economic potential. The destitution that rapidly came to characterize the lives of the indigenous Ainu population was attributed not to the specifics of colonial policy, but to the innate inferiority of the *dojin* (native) population. The dehumanization of the Ainu began with the view that the Ainu either were not there, or were savages, or both. In a process that would be repeated elsewhere in the empire, the Ainu were gradually constructed as a primitive and racially immature 'other' in a discourse that justified and rendered the colonial project inevitable. The colonial relationship with the Ainu, and their categorization as primitive savages, also provided an initial context in which images of indigenous inferiority could be contrasted with those of a modern, civilized Japan.

It was within the context of the political, economic and social processes that developed under colonial rule in Hokkaido, Korea and Taiwan that the new Japanese identity was most fully expressed. If a strongly collectivistic nationalism allowed the Japanese to partake of a modern and progressive identity, the existence of empire confirmed their own manifest superiority *vis-à-vis* the peoples of Asia. Likewise, if industrial and technological progress were the indices of civilization and enlightenment, then a lack of material development provided indisputable evidence of inferiority. It was this lack of both a martial spirit and the institutions of modern industry that persuaded many Japanese that the peoples of East Asia could only achieve a civilized state through exposure to the work habits and martial values that had produced a powerful Japan. The presumed correlation between economic development and the inherent and differing capacities of human societies led Fukuda Tokuzo, in 1902, to conclude that the transformation of Korea from a preindustrial society to a modern capitalist society could only be accomplished through Japanese intervention (Hatada 1972: 34–5; Yamabe 1978: 262). Other commentators, however, were less sanguine about the civilizing impact of Japanese rule. Thirty years later, and despite more than two decades of imperial benevolence, Koreans would still be regarded as by nature 'unsuited for work in a modern industrial society' (Osaka-shi, *et al.* 1933: 32–3; Zensei 1930: 176–7).

Core narratives of progress and civilization, of which social-scientific discourse formed an important part, further assisted in the ordering of popular knowledge of the excluded 'other'. An extremely popular vehicle for the celebration of modernity, civilization and, subsequently, imperial expansion was the *hakurankai* (national expositions). Modelled after the first international exposition held at Crystal Palace in 1851, Japanese variants were held in 1877, 1881, 1890, 1895 and 1903. Designed by the noted anthropologist Tsuboi Shōgorō, the Jinruikan (Hall of Mankind) was conceived of as the centrepiece of the Fifth Industrial Exposition, held in Osaka in 1903. Tsuboi's plan to exhibit the 'races' of the world in their 'natural' settings for the education of the general public encountered rigorous opposition from Chinese, Koreans and Ryūkyūans, who objected to representations of their cultures as frozen in the past. The stark imagery of an irrational and primitive Asia, in contrast to a modern, civilized Japan, was nonetheless retained in the form of exhibits detailing the lives of Ainu, Taiwanese aboriginals and Malays.

The popular discourse of the primitive 'other' was also sustained by the imagery of the Japanese civilizing mission. Everything else was relegated to the background, with the indigenous populations of Hokkaido, Taiwan and Korea classified as stagnant, degenerate and incapable of appreciating the resources they possessed. Representations of this type were evident at both the Takushoku Hakurankai (Colonial Exposition) of 1912 and at the Natural History Museum in Sapporo. The latter contained life-size waxwork reproductions depicting the Japanese 'exploration' of Hokkaido in 1870. The impression conveyed was of an entire territory unappreciated and unused by its original inhabitants. The 'new' history of Hokkaido, cast in images of a redemptive Japanese project and tethered to invidious stereotypes of racial infantilism and primitivism, was there for all to behold. The set of deterministic assumptions concerning the capacities of subordinate populations that informed the Hakurankai and museum exhibitions of this type fused popular and social-scientific understandings of the 'other' within an overarching discourse of race. By providing detailed and scientifically verified information about the racial character, behaviour and habits of the 'other', the social sciences offered both a justification for paternalistic control and an archival resource that colonial administrators could draw upon.

Within the colonial context itself, racialized discourses informed both policy formulation and administrative practice. Inequality was attributed to differences in national or racial characteristics – differences that marked some peoples as unfit to survive the struggle for survival in a modern industrial society. As such, their exclusion from the national community was judged natural and inevitable. In *The Japanese Nation*, written in 1912, soon after his appointment as Professor of Colonial Studies at Tokyo Imperial University, Nitobe Inez described the 'hairy Ainu' as a Stone Age population. Nitobe's depiction of the Ainu as somehow existing beyond the confines of human history, and therefore doomed to extinction, paralleled conclusions drawn some years earlier by Basil Hall Chamberlain:

> … so little have they (Ainu) profited from the opportunities offered to them during the last one thousand years or two thousand years, that there is no longer room for them in the world.
>
> (Chamberlain 1887: 43)

Nitobe's assessment of the Ainu also bears comparison with a similar account of the Korean people written after a visit to the peninsula. In representing the inhabitants as moribund and incapable of adapting to current realities, Nitobe draws a clear distinction between the neglect and forlornness of the Korean 'present' and, at least by implication, the promise of a progressive future under Japanese governance:

> The very physiognomy and living of these people are so bland, unsophisticated and primitive, that they belong not to the twentieth or the tenth – nor indeed to the first century. They belong to a prehistoric age … the Korean habits of life are the habits of death. They are closing the lease of their ethnic existence. The national course of their existence is well-nigh run. Death presides over the peninsula.
>
> (Nitobe 1909: 214, 216)

The marginalization of subordinate populations, as either colonial subjects or migrant labour drawn to the metropolitan core, was interpreted almost exclusively within an overarching discourse of race. Kawamura Minato has argued in this context that by the late 1920s mass 'orientalism', in which images of colonial and other inferior populations were contrasted with a progressive and modern Japan, had become an integral part of commonsense understanding. Imagery of this type would later become a regular feature in novels and children's comic strips, the most popular of which was Shimada Keizo's *Bōken Dankichi* (Dankichi the Adventurer), which, between 1933 and 1939, serialized the adventures of a Tintin-like protagonist among the primitives of the South Seas. Whereas the savagery of the islanders in *Bōken Dankichi* was offset by their comically exaggerated features, in the exploits of the common soldier, *Nora-kura* (Black Mutt), the (Chinese) enemy was degraded to the level of barnyard animals (Kawamura 1993:119).

It was in the sphere of international relations, particularly between

Japan and the other imperial powers, that a two-tiered and apparently contradictory narrative of race was articulated (Shimazu 1989: 93). It was a conceptualization that, on the one hand, assumed a common destiny for the peoples of Asia and was predicated on an inevitable conflict between the 'white and yellow races' (Oyama 1966: 341). The Japanese were thus identified as sharing the same racial origins as Chinese and Koreans. On the other hand, this European-derived narrative of race did not preclude the existence of a further definition which identified race with nation, and which distinguished imperial Japan, in equally deterministic terms, from its Asian neighbours. This perspective, founded upon the assumed incapacity of subordinate populations to manage their own affairs, reaffirmed a sense of national purpose and racial superiority among the Japanese people, irrespective of their class position at home. The subdivision of the human species that these assumptions affirmed also imposed a set of obligations on Japan as *Tōyō no Meishu* (The Leader of Asia). These obligations included not only raising colonial peoples to a level commensurate with their 'natural' abilities, but also preserving the essential and superior qualities of the Japanese within a carefully delineated hierarchy of race (Takeda 1938: 121).

[handwritten annotation: Japanese belonged to Asian ppl but were "superior".]

References

Balibar, E. (1990) 'Racisme et Nationalisme', in E. Balibar and I. Wallerstein (eds), *Race, Nation, Classe*, cited in M. Edwards (trans.), 'Paradoxes of Universality', in D.T. Goldberg (ed.), *Anatomy of Racism*, Minneapolis: University of Minnesota Press.

Barshay, A. (1988) *State and Intellectual in Imperial Japan: The public man in crisis*, Berkeley: University of California Press.

Chamberlain, B.H. (1887) *The Language, Mythology and Geographical Nomenclature of Japan, Viewed in the Light of Aino Studies*, Tokyo: Tokyo Imperial University.

Chubachi, M. and Taira, K. (1976) 'Poverty in Modern Japan: Perceptions and realities', in H. Patrick (ed.), *Japanese Industrialization and its Social Consequences*, Berkeley: University of California Press.

Fujino, Yutaka. (2001) *'Inochi' no Kindaishi: 'Minzoku Jōka' no nan no motoni Hakugai sareta Hansenbyō Kanja*, Kyoto: Kamogawa Shuppan.

—— (2006) *Hansenbyō to Sengo Minshushugi: Naze Kakuri wa Kyōka Saretanoka*, Tokyo: Iwanami Shoten.

Fujitani, T. (1993) 'Inventing, Forgetting, Remembering: Toward a historical ethnography of the nation state', in H. Befu (ed.), *Cultural Nationalism in East Asia*, Berkeley: University of California.

Gilroy, P. (1990) 'One Nation Under a Groove: The cultural politics of 'race' and racism in Britain', in D.T. Goldberg (ed.), *Anatomy of Racism*, Minneapolis: University of Minnesota Press.

Gluck, C. (1985) *Japan's Modern Myths*, Princeton: Princeton University Press.

Greenfeld, L. (1992) *Nationalism: Five roads to modernity*, Cambridge: Harvard University Press.

Hane, M. (1982) *Peasants, Rebels, and Outcastes: The underside of modern Japan*, New York: Pantheon Press.

Hatada, T. (1972) *Nihonjin no Chōsen Kan*, Tokyo: Keiso Shobo.

Harada, T. and Kang, J. (1985) *Kōza Sabetsu to Jinken [4] Minzoku*, Tokyo: Yuzankaku.

Hayashida, C.T. (1976) *Identity, Race and the Blood Ideology of Japan*, unpublished Ph.D thesis, University of Washington.

Irokawa, D. (1986) *The Culture of the Meiji Period* (M. Jansen ed. and trans.), Princeton: Princeton University Press.

Ishii, R. (1937) *Population Pressure and Economic Life in Japan*, Chicago: Chicago University Press.

Ito, M. (1982) *Kazoku Kokka no Jinruigaku*, Tokyo: Minerva Shobo.

Justice Research Organization of the Japan Law Foundation (2005), *Final Report of the Verification Committee Concerning Hansen's Disease Problem*, Tokyo.

Kada, T. (1940) *Jinshu Minzoku Sensō*, Tokyo: Keio Shobo.

Kanai, K. (2003) *Chūsei no Raija to Sabetsu*, Tokyo: Iwata Shoin.

Kato, H. (1955) 'Kokutai Shinron', in *Meiji Bunka Zenshu*, Tokyo: Nihon Hyoron Shinsha.

Kawamura, M. (1993) 'Taishū Orientarizumu to Ajia Ninshiki', in M. Kawamura (ed.) *Kindai Nihon to Shokuminchi [7]; Bunka no naka no Shokuminchi*, Tokyo: Iwanami Shoten.

Kawamura, N. (1990) 'Sociology and Socialism in the Interwar Period', in J.T. Rimer (ed.), *Culture and Identity: Japanese intellectuals during the interwar years*, Princeton: Princeton University Press.

Kikuchi, I. (1972) 'Hozumi Nobushige to Shakai Ken', *Nihon Gakushi-in Kiyo* 30, 1: 21–42.

Kume, K. (1935) *Kyūjyūnen Kaikoroku*, Tokyo: Waseda Daugaku Shuppanbu.

—— (1985) *Tokumei Zenken Taishi Beiō Kairan Jikki*, Tokyo: Iwanami Shoten.

Lauren, P.G. (1988) *Power and Prejudice: The politics and diplomacy of racial discrimination*, Boulder: Westview Press.

Leupp, G. (1995) 'Images of Black People in Late Mediaeval and Early Modern Japan', *Japan Forum* 7, 1: 1–13.

Miles, R. (1993) *Racism After 'Race Relations'*, London: Routledge.

Nitobe, I. (1909) *Thoughts and Essays*, Tokyo: Teibi Publishing Company.

—— (1912) *The Japanese Nation: Its land, its people, its life: With special consideration to its relations with the United States*, New York: G. Putnam's Sons.

Niunoya, T. (2001) 'Chūsei no Hinin to "Rai" Sabetsu', in Okiura, K. and Tokunaga, S. (eds), *Hansenbyō: Haijo Sabetsu Kakuri no Rekishi*, (pp. 75–91) Tokyo: Iwanami Shoten.

Nolte, S.H. (1987) *Liberalism in Modern Japan*, Berkeley: University of California Press.

Osaka-shi, Shakai-bu, Rōdō-ka (1933) 'Shakai-bu Hōkoku dai 177', *Chōsenjin Rōdōsha no Kinkyō*, Osaka.

Oyama, A. (ed.) (1966) *Yamagata Aritomo Ikensho*, Tokyo: Hara Shobo.

Pyle, K.B. (1969) *The New Generation in Meiji Japan*, Stanford, Calif: Stanford University Press.

Sawano Masaki (1994). *Raisha no sei: Bunmei Kaika no Jōken toshite*, Tokyo: Seikyusha.

Shimao, E. (1981) 'Darwinism in Japan', *Annals of Social Science* 38: 93–102.

Shimazu, N. (1989) 'The Japanese Attempt to Secure Racial Equality in 1919', *Japan Forum* 1, 1: 93–100.

Stepan, N. (1982) *The Idea of Race in Science: Great Britain 1800–1960*, London: Macmillan.

Takeda, Y. (1938) 'Naichi Zaijyū Hantōjin Mondai', *Shakai Seisaku Jiho* 213: 99–136.

Takeuchi, K. (1987) 'How Japan Learned About the Outside World: The views of other countries incorporated in Japanese school textbooks 1868–1986', *Hitotsubashi Journal of Social Sciences* 19: 1–13.

Tanaka, S. (1993) *Japan's Orient: Rendering pasts into history*, Berkeley: University of California Press.

Weiner, M. (1989) *The Origins of the Korean Community in Japan, 1910–1923*, Atlantic Highlands: Humanities Press.

——(1995) 'Discourses of Race, Nation and Empire in Pre-1945 Japan', *Ethnic and Racial Studies* 18, 3: 433–56.

Yamabe, K. (1978) *Nikkan Heigō Shoshi*, Tokyo: Iwanami Shōten.

Yasuda, H. (1992) 'Kindai Nihon ni Okeru "Minzoku Kannen no Keisei"', *Shiso to Gendai* 31: 61–72.

Yoshino, K. (1992) *Cultural Nationalism in Contemporary Japan*, London: Routledge.

Yun, K.C. (1993) 'Minzoku Gensō no Satetsu', *Shiso*, December: 4–37.

Zaidan Hojin Nichibenren Hōmukenkyū Zaidan Hansenbyō Mondai ni kansuru Kenshōkaigi (2005) *Hansenbyō Mondai ni kansuru Kenshōkaigi Saishū Hōkokusho* (http://www.jlf.or.jp/work/hansen_report.shtml#saisyu).

Zensei, E. (1930) 'Chōsenjin no Naichi Tokō', *Gaiko Jiho* 607: 173–7.

2 The Ainu

Indigenous people of Japan

Richard M. Siddle

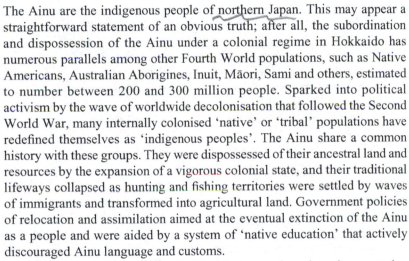

The Ainu are the indigenous people of northern Japan. This may appear a straightforward statement of an obvious truth; after all, the subordination and dispossession of the Ainu under a colonial regime in Hokkaido has numerous parallels among other Fourth World populations, such as Native Americans, Australian Aborigines, Inuit, Māori, Sami and others, estimated to number between 200 and 300 million people. Sparked into political activism by the wave of worldwide decolonisation that followed the Second World War, many internally colonised 'native' or 'tribal' populations have redefined themselves as 'indigenous peoples'. The Ainu share a common history with these groups. They were dispossessed of their ancestral land and resources by the expansion of a vigorous colonial state, and their traditional lifeways collapsed as hunting and fishing territories were settled by waves of immigrants and transformed into agricultural land. Government policies of relocation and assimilation aimed at the eventual extinction of the Ainu as a people and were aided by a system of 'native education' that actively discouraged Ainu language and customs.

While clearly supported by the historical record, such an interpretation does not resonate widely in Japan. Official and popular history views the creation of Hokkaido as an exercise in 'development' (*kaitaku*), not colonisation. Given the politicisation of the category 'indigenous peoples' and an international movement for indigenous rights centred on the United Nations, the state has resisted, largely successfully, any acknowledgment of the Ainu in these terms. For ordinary Japanese, the commonsense Nihonjinron master narrative of national homogeneity (Yoshino 1992, Befu 2001) denies the Ainu an existence as a separate ethnic minority – they are regarded as either completely assimilated or biologically extinct. Kitsch displays at Hokkaido tourist attractions do little to counter the notion that the Ainu are, at best, an anachronism.

Nevertheless, the Ainu have refused to passively acquiesce to the dominant stereotype of them as a 'dying race' (*horobiyuku minzoku*) that has been proclaimed by officials, scholars and educators since the late nineteenth century. At the beginning of the twenty-first century, the cultural symbols of a revitalised and contemporary Ainu identity have become prominent as Ainu activists press their claims on the basis of their distinct indigenous ethnicity. After an overview of their origins and history, this chapter will describe the Ainu struggle for rights and identity as indigenous people that has been underway since the 1960s and peaked with the enactment of the controversial and divisive Ainu Cultural Promotion Act in 1997.

HISTORICAL OVERVIEW OF AINU–JAPANESE RELATIONS

It is difficult to pinpoint the origins of the Ainu people with certainty. Archaeological evidence from Hokkaido points to longstanding cultural continuities with the peoples of maritime Siberia and the Amur River basin, as well as links with Honshu and the south (Yamaura and Ushiro 1999). It is clear that at least two culturally distinct populations coexisted in Hokkaido from about the eighth to the thirteenth centuries: the Satsumon in the southern and central regions and the Okhotsk along the northern and eastern coasts. As yet, little is known about how these two groups interacted.

The historical record begins with the expansion of the Yamato or *ritsuryō* state into the north of Honshu from the eighth century. For a long time it was accepted that the Ainu were the remnants of the aboriginal inhabitants of northern Japan who had been pushed ever northwards until finding a final refuge in Hokkaido. These people were known as the Emishi (literally, 'barbarians' who were not under Japanese political authority) in Japanese records between the eighth and twelfth centuries. More recent scholarship, however, indicates that the picture was far more complex than this. The Emishi were a diverse grouping, and differed culturally in many respects from the populations of Hokkaido. They raised horses and cultivated rice, for instance, practices unknown in Hokkaido in this period. On the other hand, the far north (present day Aomori and northern Iwate prefectures) has place names derived from the Ainu language and documentary records of Ainu communities that maintained a separate identity into the seventeenth century. Whatever the extent of diversity, by the thirteenth century this area and its original inhabitants were firmly part of the medieval Japanese state, and the northern barbarians that appear in Japanese documents were unambiguously the indigenous native peoples across the Tsugaru Straits in Hokkaido, a land the Japanese knew as Ezogashima.

It is around the same time that a clearly identifiable Ainu culture replaced that of the Satsumon and Okhotsk in Hokkaido, drawing upon elements of both. Bear ceremonialism, for instance, a key element of Ainu culture, featured prominently among the Okhotsk. The Ainu also inhabited the southern half of Sakhalin and the Kurile archipelago. These populations, while recognisably Ainu, differed culturally and linguistically from those in Hokkaido, which in turn displayed regional variations of culture and dialect.

The whole region was rich in natural resources, especially fish such as salmon and herring. The interior of Hokkaido had large herds of deer, while the Okhotsk Sea costs supported a variety of sea mammals in the north. A total population of perhaps 40,000 Ainu subsisted primarily by hunting, fishing and gathering wild plants, although simple cultivation was also known in Hokkaido. The Ainu never existed in isolation, and were incorporated into trading networks that extended south into Japan and north into maritime Siberia and the Amur River basin. Communities formed along the coasts and inland along the river systems of Hokkaido, with clear hunting and fishing territories (*iwor*).

Social organisation of the Ainu was based on both patrilineal and mat-rilineal kingroups, with clear status distinctions. Each community had a leader (*kotankorokur*), selected on the basis of both inheritance and ability, who took a leading role in trade and mediated disputes based on customary law. The Ainu way of life, like that of all native peoples, was characterised by an inseparable and complex spiritual relationship with the land and phenomena of the natural world. The central religious rite was the *iyomante*, in which the spirit of a bear was 'sent back' to the realm of the gods, although there is debate over when the ceremony developed to its present form. A rich oral literature developed, with marvellous heroic epics (*yukar*) and folktales (*wepeker*), and what survives hints at a complex and stratified society involved in both trade and warfare with its neighbours (for Ainu life and culture before colonisation, see Munro 1963; Watanabe 1973; Fitzhugh and Debreuil 1999).

Trade and warfare

For the Japanese (usually known in the literature as Wajin), who regarded the inhabitants of the northern regions through the prism of Chinese notions of civilisation and barbarism, the inhabitants of Ezogashima were little more than a variety of demon. These barbarians, however, controlled natural resources that the Japanese desired, and a flourishing trade developed in furs and sea products. Exiled criminals and Japanese fleeing from warfare crossed over the Tsugaru Straits.

By the fifteenth century, Japanese trading settlements were dotted around the tip of the Oshima peninsula in southern Hokkaido. Ainu (known at this time as Ezo) and Wajin in this region had come to rely on each other. The Wajin needed the Ainu to harvest and exchange the natural products of the region, while the Ainu relied on the trading relationship for iron, rice and other items of daily life. Japanese trade goods were incorporated into Ainu society as symbols of wealth and power (for the development of trade and Ainu–Japanese relations during the early modern period see Takakura 1960; Howell 1995, 2005; Siddle 1996; Walker 2001).

In 1456, friction between the Ainu and the newcomers flared into conflict after a Wajin blacksmith killed an Ainu in a quarrel over a blunt knife. The following year, Ainu led by Koshamain destroyed all but two of the Wajin settlements and almost drove the Wajin out of Ezogashima altogether, initiating a century of intermittent warfare. A feature of Ainu–Wajin conflicts was the use of treachery (*damashi uchi*) by the Japanese side; drawing on Ainu customs of negotiation and compensation to settle disputes, the Wajin would hold feigned peace talks at which Ainu leaders were ambushed and killed (Tabata 1993). Such incidents occurred in 1515, 1529 and 1536. In 1514 the Kakizaki family had emerged as the leader of the Japanese in southern Hokkaido, and in 1551, Kakizaki Suehiro, convinced that continued warfare was not beneficial for trade, sought an accommodation with the local Ainu. The resulting agreement split the profits of trade between Ainu and Wajin leaders, but it gave Kakizaki monopolistic control over trade and established Japanese territorial control over a small area of southern Hokkaido.

In 1599 the Kakizaki family took the name of Matsumae, and in 1604 their marginal domain was incorporated into the Tokugawa state. The black seal edict of Tokugawa Ieyasu that legitimised the Matsumae domain, following an earlier edict of Hideyoshi in 1593, limited Matsumae political authority to their territory. The rest of the island and surrounding areas remained foreign land, known as Ezochi (Ainu-land). The legitimacy of the domain rested on its role as the gatekeeper to the north and intermediary in the Ainu trade, recognised by the granting of a trade monopoly to the Matsumae. While the Matsumae domain possessed rich fishing grounds, there was little agricultural potential and this trade was vital for the domain economy. Rice (over 55,000 bales annually) and other foodstuffs had to be imported to Matsumae, and the products of Ezochi were shipped back in return.

To impose control on trade, the Matsumae set up a series of trading posts, known as *akinaiba*, in Ainu territory and discouraged the Ainu from freely trading where and when they wished. Products from the trading posts were exchanged with Honshu traders, who were limited to certain ports where they were subject to control and taxation. After 1644 Ainu boats were no longer to be seen in Tohoku ports, an indication of the success of Matsumae attempts to monopolise trade. By this time, the domain was becoming increasingly dependent on traders from Honshu, especially those of Omi (modern Shiga Prefecture). Omi trading houses such as Ryohamagumi and Yawatagumi began setting up branch offices in Matsumae from the 1630s. Motivated by risk and profit, the traders began to increasingly exploit the Ainu. The size of the *ezotawara*, the special small rice bales used in the Ezo trade for convenience of transportation, was reduced, while rates of exchange were maintained, in effect raising prices for one of the staple Wajin goods on which Ainu around the trading posts had become dependent. Trade relations had led to Ainu settlements in these areas forming into larger groupings under the control of powerful leaders who gained their wealth and status from the trade. As tensions mounted, disputes between groups sometimes escalated into armed conflicts. Japanese historical sources indicate that the feud between two powerful Ainu groups, the Menashkur and the Shumkur, which took place between 1648 and 1668 in what is now the Hidaka region, was a major source of political instability. Although the trading and gold-panning interests of the Matsumae were threatened, they could do little more than offer to mediate.

Major conflict erupted in 1669. Led by Shakushain (Samkusainu), leader of the Menashkur Ainu of Shibechari (modern Shizunai), many Ainu attacked trading posts and vessels over much of Ezochi, killing hundreds of Wajin. A few hundred Ainu then marched west to confront the Matsumae near their domain. Here, however, they were defeated, and a pacification campaign sent after Shakushain later in the year resulted in the Ainu leader's assassination during feigned peace negotiations.

While there is a tendency among contemporary Ainu and their supporters to interpret this conflict as an 'ethnic' war of liberation, the historical evidence suggests otherwise. Rather than reifying Ainu ethnicity as an *a priori* fact, a given 'reality' that affected relations between 'Ainu' and 'Japanese', it is necessary to understand it as a creative dimension interwoven into the very fabric of such interactions, and further transformed by them. As David Howell (2005) has argued, Ainu identity was consciously manipulated by the Matsumae authorities in Ezo through the use of ceremonial (such the *uimam* ceremony, in which trade was conducted under the disguise of the presentation of tribute) and through the maintenance of rigid boundaries (with prescriptions being placed on the adoption of Japanese clothing and hairstyles).

According to contemporary historical records (admittedly Japanese), the war of 1669 was an attempt by Shakushain to break the Matsumae monopoly and regain control over trade with Honshu. To further complicate the 'ethnic' dimension, Japanese and Ainu fought on both sides, including a certain Shōdayū, who is referred to as a son-in-law of Shakushain, indicating that important Japanese allies were even incorporated into the Ainu kinship system. Certainly, the Matsumae did not appreciate Shōdayū's involvement, and burned him at the stake (Walker 2001: 67).

As a result of the Ainu defeat, the previously autonomous regional groups in western and central Hokkaido fell under Matsumae control. This even included the Ainu of Ishikari, led by Haukase, who had refused to participate in the fighting. Ainu in the outlying areas to the north and east, however, still remained independent or maintained a tribute relationship with Matsumae. With the rise in Matsumae dominance after the war, the trading posts and trade vessels began to penetrate into their territories as well, reaching Karafuto (Sakhalin) and the Kuriles. In 1774 Kunashiri became the trading territory of the merchant Hidaya Kyūbei, originally from Honshu, although the establishment of permanent commercial operations in this area was impossible until 1782 due to the intransigence and power of the local Ainu leaders.

From the early eighteenth century, the coastal trading territories, now numbering around seventy and known as *basho*, began to come under the direct control of mainland traders. Domain expenses were increasing and the Matsumae were deeply in debt to the merchants. The Matsumae hoped that letting merchant contractors operate the *basho* after paying a fee would increase trade volume and profits, and therefore tax receipts. This arrangement gradually developed over the course of the eighteenth century and has come to be known as the *basho ukeoi* (subcontracted trading post) system. To pay these taxes and fees (along with forced 'loans' to the Matsumae of which there was little chance of repayment), the traders had to move away from barter trade to a more rationalised system. This was aided by the expansion of mainland agriculture, which led to a subsequent increase in demand for fish fertiliser and an interest in the fisheries of Ezochi. These developments were made possible by the systematic exploitation of fishing grounds, using merchant capital, technology and management and Ainu labour. This was a gradual process that did not reach full development until the nineteenth century. Contractors introduced advanced fishing methods and equipment, built processing facilities and barracks for the Ainu labourers, and shipped the products directly to markets in Kansai (Howell 1995). Risks were high, and high fees and forced loans to the Matsumae put pressure on the contractors to make the highest profits possible. One result was cruel treatment of the Ainu.

Emphasis had shifted from obtaining the products of Ainu labour through trade to the direct exploitation of that labour itself. Ainu around the *basho*, who were dependent on Wajin goods and whose leaders derived authority from their relationship with the *basho*, were coerced into working for rations and goods. Conditions were varied, but were often harsh in the worst *basho*. In 1789, after some years of suffering an exceptionally cruel regime, Ainu attacked and killed seventy-one Wajin on Kunashiri and in the Nemuro area. This final act of armed resistance was eventually suppressed by the

Matsumae, with the help of local Ainu leaders under their control. After an investigation, thirty-seven Ainu were executed at Nokkamappu. This turned into a messy affair, as the condemned Ainu refused to be quietly beheaded in turn and had to be butchered in the stockade.

The appearance of Russians in the north around this time meant that Ezochi and the Ainu became a matter of utmost concern in Tokugawa political circles. In 1792 Russians led by Adam Laxman landed at Nemuro, requesting the opening of trade relations with Japan. Although Laxman was rebuffed, the Russian presence became impossible to ignore. Arguments for the annexation of Ezochi became increasingly influential. In 1798 the Bakufu sent a large expedition to Ezochi, including Sakhalin and the Kuriles, and in 1799 they overrode Matsumae objections by annexing part of the region. By 1807 all Ezochi had been placed under direct Bakufu control through offices established in Matsumae and Hakodate. This was the first time centralised Japanese political authority was extended to the whole region, but Ezochi was too vast and rugged to administer in the same way as other Tokugawa lands. The Bakufu stationed garrisons around the coast and intervened in the Ainu trade to alleviate the worst injustices, but most Wajin still lived in the Matsumae domain or at the fishing stations. One change, however, was the introduction of a policy that aimed to 'civilise' the Ainu by converting them (often forcibly) to Japanese customs and lifestyle.

When the Russian threat receded, the Bakufu abandoned Ezochi and handed it back to the Matsumae in 1821. The border area reverted to its previous ambiguous status. The Matsumae and merchants were keen to reassert their economic control in Ezochi and their authority over Ainu labour in the fishing stations. The assimilation policy was scrapped, and forced labour and resettlement became a feature of Ainu life. Ainu labour was used for roadbuilding, transportation and servicing the fisheries, in addition to direct economic production. Ainu were brought down from the mountains to work on the coast, or were transferred between *basho* run by the same trader. The sexual exploitation of Ainu women by Wajin migrant workers became commonplace. The recruitment of labour was accomplished by the use of physical coercion if necessary, leaving the elderly and infirm behind. These practices were all recorded in detail in the journals of a sympathetic Japanese explorer, Matsuura Takeshiro (1818–88), who conducted six official surveying missions in Ezochi and Karafuto.

Diseases introduced by the migrant workers contributed to the destruction of Ainu society (Walker 2001: 177–203). As the Ainu ceased to be the main economic producers of Ezochi, the movement of immigrants increased, encouraged by the easing of travel restrictions and tolls. As a result, by the 1850s the strict distinction that had previously been maintained between Matsumae and Ezochi had begun to break down. In 1855 the Bakufu reasserted control over the area, after the Treaty of Shimoda established the Russo–Japanese border between Etorofu and Uruppu.

Colonisation and dispossession

With the Meiji Restoration of 1868 and the establishment of the Kaitakushi (Colonisation Commission) in 1869, Ezochi was renamed Hokkaido and transformed into an internal colony of the new Japanese state, a strategic 'empty land' to be settled by immigration and developed along capitalist lines. Both of these policies required the dispossession of the Ainu as a prerequisite. This dispossession was initiated with the appropriation of Ainu land as *terra nullius* by the Kaitakushi under the Land Regulation Ordinance (Jisho Kisoku) of 1872. With this legal (in Japanese eyes) mechanism, the formal dispossession of Ainu resources was complete. The Ainu were forced into chronic destitution. From the mid-1870s, officials began entering Ainu into the system of household registers (*koseki*), the basic administrative apparatus through which the emerging modern state established surveillance and control over its subjects. From the start, though, Ainu households were distinguished as those of a different kind of subject by the designation 'former native' (*kyūdojin*).

Mass immigration, a market economy and a colonial administration created a new colonial society in Hokkaido. The salmon and deer upon which the Ainu depended were soon depleted by uncontrolled exploitation. Land was surveyed and partitioned for settlement. The authorities began in the 1880s to round up and relocate Ainu communities to clear them out of rich lands designated for agricultural settlement, and to make them easier to control. Also relocated were communities from Sakhalin (after the Russians took control in 1875) and the Kuriles (in 1884). Life in the 'reservations' was grim, and in some cases the communities were even moved on again. By the end of the century, the 17,000 Ainu accounted for around 2 per cent of the population of Hokkaido (for colonial and Ainu policy in this period, see Siddle 1996: 51–112).

For the officials and educators concerned with Ainu policy, and for the bulk of impoverished Japanese immigrants who moved into the ancestral lands of the Ainu, destitution and social breakdown among the 'natives' (*dojin*) were attributed not to specific colonial policies but to the innate propensities of the Ainu themselves. It made sense to most that the Ainu were a 'dying race' losing the 'struggle for survival', especially since social Darwinism enjoyed the status of scientific truth in Meiji Japan. Conversely, the speed with which Japan embraced Western ideas and embarked upon expansion and development in Hokkaido proved the superiority of the 'Japanese race'. The innate inferiority of the Ainu therefore justified, as well as explained, their subordination. By 1918, for the former governor of the colony of Karafuto (southern Sakhalin, controlled by Japan 1905–45), this supposed inferiority also sanctioned the exclusion of the Ainu from the national community, as his fondness for eugenics blurred the boundaries of 'race' and nation:

> Our country is proud of the purity of our ancient stock, and the long-term preservation of the purity of the stock (*shuzoku junsui*) is our nationalism … If interbreeding with Ainu introduces Ainu blood into Japanese it will violate the movement to preserve our national essence (*kokusui*).
>
> (Hiraoka 1918: 6)

The subsequent 'native policy' that developed attempted to manage and control the 'Ainu problem' (*Ainu mondai*) by resettling Ainu away from productive land earmarked for immigrants and by establishing a separate and inferior system of 'native education'. The aim was to forcibly assimilate the Ainu as speedily as possible, though for the many officials and scholars who subscribed to a social-Darwinist view of human societies, this was seen as an impossible task. A humanitarian movement to halt the physical extermination of the 'dying race' resulted in the enactment of a Former Natives Protection Act (*Hokkaido Kyūdojin Hōgo Hō*) in 1899. Under this Act, the Ainu were granted small plots of land in an attempt to turn them into farmers. By the beginning of the twentieth century, the activities of scholars, educators, colonial officials and journalists ensured that the image of an inferior 'dying race' informed both government policy and public opinion.

Some Ainu, with the help of missionaries, were able to overcome disadvantage and severe discrimination to gain an education and become leaders in their communities, but they internalised the attitudes that informed and perpetuated the structures of domination within which they were enmeshed. Young Ainu like Iboshi Hokutō, Chiri Yukie and Ega Torazō understood their desired goal – for all Ainu to become loyal subjects of the emperor – as being hindered by backward customs, a lack of education and the evils of alcohol. A number of self-help organisations were set up in Hokkaido, many with the support of missionaries or the social welfare sections of local government. The most important was the Ainu Kyōkai, founded in 1930, which provided a forum for all Hokkaido Ainu to come together.

Japanese bureaucrats enthusiastically promoted biological assimilation through intermarriage. Ainu blood, they argued, would mingle with that of the *Yamato* race, and this process of 'fusion' represented 'progress' for the Ainu. In this instance, eugenics was used as an argument not to prevent the birth of 'hybrids' but to promote it; 'based on the principles of eugenics, mixed-blood children take after the superior race and are born almost as Japanese' (Kita 1933: 27; Siddle 1996: 94–7). In reality, attempts to encourage intermarriage were doomed from the start because of strong prejudicial attitudes held by most Japanese, who continued to view all Ainu as innately inferior. Those Ainu women who did further the agenda and marry Japanese men were often physically and mentally abused. Kyōko Sugimura, married at 17 to a Japanese man eight years older, became suicidal due to frequent beatings and taunts; pointing to his arm, her husband would say 'this is human skin – your hairy skin is that of a beast' (Takahashi 1981: 39).

After defeat in 1945, Japan was occupied by American forces under General Douglas MacArthur. A new American-authored constitution was drafted in 1946 and came into force the following year. For the first time, Japanese were granted a range of guaranteed political, civil and social rights and freedoms. The year 1952 saw the end of the Occupation and the beginning of Japan's spectacular economic growth. For the Ainu, though, little changed. Most remained severely disadvantaged in the face of continuing discrimination. From the 1960s the state redefined the Ainu problem as one of economic deprivation on the margins of society, and it instituted some small-scale welfare policies. Assimilation was still regarded as the only solution. As in the pre-war period, essentialised notions of inferior Ainu 'blood' served to deny Ainu individuals the opportunities afforded to ordinary Japanese in the period of high economic growth. Individual Ainu within their local communities could not escape their categorisation by Japanese neighbours – 'however mixed you are, if you have even only a little Ainu blood you are Ainu' was how one described it (Gonai and Wakabayashi 1972: 201) – and therefore the consequences of that categorisation in terms of severe discrimination at school, in marriage and in the workplace. Such prejudice was localised and varied in intensity between communities (Siddle 1995: 73) but was a reality for most Ainu. On the other hand, the emerging myth of monoethnic Japan denied any recognition of, let alone respect for, a group identity that could form a basis for political action or feelings of self-worth. Moving away from Hokkaido so that one could 'pass' in the anonymity of the working-class ghettos of Japan's large cities was the only alternative for many.

Ironically, one of the few ways to make ends meet for those Ainu who remained in Hokkaido was to peddle sad and tacky parodies of 'Ainu culture' as exotic tidbits for a new generation of mainland Japanese tourists. Tourism aroused complex emotions among Ainu, many seeing it as degrading or as encouraging the reproduction of prejudice. The production of tourist art had, in fact, been going on for a long time. Even during the days of the *basho* some Ainu had carved articles for sale, and the carving of bears had been encouraged as a self-help exercise in communities like Chikabumi in the pre-war period (Debreuil 1999). Nevertheless, such 'relic[s] of a not quite dead culture' (*Economist* 1978: 69) did little to counter the rising swell of Nihonjinron narratives of ethnic homogeneity that conveniently elided the recent memories of Japan's failed multiethnic empire.

ETHNIC MOBILISATION, IDENTITY POLITICS AND INDIGENOUS RIGHTS

The situation began to change from the late 1960s, when a wave of radical citizen protest in Japanese society inspired young Ainu and inaugurated a new Ainu politics (see Siddle 1996: 147–89). A number of activist groups inspired both by domestic radicalism and militant indigenous groups overseas, such as the American Indian Movement that was involved in the 1972 siege of Wounded Knee, emerged to confront the agents of discrimination, organising effective campaigns against scholars and tourist operators. They also challenged the co-opted position and conservative leadership of the official Ainu organisation, the Utari Kyōkai (Utari is an Ainu word for themselves that is seen as lacking the negative connotations attached to the term Ainu). The Utari Kyōkai traces its lineage back to the Ainu Kyōkai and self-help movement of the 1930s, and for most of the post-war period it provided the interface between Ainu and the state by administering funds earmarked for Ainu welfare policies.

The increasing salience of the *Ainu mondai* (Ainu problem) in the early 1970s, aided by acts of urban terrorism carried out by Japanese radicals in the name of Ainu liberation (no Ainu were actually involved), initiated a response from the state in the form of a specific welfare policy for Ainu communities, modeled after the Dōwa Special Measures Law, and known as the Utari Taisaku (Utari Countermeasures). Implemented from 1974, this is administered through the Utari Kyōkai and is reviewed every seven years.

But the new Ainu politics was about much more than welfare. Ainu activists explicitly rejected the state's rhetoric and policy of assimilation, although this had been accepted by earlier generations of Ainu leaders. While on the one hand, the political struggle focused on confronting prejudice and increasing access to the wealth and resources of Japanese society, on the other hand, it was (and continues to be) a struggle over identity. In a reversal of the flight of Ainu youth from Ainu identity, young men and women actively sought out their roots, interviewing elders, reviving crafts and rituals and constructing new ceremonies to celebrate the heroes of a new Ainu history that challenged the comfortable master narrative of Hokkaido 'development'. Ainu were challenging the dominant notion of an inferior 'dying race' and attempting to create a contemporary Ainu cultural identity.

This effort contributed towards a 'cultural revival' among the Ainu. The notion of a 'revival' is perhaps misleading because of its implication of an unbroken continuity, however tenuous, between pre-modern Ainu culture and the present. This continuity is not the case. Ainu communities have been fundamentally transformed by their incorporation into the market economy. Ainu are as far removed from the 'traditional' way of life, the social world of the *kotan* (village community), as their Japanese neighbours are from the idealised castle towns of the *jidaigeki* samurai drama on popular TV. 'Ainu culture' is a modern abstraction. This is not to say, though, that it is somehow 'false'. Ethnic and nationalist politics in contemporary states involves the reification of everyday (or past) social practices as 'culture' and the selective use of certain cultural elements as symbolic boundary markers (Eriksen 1993: 101–4). Ainu are merely pursuing the same strategies as did Meiji Japanese nation builders, although in a perhaps more visible way (Siddle 2006). Not anything goes, of course, and the acceptance of these cultural markers depends on their ability to resonate with the imagined past. In the early days of cultural revival, a few Ainu elders criticised some of the recreated rituals and ceremonies of the Ainu movement as inauthentic (Siddle 1996: 174). But other Ainu accepted them, and the cultural markers of Ainu identity today include language, dance, ritual and oral literature alongside aspects of material culture such as clothing and handicrafts. Ainu cultural identity can thus be symbolically 'performed' at both formal occasions such as political rallies or festivals and at informal parties or family gatherings. Alternatively, it can be presented in commodified form to tourists.

This reaffirmation of 'Ainuness' did not just fulfil individual psycho-logical needs (though that is clearly important – see, for instance, Tsuda 1999), but was overtly politicised in that specific rights were now demanded on the basis of this separate cultural identity as a 'people' (*minzoku*) – or, more specifically, as an *indigenous* people (*senjū minzoku*). This specific form of identity – indigenous people – owes less to anthropology than to international law and human rights movements. International law has developed a body of instruments to protect the rights of minorities. Indigenous leaders have argued that these do not adequately reflect the special circumstances and needs of aboriginal peoples who have been marginalised within their own homelands by colonial invasion. Borrowing from the successful Third World nationalist liberation struggles, they see aboriginal peoples as 'first nations' who have yet to be decolonised. The resulting movement within the United Nations has pushed forward the concept of a special category of 'indigenous rights' enshrined in a draft Declaration on the Rights of Indigenous Peoples. Alongside sections that protect the cultural identity and practices of indigenous peoples are more fundamental, and controversial, rights of political empowerment in the form of self-determination.

During the late 1980s and early 1990s, most Ainu appeared united with the Utari Kyōkai in pressing for the implementation of the so-called 'Ainu New Law' (*Ainu Shinpō*), a draft law adopted by the Utari Kyōkai in 1984 that became the agenda for Ainu demands against the state. This draft enshrined key rights and guarantees to enable Ainu to gain full citizenship, including guaranteed political participation, economic benefits in the form of a 'self-reliance fund' based on the principle of compensation for historical dispossession and to be administered by Ainu themselves, and the rights to cultural identity, in particular the use and revitalisation of the Ainu language. Since 1987, when Ainu began to participate in the United Nations Working Group on Indigenous Populations in Geneva, these rights have been increasingly understood and presented within the context of the ongoing attempt to define and establish 'indigenous rights' in international law.

The Japanese state has only given ground reluctantly. Indeed, it only officially recognised the existence of the Ainu as an 'ethnic minority' (*shōsū minzoku*) in 1991, in its third periodic report to the United Nations on the implementation of the International Covenant on Civil and Political Rights (ratified by Japan in 1979). In its first report, in 1980, the government stated flatly that minorities as defined under Article 27 of the Covenant 'did not exist in Japan' (Utari Kyōkai 2001: 284). But while recognition of the Ainu as an ethnic minority represented progress, it would still take until 2008 before the Japanese government finally felt ready to acknowledge that the Ainu are also an 'indigenous people' (*senjū minzoku*). One possible reason for this involves Japan's long-running territorial dispute with Russia over the sovereignty of the Northern Territories (four islands in the Kurile chain invaded by Russia in 1945 that have long been a focus for Japanese nationalism), a legacy of Japan's colonisation of the north. Anything that could weaken Japan's claim to the islands, such as even the recognition that the Ainu are in fact the indigenous people of this area, is one presumed reason for Japan's strong opposition to the very concepts of indigenous rights, though this has never been officially acknowledged (Dietz 1999: 364).

1997 – Nibutani Dam and the Cultural Promotion Act

The year 1997 was pivotal for Ainu politics. In a landmark decision by the Sapporo District Court on 27 March 1997, the Japanese judiciary recognised that not only does the legal category of indigenous peoples exist, but that the Ainu fit that definition. This decision marked the end of a case brought by two Ainu activists from the village of Nibutani, Kayano Shigeru and Kaizawa Tadashi, against the Hokkaido Development Agency, in which they argued that the forcible appropriation of their land (including sacred sites) to construct a dam was illegal. After a lengthy series of hearings in which the historical narrative of Ainu dispossession played a central role, the court agreed. In finding in favour of the Ainu plaintiffs, the 'Nibutani Dam' ruling clearly recognised the rights of minority group members to enjoy their culture, and argued that the situation of indigenous minorities was distinctive and 'requires greater consideration' (Levin 2001: 488).

The ruling was clearly a landmark in terms of the Ainu struggle. It simultaneously overturned the master narrative of monoethnicity, recognised the Ainu as an indigenous people and demanded that the state recognise and respect minority cultures (for a detailed analysis see Levin 2001; Stevens 2001). Nevertheless, it was only a partial victory. While accepting that the Ainu are an indigenous people, the court acknowledged the indigenous people's movement primarily in terms of respect for cultural identity and practices, without going so far as to endorse rights to self-determination in political matters, land, resources and so forth. And though the court recognised the Ainu as an 'indigenous people', this definition is still not accepted by the state in other contexts.

What contributed to the impact of the Nibutani Dam ruling was that it came at a crucial stage of the Government's drafting of new legislation for the Ainu. A favourable environment for consideration of Ainu demands had finally emerged following the political realignment of 1993–4 that saw the Liberal Democratic Party (LDP) removed from power and replaced by a short-lived administration under Socialist Prime Minister Murayama Tomiichi, and the presence for the first time of a prominent Ainu, Kayano Shigeru, as a member of Japan's House of Councillors. Encouraged by their success in Nibutani, the Utari Kyōkai assented to the drafts presented to them by the Government, and on 1 July 1997 the Ainu Cultural Promotion Act (CPA) became law.

This 'Ainu New Law', however, bears little resemblance to that which Ainu activists had been campaigning for since 1984. The short-term effects of this legislation on the Ainu movement have been widely seen as ambivalent or negative (for an extended discussion see Stevens 2001; Siddle 2002; Ogasawara 2002). While the aim of 'promoting' and protecting Ainu culture in a multicultural Japan appears laudable, what it means is that the state now approves of Ainu culture as a commodity to be enjoyed by all Japanese, but is not prepared to grant the Ainu any specific or meaningful rights to overcome the legacies of their material and ideological marginalisation. In reality, it disguises some disturbing implications for Ainu identity and citizenship. The state has arrogated to itself the power to define what comprises 'authentic' Ainu culture, while at the same time reifying it in a 'traditional' form. By tying Ainu identity specifically to this fossilised notion of traditional culture ('real' Ainu are only those who can speak Ainu and carve, dance or weave) and regarding it as threatened, the state has left ordinary Ainu struggling to square this imposed 'authenticity' with the lived reality of their everyday lives. The agencies and programmes established under the CPA for cultural promotion have been very effective at co-opting the Ainu leadership. By focusing on 'culture', the state has attempted to depoliticise the 'Ainu problem' and disconnect it from the international struggle for indigenous rights. On the domestic front, it is now a matter of state-sponsored culture and education, backed up by welfare programmes for a disadvantaged social group. But the government can also present itself at the UN and elsewhere as proactive and progressive in its Ainu policy.

The introduction of the CPA means that indigenous rights are effectively off the agenda. This was made explicit in the consultation process that preceded the CPA (a process, incidentally, from which the Ainu were almost completely excluded), when indigenous rights were categorically rejected as a conceptual basis for the legislation. In the words of the official report of the ad hoc Council of Experts in April 1996, 'the issue of the right to self-determination ... cannot be made the basis for the development of a new policy for the Ainu people' (Utari Kyōkai 2001: 243). Officials quashed all attempts to definitively categorise the Ainu as an indigenous people. The state conceded only what it was prepared to give. Ainu participation in the drafting of the CPA was minimal. For its critics, rather than reflecting a genuine new relationship between the Ainu and the state, the CPA shows instead that the paternalistic control and management of the Ainu people remains a basic premise of Ainu policy in a way little changed since the Meiji period. The 1899 Protection Act is no more, and the rhetoric may indeed have changed from social-Darwinist arguments for the protection of a 'dying race' to an official respect for Ainu culture and multiculturalism, but the structures of oppression and their agents – officials and scholars – remain the same.

On the other hand, an alternative reading of the CPA is that it is not a sinister device to disable the Ainu movement (Tsunemoto 1999; Stevens 2001). Supporters argue that this is a necessary first stage towards establishing a new relationship that can go forward to achieve the Utari Kyōkai's stated aim of 'coexistence' (*kyōsei*). The formal acquisition of cultural rights is an important first step to the full practice of the political, civil and social rights guaranteed under the 1946 constitution. It was in such a spirit that the CPA was widely greeted in the press as 'epoch-making' (*kakkiteki*) legislation in 1997. These supporters of the process also point to the Japanese government's vote in favour of the UN Draft Declaration of the Rigths of Indigenous Peoples in September 2007, and its even more recent (June 2008) official recognition of the Ainu as an indigenous people in the run-up to the 2008 G8 Summit in Hokkaido, as major steps forward and a vindication of this gradualist approach. It is still too early to tell, however, if this belated recognition is anything more than a symbolic gesture given the extreme caution that Japanese representatives still display towards the whole issue of indigenous rights at the UN.

Ainu in the twenty-first century

Being Ainu in twenty-first-century Japan can mean different things. There are still many individuals ascribed an Ainu identity on the basis of descent who prefer to hide or deny it wherever possible, and others who use an Ainu identity instrumentally to gain welfare benefits or work in the tourist trade. Then there are others who positively identify themselves as Ainu. But as more and more Ainu marry Wajin, increased social mobility alters the demographics of Ainu communities, and discrimination becomes less overt, motivating the young to maintain an Ainu identity has become an urgent issue. As a result of these factors, the size of the Ainu nation is not clear. The official population figure for Hokkaido was given as 23,767 in 1999 (Hokkaido Kankyō Seikatsu Bu 2000: 3), but since the Japanese census provides no options to positively proclaim an Ainu ethnic identity, it is not possible to be definitive.

Ainu politics has lost momentum since the enactment of the CPA. Tensions between radical Ainu and the Utari Kyōkai have resurfaced. Many of the Utari Kyōkai leaders are wealthy Ainu who have made good in Japanese society and are incorporated into local networks of political patronage. The Association management also includes staff seconded from the Hokkaido Government. While in international forums such the United Nations Working Group on Indigenous Populations they call for the full implementation of a radical agenda of indigenous rights, at home they pursue more traditional patterns of Japanese interest-group politics. The much smaller number of radical activists, even though most are also members of the Utari Kyōkai, espouse their alternative agendas within a number of fragmented groups, often with overlapping membership, but with little real power inside Japan. Examples include the Ainu Kaihō Dōmei (Ainu Liberation League), which grew out of the New Left movement of the 1970s and has participated in campaigns of direct action against scholars, and the Ainu Moshiri no Jijiku o Torimodosu Kai (Association to Restore the Autonomous Ainu Homeland), which demands the return of the disputed Northern Territories as a homeland for the Ainu, the indigenous people of the islands. Court actions have been brought since 1997 against both the state and scholars in attempts to regain some momentum and recreate the success of the Nibutani Dam case, but without significant success (Siddle 2002: 416–20). Some activists are becoming more involved in the global indigenous movement and the study of international law, presenting an alternative Ainu voice at the UN and indigenous gatherings (Dietz 1999: 364). For the majority Japanese population, indifference and a lack of knowledge remain the norm. A 2003 government survey (Naikaku Fu Daijin Kanbō Seifu Kōhō Shitsu 2003: 62–7) reported that two-thirds of the Japanese public had no knowledge of human rights issues concerning the Ainu, and of the 34 per cent who did, the Ainu problem was understood primarily in terms of the government agenda of cultural preservation (48.1 per cent) and the need for a policy of cultural promotion (72.7 per cent).

Serious issues remain, while new challenges have surfaced. Ainu remain disadvantaged; they fared worse than most in the recession of 1990s, with 31 per cent describing severe hardship in 1999, double the proportion of a 1993 survey, while another 49.6 per cent reported some economic difficulties (Hokkaidō Kankyō Seikatsu Bu 2000: 29). Tourism continues to play an ambiguous role, both creative and destructive of Ainu culture and with the potential to empower individuals while simultaneously denying them a contemporary modern identity (Debreuil 1999; Hiwasaki 2000). In a similar fashion, despite its drawbacks the CPA has stimulated cultural production. Independent groups of younger Ainu are actively pursuing cultural projects, both traditional and contemporary, and interacting ever more widely with other indigenous peoples (Dietz 1999: 364–5). The Ainu language refuses to die (see Maher 2001). But the new century has also seen the passing of many of the Ainu elders, male and female, who provided the last direct link to a time when the Ainu language and culture were an everyday lived experience, and who provided a repository of knowledge for younger activists to draw upon. The death in May 2006 of Kayano Shigeru – leading authority on Ainu culture and language, national politician, Nibutani Dam activist and the most prominent Ainu of his generation – perhaps marks the end of an era.

Author's note: This chapter updates the version in the first edition (Siddle 1997) and incorporates further material that originally appeared in Citizenship Studies *(Siddle 2003). I am grateful for permission to reproduce it here. Since the first edition in 1997, there has been an increase in English-language scholarship on the Ainu, including some important work on early modern Hokkaido (Walker 2001; Howell 2005) and a major volume from the Smithsonian (Fitzhugh and Debreuil 1999). Accordingly, wherever possible I have referred the reader to these in preference to less accessible Japanese language sources.*

References

Befu, H. (2001) *Hegemony and Homogeneity: An anthropological analysis of Nihonjinron*, Melbourne: Trans Pacific Press.
Debreuil, C. (1999) 'Ainu Journey: From tourist art to fine arts', in W. Fitzhugh

38   R.M. Siddle

and C. Debreuil (eds), *Ainu: spirit of a northern people*, Washington: Smithsonian.
Dietz, K.L. (1999) 'Ainu in the International Arena', in W. Fitzhugh and C. Debreuil (eds), *Ainu: spirit of a northern people*, Washington: Smithsonian.
Economist (1978) 'The Smooth Men and the Hairy', September 30, 1978, p. 69.
Eriksen, T.H. (1993) *Ethnicity and Nationalism: Anthropological perspectives*. London: Pluto Press.
Fitzhugh, W. and C. Debreuil (1999) *Ainu: spirit of a northern people*, Washington: Smithsonian.
Gonai, M. and M. Wakabayshi (1972) *Ashita ni Mukatte: Ainu no hitobito wa uttaeru* (Facing Tomorrow: An Ainu appeal), Tokyo: Maki Shoten.
Hiraoka, S. (1918) 'Ainu Jinshu Shobun Ron' (On the Disposal of the Ainu Race), appendix in T. Aoyama, *Kyokuhoku no Bettenchi* (The Different World of the Extreme North), Tokyo: Nippon Seinen Tsushinsha.
Hiwasaki, L. (2000) 'Ethnic Tourism in Hokkaido and the Shaping of Ainu Identity', *Pacific Affairs* 73(3): 393–413.
Hokkaidō Kankyō Seikatsu Bu (2000) *Heisei 11-nen Hokkaidō Utari Seikatsu Jittai Chōsa Hōkokusho* (Report on the 1999 Survey into Ainu Living Standards), Sapporo: Hokkaidō.
Howell, D. (1995) *Capitalism from Within: Economy, society and the state in a Japanese fishery*, Berkeley, Los Angeles and London: University of California Press.
—— (2005) *Geographies of Identity in Nineteenth-Century Japan*. Berkeley, Los Angeles and London: University of California Press.
Kita, K. (1933) 'Dojin Hogo no Enkaku to Hogohō no Seishin' (A History of Native Welfare and the Spirit of the Protection Act), *Hokkaidō Shakai Jigyō* 15: 21–9.
Levin, M. (2001) 'Essential Commodities and Racial Justice: Using constitutional protection of Japan's indigenous Ainu people to inform understandings of the United States and Japan', *New York University Journal of International Law and Politics* 33(2): 419–526.
Maher, J. (2001) '*Akor Itak* – Our Language, Your Language: Ainu in Japan', in J.A. Fishman (ed.), *Can Threatened Languages be Saved? Reversing Language Shift Revisited: A 21st century perspective*, Clevedon: Multilingual Matters.
Munro, N.G. (1963) *Ainu Creed and Cult*, London: Routledge and Kegan Paul.
Ogasawara, N. (2002) 'Ainu Bunka hō Shikō kara go Nen' (Five Years Since the Enactment of the Ainu Culture Law), *Sekai* 707 (November), 284–91.
Naikaku Fu Daijin Kanbō Seifu Kōhō Shitsu (2003) *Gekkan Yoron Chōsa* (Public Opinion Monthly), 35(7) (July).
Siddle, R. (1995) 'The Ainu: Construction of an image', in J. Maher and G. Macdonald (eds), *Diversity in Japanese Culture and Language*, London and New York: Kegan Paul International.
—— (1996) *Race, Resistance and the Ainu of Japan*, London and New York: Routledge.
—— (1997) 'Ainu: Japan's indigenous people', in M. Weiner (ed.), *Japan's Minorities: The illusion of homogeneity*, London and New York: Routledge.
—— (2002) 'An Epoch-Making Event? The 1997 Ainu Cultural Promotion Act and its impact', *Japan Forum* 14(3): 405–23.
—— (2003) 'The Limits to Citizenship in Japan: Multiculturalism, indigenous rights and the Ainu', *Citizenship Studies* 7(4): 447–62.
—— (2006) 'The Making of Ainu Moshiri: Japan's indigenous nationalism and its

cultural fictions', in N. Shimazu (ed.), *Nationalism in Japan*, London and New York: Routledge.

Stevens, G. (2001) 'The Ainu and Human Rights: Domestic and international legal protections', *Japanese Studies* 21(2): 181–98.

Tabata, H. (1993) 'Some Historical Aspects of Ainu-Japanese Relations: Treachery, assimilation and the myth of Ainu counting', in N. Loos and T. Osanai (eds) *Indigenous Minorities and Education: Australian and Japanese perspectives of their indigenous peoples, the Ainu, Aborigines and Torres Straits Islanders*, Tokyo: Sanyūsha.

Takahashi, M. (1981) *Zoku Hokkaidō no Onnatachi: Utari hen* (Women of Hokkaido Continued: the Ainu), Sapporo: Hokkaidō Joseishi Kenkyūkai.

Tsuda, N. (1999) 'A Personal Rebirth through Ainu Traditional Basketry', in W. Fitzhugh and C. Debreuil (eds), *Ainu: spirit of a northern people*, Washington: Smithsonian.

Tsunemoto, T. (1999) 'The Ainu Shimpo: A new beginning', in W. Fitzhugh and C. Debreuil (eds), *Ainu: spirit of a northern people*, Washington: Smithsonian.

Utari Kyōkai (2001) *Kokusai Kaigi Shiryō-shū* (Materials from Overseas Conferences). Sapporo: Shadan Hōjin Hokkaido Utari Kyōkai.

Walker, B. (2001) *The Conquest of Ainu Lands: Ecology and culture in Japanese expansion*, Berkeley, Los Angeles and London: University of California Press.

Watanabe, H. (1973) *The Ainu Ecosystem*, Seattle and London: University of Washington Press.

Yamaura, K. and H. Ushiro (1999) 'Prehistoric Hokkaido and Ainu Origins', in W. Fitzhugh and C. Debreuil (eds), *Ainu: spirit of a northern people*, Washington: Smithsonian.

Yoshino, K. (1992) *Cultural Nationalism in Contemporary Japan: A sociological enquiry*, London and New York: Routledge.

3 'Mixed-blood' Japanese

A reconsideration of race and purity in Japan

Robert A. Fish

Studying the history of 'mixed-blood' Japanese in modern Japan in many ways resembles a surreal version of the 1970s television game show *To Tell the Truth*. In this game, three individuals would start the game by proclaiming 'I am X,' and then the two imposters would attempt to trick the celebrity judges into believing they were actually 'X.' In this slightly surreal version, the three contestants, each claiming to be a 'mixed-blood' Japanese, would stick to the following scripts, all delivered in fluent Japanese:

Contestant One: I grew up in Tochigi Prefecture, the daughter of a Caucasian-American mother and Japanese father, and I developed a close relationship with my paternal grandmother. At the age of 15, I received a scholarship to attend high school in the United States, and proceeded to spend the next ten years primarily there. Returning to Japan during my twenties to pursue my musical career, I have achieved recent success, including an appearance on Japan's traditional New Year's show, *Kohaku* (Red and White Song Battle), in which I sang my popular ballad as a tribute to my grandmother in rural Japan. Although I did struggle to learn English in my teenage years, Japanese is my language of choice.

Contestant Two: Raised primarily by my African-American father and first my birth mother then a second Japanese girlfriend of his until the age of 3, I was turned over to the Elizabeth Saunders Home, an orphanage primarily for 'mixed-blood' children, when my father returned home to the southwest of the United States. As an adult, I have lived a middle-class life as a small businessman, and I have two children. I have never left Japan and do not speak English. I had an opportunity to visit the United States in the mid-1960s. However, having read the newspapers at that time, I did not go – I was afraid of prejudice.

Contestant Three: I was abandoned in the bathroom of a Yokohama city bus station.

As intimated by the true examples above, 'mixed-blood' Japanese in modern Japan have had widely varying life experiences – ranging from lives in elite society, through enjoying and enduring the comforts and trials of middle-class life in the world of the salary man employed at one of Japan's mega corporations, to homelessness and poverty.[1] Despite the diverse reality of 'mixed-blood' Japanese, few labels of a group in Japan come so packed with tagged meanings for the English-speaking world. Immediately for most, including Japan specialists, such labels conjure up traditional images of an 'outsider' group in 'homogeneous Japan,' of the importance of pure-bloodedness in Japanese identity, and of a group being victimized by discrimination. As John Dower described the group born during the Occupation of Japan (1945–52), they 'became one of the sad, unspoken stories of the occupation – seldom acknowledged by their foreign fathers and invariably ostracized by the Japanese.'[2] This widely held image, however, does not arise from careful study of the history of this diverse group. Rather, as John Lie (accurately) bemoaned in reviewing the original edition of this book, 'mixed-blood' people have been a mostly 'neglected group' in the scholarly literature.[3] This chapter shall start to address this situation through providing a broad overview of the history of 'mixed-blood' people in Japan, with particular emphasis on their early post-war experience – a pivotal period in their history (and the dominant source of the image of 'mixed-blood' Japanese as a group chronically ostracized from Japanese society).

Careful study shows that this group has followed a different historical arc than most, if not all, of the other 'minority' groups addressed in this volume – in particular since this is the only group identified primarily based on phenotype. Three specific historical circumstances largely shaped the position of 'mixed-blood' Japanese in post-war Japan. The first of these circumstances is the position of Japan in relation to global intellectual currents during the Enlightenment – the period that provided the strongest basis for phenotype-based racism in the modern world.[4] The second circumstance is the legacy of the nature of, and intellectual justifications for, Japanese imperialism in the early twentieth century, which fundamentally influenced the position of 'minority' groups and the understanding of issues of inclusion and difference (as well as racism) in post-war Japan in a manner that differs in important ways from these issues in other portions of the globe. The final circumstance is that the issue of 'mixed-blood' Japanese was most widely discussed in the ten years immediately after the end of World War Two, and it is this discussion (as well as the 'mixed-blood' Japanese born during these years) that in many ways defines our understanding of 'mixed-blood' people in Japan. The economic position of Japan during this era, combined with dominant geopolitical ideas regarding the nature of human rights and equality at that time, fundamentally influenced the position of 'mixed-blood' Japanese in post-war Japan. This chapter shall focus most specifically on this early post-war group and the debate surrounding their position in Japanese society.

The term 'mixed-blood Japanese' has been used so broadly as to become meaningless without some commentary. At various times, the definition of this term has been based on the national origins of parents, at others times it has been based on phenotype, and at still others it has been based on some combination of the two. The dominant popular usage, however, has been to refer to people who appear to be the offspring of one parent of East Asian origin and one parent of non-East Asian origin. These people can be identified by some type of phenotypic marker, and they maintain permanent residence in Japan. Even using this definition, creating an appropriate label for this group, as psychologist Stephen Murphy-Shigematsu has argued, can be nearly impossible.[5] Terms ranging from 'international children', to the Japanese term *hāfu*, to 'multi-ethnic' Japanese have been used. However, the term 'mixed-blood,' although antiquated in Japan, is most widely used in scholarship and also provides a reminder of the importance of the idea of 'blood' in identifying this diverse group in Japan, so shall be used in this chapter.

BRIEF HISTORY OF 'MIXED-BLOOD' PEOPLE IN JAPAN

While 'mixed-blood' Japanese did not become a widely recognized group until after World War Two, they existed from the time the first European missionaries and traders arrived in Japan. Research regarding 'mixed-blood' people in Japan before the end of World War Two is extremely thin, but the little we know about this history sheds some light on the post-war history of this group and clarifies our understanding of the position of minorities in post-war Japan.

Gary Leupp, who studied the history of interracial intimacy during the late Sengoku (*c.* 1560–1600) and Tokugawa era (1600–1868), argues that

> [D]uring the *sakoku* period alone, the circumstances surrounding European men's relations with Japanese women and their children evolved significantly. In all, we can characterize the Japanese attitude towards such children as tolerant and compassionate. From the sixteenth through nineteenth centuries, western sources indicate that half-European children were fully accepted into Japanese society.[6]

As Leupp shows, the story is not a simple one of acceptance; at times around the 1630s, when there was a strong push by the Tokugawa *bakufu* to ban Christianity, there were even laws demanding the deportation or execution of all 'mixed-blood' children. Of more importance in our overall understanding of the position of minorities in Japanese society is that 'in general, during the Tokugawa period, Japanese did not divide the world into regions of "fair" and "dark" races, as Europeans did, but rather into "we Japanese" and "others."'[7]

In understanding the development of attitudes toward minority groups in Japan, three important points bear mentioning. The first point is that because of the limited contact Japan had with those of European or African descent, the numbers of 'mixed-blood' people in Japan during this era was of little consequence, and in most of Japan this group was non-existent. Second, possibly as a result of the small number of visual minorities in Japan during this era, no widely held belief system based on characterizing people by phenotypic differences developed. Finally, it is vital to note that during this era of relative isolation, the basic philosophy of Euro-American phenotype-based racism developed within the context of the Enlightenment and the first wave of overseas imperialism. Enlightenment thinkers attempted to classify all aspects of the world, both natural and social. A dominant aspect of this classification was the classification of humans based on phenotypic characteristics. The philosophical roots of much of Western skin-based racism, it has been argued, can be found in Enlightenment thinking.[8] The development and strengthening of skin-based racial hierarchies, with fairer-skinned people viewed as superior to darker-skinned people, coincides not just with the Enlightenment but also with the first and second waves of European (and later American) overseas imperialism, with race-based hierarchies serving as a philosophical justification of European colonial domination.

Japan was, at most, an observer in these two global developments. During the Enlightenment era, in which classifying human populations based on phenotype played an important role in the European intellectual world, such philosophies did not have a significant impact on the vibrant intellectual world of Tokugawa Japan. While European intellectual currents, including European theories of race, significantly influenced Japanese thinkers, especially after 1868, the manner in which they were integrated into Japanese intellectual life differed significantly from Europe in terms of their importance in ideas about Japanese self-identity and race.

Perhaps most importantly, in terms of international intellectual currents influencing Japanese ideas about 'race,' late nineteenth and early twentieth-century imperialism played a crucial role. It is during this period that the 'great race' to imperialize the non-European world occurred, further strengthening the role of racial hierarchies in American and European (as well as African) social constructs and philosophies. 'Racial science' and 'social Darwinism' became dominant justifications for the European domination of the world. Japan was neither immune nor oblivious to these intellectual currents. Further, especially after the Russo–Japanese War of 1905, Japan became one of the most important players in the imperial game.

While phenotype-based racism and racial classification were central to Euro-American imperialism, their role was far more oblique in the Japanese version. Rather, while national definitions of human classification played a central (albeit highly complex) role in Japanese imperialism, classifications based on the 'light/dark' dichotomy that were so important in the Euro-American intellectual and political ideology never became a defining influence on dominant self-constructions of Japanese national self-identity.

Further complicating the picture is the nature of the 'mixed-blood' population in Japan during the pre-war and wartime eras – a topic that has not been studied yet in any depth. This population was never statistically significant, nor was it large enough to draw any significant notice from the government or the popular press. The 'mixed-blood' population in Japan at this time was primarily composed of the offspring of socially well-regarded and financially well-off parents. These offspring included the children of missionaries, leading businessmen (both Japanese and foreign), teachers, and scholars. During this era, when Japanese people worried about the degradation of Japanese identity through 'blood impurities' or through other means they were preoccupied with arguments of eugenics, and they were far more likely to be concerned about the offspring of Japanese and Koreans than those of European, African, or Indian descent. In short, the 'mixed-blood' population, as it was to be understood in the post-war era, was of little or no significance in Japanese conceptions of self-identity, and likely of little consequence in terms of its size, during the Meiji, Taisho, and Showa eras through to the end of World War Two.

That insignificance changed, at least in perception, with the arrival of the Occupation forces in September 1945. The post-war era created three distinct changes in the nature of the 'mixed-blood' population. First, although never a statistically significant portion of the overall Japanese population, numbers grew, and, particularly in prefectures with large military bases such as Kanagawa, the population grew significantly in visibility. Second, and more importantly, many members of the Japanese public perceived that the population was much larger than it was in reality, with some estimating that the numbers were in the hundreds of thousands and growing. Third, in a distinct change from the pre-war era, a large proportion of the 'mixed-blood' population that remained in Japan was born to members of lower socioeconomic classes, and a large proportion lived in single-mother households.

As a result of these three factors, Japanese society reconsidered the position of 'mixed-blood' people in Japan in multiple ways in the first quarter century after the end of the War, with certain specific moments forcing the issue into the public domain. The discussion of 'mixed-blood' children was intense during the Occupation (1945–52) and the early 1950s. Discussion reached a particularly fevered pitch in 1952–3, when the first group of 'mixed-blood' children were preparing to enter elementary school, and, simultaneously, the legislature (and, to a lesser extent, the general public) were debating the proper way to aid the significant number of 'mixed-blood' children in need of social welfare services.

Contemporary viewpoints and opinions in the early 1950s about 'mixed-blood' children varied widely. However, most Japanese agreed that 'mixed-blood' children were in some way different – the question was, what were the implications of that difference for Japan and for the children themselves, and how did this type of phenotype-based difference build into larger Japanese historical concerns over identity and difference?

The emphasis on and perception of difference is not at all surprising. Historically, Japan had dealt with issues of diversity throughout its colonial period, but rarely involving people with such stark phenotypical difference. After all, when looking at a pre-war photograph, one would often be hard-pressed to pick out the Chinese or Korean living in Japan based on facial features alone, but most people could identify a 'mixed-blood' child with relative ease.

Nonetheless, Japan's legacy as a multiethnic empire helped shape post-war ideas about Japanese identity, influencing attitudes and actions towards the post-war 'mixed-blood' children. Oguma Eiji, who has perceptively analyzed the influence of pre-war racial ideologies on post-war conceptions of Japanese self-identity, argues that the image of Japan as a homogenous nation, defined as belief in the myth that 'the Japanese nation has consisted, and today still consists, of only the Japanese nation, which shares a single, pure origin, and a common culture and lineage,' was fairly widespread in early post-war Japan.[9] This myth, however, was often entwined in an anti-imperialist wrapping. As Oguma explains,

> a number of theorists emerged who argued for a peace-loving homogeneous state to replace the prewar militaristic multinational empire. The self-image of Japan as an island nation that contained no aliens, and was therefore peaceful and tranquil, proved to be very attractive to a people tired of war. In this discourse, the Emperor came to symbolize the unity of this peaceful island nation.[10]

This image of peaceful homogeneity creates a situation in which 'mixed blood' Japanese would be treated as outsiders, but that outsider position would not necessarily come prepackaged with hate, since it arose out of a self-identity couched in terms of peace. The important question was, to what extent would this identity of 'homogeneity' impact on the actual lives of 'mixed-blood' Japanese?

By 1953, the Japanese government had developed an official policy that vigorously promoted treating 'mixed-blood' children as Japanese, encouraging full integration into public schools, providing special measures to aid in potential problems in schools, and providing specific support to combat racism. However, as the ideals of a government policy and the messy reality of life differ, we can learn much about the history of this group through studying the debate leading up to adoption of this integration policy, as well as through examination of the lives of the 'mixed-blood' Japanese living within Japanese society.

While almost all in Japanese society viewed the 'mixed blood' children as in some way 'different,' as would be predicted by the acceptance of the myth of homogeneity, Japanese people responded to 'mixed-blood' Japanese in diverse ways. One response was to fear the effects of the 'mixed-blood' population on the Japanese race, often leading to anger towards and rejection of the children and their guardians. A second broad reaction was one of sympathy for the children, and advocacy of some type of response to their situation in order to help them succeed, while still maintaining an emphasis on their 'difference.' A third response, and the one ultimately legislated, was to implicitly acknowledge their physical difference, but to attempt to ignore it and emphasize their 'Japaneseness.'

Within the Diet, debate about 'mixed-blood' children began in 1946, and reached its peak in 1952–53, when the policy about schooling of 'mixed-blood' children was decided. These legislative debates encompassed all three of the attitudes outlined above. Racist (particularly anti-black) arguments entered the debate in the Diet. In the most negative statement about 'mixed-blood' children mentioned on the floor of the Diet, Koyama Shinjirō, the head of the General Affairs Section of the Ministry of Welfare, wondered 'what kind of influence will the recent mixed-blood, especially black mixed-blood issue, which, in reality, the Japanese people have not experienced in such large quantity from the very beginning, have on the intrinsic nature of the Japanese people?'[11]

The fears about the effect of 'mixed-blood' children on Japanese ethnicity spread beyond the halls of the Diet. A third-year junior high school student in Aomori Prefecture (which had cited inaccurate statistics that over 100,000 'mixed-blood' children were in Japan) wrote, 'If things continue as they are, I am worried that won't the number of mixed-blood children in Japan increase a lot? Won't the current Japanese ethnicity end up becoming a crossbreed (mixed-blood child) of Americans and Japanese through the soldiers and prostitutes?'[12] From the halls of power to the halls of junior high schools in rural northeastern Japan, a stream of racist thought concerned about the weakening of the 'Japanese race/ethnicity' reared its head.

Although the perception exists that these ideas were endemic to Japanese society at the time and shaped the lives of 'mixed-blood' people, such openly racist sentiments towards 'mixed-blood' children represented a minority viewpoint in Japan. Within Japan, this perception can be closely traced to presentations of the 'mixed-blood' issue in popular culture, especially film, and, to a lesser extent, in popular memoirs and newspapers.[13] However, many questioned the relationship between these images and reality. As the mother of one 'mixed-blood' child in Yokohama noted, 'In terms of mixed-blood children, it seems that journalism about them adopted a great deal of nervousness, but, in my case, I think that it seems like there have not been any problems.'[14] Dr Takaki Shirō, head of the Child Mental Health Department of the National Mental Health Research Center, even went so far as to argue that the attention given to the issue made things worse. He lamented, 'I dislike it that too much has been made of the mixed-blood children problem since the end of the war. Isn't it the case that through this attention the feeling has been created that the pure Japanese race has been defiled? The fact that the count of mixed-blood children has been exaggerated may also have helped [create this feeling].'[15]

The most common sentiment expressed by those in power was not negative towards 'mixed-blood' children *per se*, but there were serious concerns expressed about their ability to function in Japanese society. Linking his concerns to his belief in the myth of the pure-blooded Japanese, Diet Member Tanaka Hisao explained: 'don't we run the risk that mixed blood children coming to a people with one pure blood, unlike the environment of America, will be looked at as a special human tragedy?'[16] In different incarnations, variations of the theme that the 'mixed-blood' children faced serious challenges were expressed by virtually all members of society whose opinion has been recorded. In the Diet, Representative Suida explained his concerns for the children's futures: 'I think that the love children made with the black men, especially when thinking about the unhappy future eyes that will be cast upon them, look the most pitiful since they will face the most persecution.'[17]

This idea that the children did not bear responsibility for their position, and therefore deserved support, acceptance, and often sympathy, pervaded both the Diet and the general public. Within the broader society, children living near military bases, when writing about 'mixed-blood' children, repeatedly emphasized the idea of these children as a group to be pitied. This attitude is exemplified by the example of Matsuda Kimiko, an elementary school fifth-year student in Tottori Prefecture, who expressed the idea poetically:

> In the neighborhood by my home a *pan pan*
> gave birth to the child of a soldier
> The child had gotten much bigger
> and when s/he sees anyone
> says granny.
> Its face looks like a soldiers
> and it has a cute face
> however, when the child gets bigger
> if it knows it is the child of a prostitute
> how will it feel?
> When I think of that time
> doesn't that child become an object of pity?[18]

Note that the poem expresses that the child will be an object of pity not because he or she is 'mixed-blood,' but because of his or her feeling when understanding that he or she is the child of a prostitute.

Two children living in Shizuoka and Kure (geographically distinct regions) use strikingly similar language to discuss the plight of the 'mixed-blood' children. Hayashi Michiko, a second-year junior high school student in Shizuoka, wrote, 'The poor children, and they bear none of the blame themselves.' Yamashiro Midori, a third-year junior high school student in Kure, explains that she 'must extend a warm and loving hand to the mixed-blood children ... because these children didn't do anything bad themselves, but their mothers and fathers bear responsibility.'[19]

In short, whether viewed at the heights of political power or through the voices of children, while Japanese society on the whole may have held the parents in contempt, little anger or hatred was directed towards the offspring. Rather, the dominant view was one of either pity or the opinion that 'mixed-blood' children were 'cute.'

Despite the wide agreement that the 'mixed-blood' children were to be pitied, there was disagreement as to the best policies for the government to pursue in relation to these children and as to the proper place for this group within the broader Japanese society. A consensus existed in the Diet and, to the extent consensus is possible, in the broader public that many of the children would need support beyond what their guardians could provide them, and that support should be forthcoming. They disagreed over how it should be provided.

Based partially on the idea that, as one legislator expressed through alluding to Madame Butterfly, the 'Pinkertons were more to blame than the Madame Butterflies,' one group argued that the United States should provide support for the children. However, even within this group, members disagreed over what that support should look like. Ideas ranged from payments from the United States government, through private child support from the fathers, to sending as many abandoned children as possible to be adopted by Americans. (A number of people argued that sending the children to America, particularly the 'half-black' children, would be a bad idea due to American racism.) Representative Yamashita, distinguishing between personal and governmental responsibility, sums up the complexities of the situation:

> [I]n terms of the national responsibility for the child itself, I feel that wouldn't the strongest aid be within the framework of Japan's juvenile social welfare system ... If we look into the national responsibility for these children, I feel that maybe we have to take responsibility for the mixed-blood children made by Japanese people left behind in Indonesia, etc. I feel that there are no Japanese people qualified to say anything [complain] to America about the mixed-blood children left in Japan.[20]

Japan faced several practical and philosophical challenges in seeking aid from the United States. On the philosophical level, while logically the fathers of many of the abandoned children could be assumed to be American, it was possible that they were Australian, British, Russian, etc. Further, as Yamashita points out, Japan would face a certain amount of hypocrisy in demanding child-support payments from the American government for 'mixed-blood' children fathered by overseas servicemen. After all, there were clearly many children fathered by Japanese servicemen throughout the former Japanese Empire, and Japan as a nation had no intention of providing any type of systematic aid for their support. On a practical level, Japan was in a relatively weak position to make demands upon the United States. While Japan had a strategic advantage because the United States wanted it to be a loyal ally in the Cold War, and proved willing to make a number of important concessions in order to secure its support, Japan could only play this hand so many times, and did not want to waste it on the relatively small problem (at least from a macroeconomic perspective) of government-financed child support for children abandoned by American servicemen. Yamashita's advocacy for seeking child support directly from the fathers was reflected in the eventual official policy of seeking out the fathers of the children.[21] As a practical matter, no effective action occurred on the governmental level to determine or secure child support payments from foreign fathers.

While legislative debates and written words can indicate the mood of the country, they do not give much insight into the actual situation of the children. Ultimately, the children as a group did not fare as well in school as would be predicted by chance. However, the problem was not so much one of racism as one of inadequate social welfare – a problem that can at least partially be tied to the delay of the discussion of the welfare of 'mixed-blood' children until after the end of the Allied Occupation of Japan. Just looking at a few representative life histories of 'mixed-blood' children before the age of five shows that many were clearly facing many challenges and handicaps not directly related to race by the eve of school entrance, and that these issues would prove difficult, if not impossible, to overcome.

Many children faced difficult circumstances. By spring of 1954, the guardians of 42 per cent of 'mixed-blood' children (1,484 guardians) were on welfare, and the ministry predicted that approximately 20 per cent more would need government support in the ensuing years.[22] Although the majority were not on welfare, the financial and family situations often created trying circumstances in which to raise children. As the Ministry of Education noted in 1955, 'Even though we can now say that they are not in particular [financial] trouble, there are many examples of mothers who must work in bars or continue living with a foreigner.' They further explain that

> [T]heir home life is quite complicated, and, even though there is much enthusiasm, many details are not taken care of, and problems like tardiness [to school] start to appear ... In any event, there are many examples in which an improvement of the home environment is necessary, and this point will become a big problem in the future.[23]

At first glance, these remarks, particularly about the women working in bars, might get dismissed as classist, sexist, or jingoistic comments of bourgeois bureaucrats. However, when the life stories on which these generalizations are based are given flesh and bones, it quickly becomes apparent that we are not looking at classism or sexism, but rather at a realistic assessment of the practical difficulties facing many of the guardians in raising their children. The Ministry of Education collected and published unedited accounts written by school teachers about 'mixed-blood' children in their first few years of school. Most of these included life histories. As will be shown in representative examples below, many were in dire situations by the time they began school.

As an example of a complication, one teacher described the third move of the school year for one 'mixed-blood' student. 'This time they were living in a separate apartment by themselves, and I would like to say it was the first home for the mother and child, but it was a room remodeled especially for a *pan pan* [prostitute who catered to the foreign soldiers].'[24] The teacher went on to explain that 'N and her school friends are not aware [of her mother's job as a prostitute]. However, in the near future as the children grow, won't they understand her mother's lifestyle? That time, and how to guide her at that time, is a problem still lingering in the future.'[25] This anecdote illustrates what the Ministry of Social Welfare meant when discussing complicated home situations. Based on government statistics, this family was neither in classifiable financial difficulty nor on welfare. In fact, without further details, it would appear that the family was moving in a positive direction. After all, the mother and child, who had always rented rooms, finally had their own apartment. From a statistical perspective, there did not seem to be a problem. However, this situation in which the mother had to prostitute herself inside the home to support N was a less than ideal environment for the child.

In a different example, one that was not all that unusual, the teacher described the child living in a small house with eight people: a great-grandmother, grandparents, an aunt (aged 15), two younger siblings (aged 3 and 5), his mother, and a stepfather. 'He calls the grandparents in the family register [the birth grandparents] daddy and mommy, and calls his birth mother older sister. He calls his birth mother's husband "Fish shop daddy" [because he owned a fish store], and it is interesting the way in which he distinguished between the two fathers.' The teacher had further explained that after the age of one, the grandmother took responsibility for the child, but the great-grandmother did most of the supervision. [26] As a reality, 'with these complications income is small, there is a lack of understanding about education, and he is just left on his own most of the time, to the extent that I think it will become trouble.'[27]

While details varied from household to household, certain scenarios, as represented by the above examples, appear with regularity. One scenario involved the mother, abandoned by the father, having to work long hours, often at night, as a bar hostess or prostitute. Because of financial difficulties, providing adequate supervision for the children while working often proved difficult or impossible. For those working as prostitutes, the additional moral approbation and complications from their jobs, including children's embarrassment over their mother's source of income, created further difficulty for the children. A second scenario involved the grandparents/grandmother acting as surrogate mother. In some instances, this proved an adequate solution. In others, for reasons of finances (the need of all household members to work full time), the ability to provide adequate care for the child was somewhat compromised. Finally, a number of mothers lived together with a series of men, often foreign soldiers, who provided their primary means of financial support. While in some cases things worked out fine, it appears that in many others, the relative instability of a constantly changing 'father' created problems by the time of school entrance. Before accounting for societal attitudes and challenges, many of the children already faced serious obstacles to school success due to difficult home situations.

The Ministry of Education, aware of this problem and fearful of societal bias against 'mixed-blood' children, had to decide on how to educate them when the first large group entered school in April 1953. When Kanagawa Prefecture announced its policy towards 'mixed-blood' children entering regular public schools in November 1952, it was '[t]he main current of thought in the Prefectural Board of Education' that, in the words of one official,

> even if during Elementary and Junior High School the children are separated from the regular schools and educated in a warm atmosphere, when they enter society they will be treated equally so they should go as soon as possible together to regular schools.

Because Kanagawa had the largest number of 'mixed-blood' children, it was anticipated that the ideas of the Prefecture and its policy of admission of the children to regular school would be followed closely by the Japanese Ministry of Education. On November 26 (thirteen days later), the Ministry of Education issued a policy similar to the one of the Kanagawa Prefectural Board of Education, explaining that 'More than being called mixed-blood children, these children hold Japanese citizenship. In thinking about the children's future, we desire that they attend public elementary schools along with majority children."[28] Tanaka, the head of the elementary and junior high school division of the Ministry of Education, explained the policy, in tentative terms, on the floor of the Diet.

> As the head of the elementary and middle school division of the Ministry of Education, in terms of the educational problems, in any event to the extent possible naturally we must educate them without prejudice and with love and understanding … it is the main thought for the most part that, for now, to the extent possible they should be educated the same as usual children in public schools.[29]

This idea of integration is consistent with the former policies of the Japanese government and Allied Occupation Government (which no longer existed). This policy is also consistent with the path taken by the national government for the provision of social welfare for 'mixed-blood' children.[30] Not coincidentally, these policies were created at the exact time that Japan was seeking increased acceptance on the international stage and official entry to the United Nations – and at a time when, in theory, the ideas of equality and human rights for all people were being touted as the ideals of modern nations, even if most nations failed to uphold them in law and practice.

While the Diet and Ministry of Education declared a policy of integrated education, and over 87 per cent of the 'mixed-blood' children would attend integrated public schools, educational leaders continued to have serious concerns about the potential problems for these children in the schools, and continually outlined the positive goals of the policy.[31] Highlighting ideas of equality, Teranaka, the head of the social affairs division of the Ministry of Education, defended the need for integrated education, despite the potential problems.

> For these mixed-blood children who carry the destiny of misfortune on their backs, I think that it is necessary that for them to be treated the same as usual Japanese children without prejudice, they be admitted to school in an unprejudiced manner together with everyone else.[32]

While the Ministry continued to emphasize the benefits of integrated schooling, they openly acknowledged, and attempted to contend with, perceived challenges of educating 'mixed-blood' children, issuing a pamphlet providing guidance to schools educating these children. The opening lines set the tone of the document. 'As a general rule, there should be no fundamental difference in the way of thinking about or methods of guiding the lifestyles of mixed-blood children in comparison to all children.' They went on to say, 'Simply, let's try to raise them with a feeling of equality and remove instances of racial prejudice.'[33] While, on the one hand, these statements can be dismissed as platitudes, on the other, they at least reflect the official position of the Ministry as communicated to actual teachers, administrators, PTA officials, and others involved in the schools. When placed in comparison to other Cold War capitalist countries' official racial policies, particularly those of the United States, the Japanese Government was actually ahead of the curve in actively encouraging equality.

That being said, the Government certainly anticipated problems. The officials themselves were not quite sure what to expect. Their concerns centered on three areas: the actions of classmates and the parents of fellow students, the concerns of the parents of the children, and the feelings of the children themselves. As they acknowledged, 'within the general society the reality is that not all people will look at the mixed-blood children with perfect understanding and attitudes.'[34] Based on this reality, they anticipated that many of the parents and guardians would have grave concerns, and, as a positive plan of action, stipulated that 'it is very important to learn the worries held by the mothers and guardians of the mixed-blood children regarding school entrance.' While acknowledging that they did not know exactly what fears the parents held, they listed a number of possibilities, such as bullying, receiving strange looks, and being shunned, and explained that 'if they [the parents or guardians] hold these concerns, we must avoid them not sending their children to school.'[35]

Despite the last-minute nature of the preparation, in April 1953 the first group of 'mixed-blood' students entered elementary schools throughout Japan. Predictably, with a group of over 1,000 students in both rural and urban areas, there were both success stories and tales of failure. The important question is, what were the trends in how this group fared in school?

Statistically, at first glance, it appears that the group suffered from a lack of academic success. Hirano Imao, a scholar of French literature and advocate for 'mixed-blood' children, argued that the children did poorly in school primarily as a result of racial discrimination.[36] Suzuki Jirō, one of the leading scholars of race and discrimination in Japan at the time, pointed out that according to the Ministry of Social Welfare, in 1962 52.7 per cent of children from 'regular' homes advanced to high school, while only 10 per cent of 'mixed-blood' children did likewise. He countered, however, that the poor showing could more effectively be explained by the effects of poverty and the realities of being raised by a single working mother in 1950s Japan than by straightforward racial prejudice.[37]

The success or failure in school of any child results from the interaction of a wide variety of factors, many not easily measured statistically. When such a large disparity exists between the success rate of 'regular' vs 'mixed-blood' students, one cannot dismiss the role of race, but we must look at the history to attempt to understand what types of factors impacted on the education of these students. Looking at the details of their experiences in school can help us understand the impact of different factors on the success of students.

To some extent, 'mixed-blood' students did experience discrimination based on appearance. As the Ministry of Education noted, 'Almost all [mixed-blood children] have had the experience of being stared at by strangers. There are also examples of children who do not like to go to the public bath or do not like when their parents take them on outings far away, etc.'[38] The important question is to what extent these types of experiences negatively impacted on their school performance, and to what extent these types of experiences carried over into the school environment. The Ministry of Education, based on their data, concluded that

> Even in cases in which things have not gone well [with classmates], more than it being because they are mixed-blood children, instead it seems that they are turned away because of their rough personalities. (It seems likely that the cause of these personalities in many cases is the complications of the mixed-blood child's family, and the teasing probably has an influence.)[39]

Despite my initial skepticism, my reading of the raw data concurs with the conclusions of the Ministry. Overwhelmingly, the children who had difficulties in school had extreme difficulties in their home life, and those who found themselves isolated often behaved in relatively antisocial ways that would have created problems for the children regardless of physical appearance.[40] Most of the children were easily integrated into the social environment of the school, bullying incidents tended to be isolated, and many children, especially those from stable homes, became leaders within their classes. No discernable patterns developed based on color (i.e. "half-white' or "half-black") or gender that correlate with predicted social outcomes/ problems in school.

Extant records show two important trends. First, while there were individual incidents at many schools, the experience of bullying or discrimination seemed more the exception than the rule in most of these students' school lives. The Ministry of Education described their 'relationship with classmates' as so: "For mixed-blood children, from the standpoint of momentary teasing, there is pretty much none who have not been bullied at all. However, there are not examples of them being looked at coldly by classmates in an enduring fashion."[41] Second, most of the students themselves (and their classmates) did not seem to internalize a strong sentiment that the 'mixed-blood' children were different until about the third grade – much later than would be the case in countries such as the United States where physical and racial difference has historically played a much stronger role in society.[42]

Perhaps as interesting historically as the fact that most of the students were not subject to extensive bullying is the nature of some of the bullying and initial problems that were encountered. Here is a fairly typical description of a moment that created a lot of worry about bullying: 'After the opening of school in April, one or two problems arose. While examining the necks and hands [of students] for cleanliness one at a time in the hallway, when I got to Y [pseudonym for the "mixed-blood" child], a boy sitting nearby said in a loud voice, "Teacher, Y-Kun is completely white, and looks like an American." After that, students said in succession, "Yeah, yeah, Y-kun is American." '[43] While details differed by case, by far the most common type of teasing (or comments perhaps not intended as teasing but that created concern on the part of the teachers) that occurred was to refer to the 'mixed-blood' child as 'American.' Most commonly, these comments came from students in the upper grades or started after the child entered his or her third year of elementary school. The importance of these trends is that children did not seem to internalize a largely racialized view of Japanese identity until later in their elementary school years. The significance placed on the use of 'American' as an epithet further highlights the importance in the minds of both teachers and the children that 'mixed-blood' children be identified as "Japanese."

While 'race,' *per se*, did not create consistent problems for students, institutionalization did. For example, one teacher, who taught three children in a 'mother–child protective institution', one of whom was a 'mixed-blood' girl, commented that 'Speaking of children in the OO institution, everyone [meaning fellow students] looks on them with a bad eye.'[44] In the case of children from an orphanage who attended public school, bullying, on the whole, was not a large problem. However, they did face significant problems socializing appropriately with the children from private households, especially in their first two years in public school. In particular, the children from the orphanage had to adjust to a different set of rules of socialization, such as how to share toys and how to react to disputes, to those that the majority of the non-institutionalized children had learned growing up in the broader society. These problems had largely dissipated by the time the children reached the third grade, at which point they had, for the most part, made significant adjustments in their behavior.[45] Of course, the entire question of the relationship of these students' negative experiences to their being 'mixed-blood' is extremely complicated, since the fact that they were 'mixed-blood' in some cases contributed to their institutionalization in the first place.[46]

As this chapter illustrates, the story of 'mixed-blood' Japanese is complicated, and should not be reduced to a simple tale of discrimination and hatred. Rather, 'mixed-blood' Japanese, especially in the post-war era, had a wide variety of life experiences, and experienced varying degrees of inclusion and exclusion from Japanese society, including enjoying many of the financial successes of Japan's period of rapid growth in the 1960s. Their story, while complex, reflects Japan's relationship to broader global economic and intellectual trends, ranging from Japan's relationship to Enlightenment thinking to the need for Japan to create policies for 'mixed-blood' people in the early 1950s, at exactly the same time that global political trends emphasized the importance of citizens' rights and equality in law, even if most of the leading powers at the time did not live up to those ideals in theory or practice.

Notes

1 Robert Fish, *The Heiress and the Love Children: Sawada Miki and the Elizabeth Saunders Home for mixed-blood orphans in postwar Japan* (Ph.D. Dissertation, University of Hawaii at Manoa, 2002), 228–30.
2 John W. Dower, *Embracing Defeat: Japan in the wake of World War II* (New York: W.W. Norton & Company, 1999), 211.
3 John Lie, Review of *Japan's Minorities: The illusion of homogeneity*, Michael Weiner (ed.) (London, New York: Routledge, 1997), in *Monumenta Nipponica* 53 no. 3 (Autumn 1998): 420.
4 David Theo Goldberg (ed.), *Anatomy of Racism* (Minneapolis: University of Minnesota Press, 1990). See especially Peter Fitzpatrick, 'Racism and the Innocence of Law,' 247–62.

5 Stephen Murphy-Shigematsu, 'Identities of Multiethnic People,' in *Japan and Global Migration: Foreign workers and the advent of multicultural society*, Mike Douglass and Glenda S. Roberts (eds) (London: Routledge, 2000). See this article for a lucid overview of the debate about terminology.

6 Gary P. Leupp, *Interracial Intimacy in Japan: Western men and Japanese women, 1543–1900* (London and New York: Continuum International Publishing Group, 2003), 208.

7 Ibid., 208.

8 Goldberg, *Anatomy of Racism*.

9 Oguma Eiji, *A Genealogy of 'Japanese' Self-Images*, David Askew (trans.) (Melbourne: Trans Pacific Press, 2002).

10 Oguma, 299.

11 Naikaku Iinkai 19 go (Nineteenth meeting of the cabinet committee), 3/13/1953.

12 Kiyono Yasutoshi, 'Minzoku no Konketsu' (Mixed-Blood Ethnicity), in *Kichi no ko*, 218.

13 Minoru Shibuya (director), *Yassa Mossa*, 1953; Fish, *The Heiress and the Love Children*, 14–24, 219–21.

14 Arinnobu Haruyo, 'Konetsuji no Haha no ki' (Record of the Mother of a Mixed-Blood Child), in *Konketsuji Shidō Kiroku II* (Record of the Guidance of Mixed-Blood Children: II), Monbushō Shotō Chūtō Kyōikukyoku (ed.) (Tokyo: Monbushō, 1955), 141.

15 Takaki Shirō, 'Seishin Eisei kara Mita Konketsuji Mondai' (The Mixed-Blood Children Issue Looked At from the Perspective of Mental Health), in *Konketsuji Shidō Kiroku II*, 151.

16 Monbusho Iinkai 12 go (Board of the Ministry of Education, Meeting 12), February 28, 1953.

17 Lower House Budget Committee Meeting Number 26, February 20, 1953.

18 Matsuda Kimiko, 'Kawaisō' (It's a Pity), in *Kichi no ko*, p. 208.

19 Hayashi Michiko, 'Ai no ko' (Love Child), in *Kichi no ko*, pp. 209–10; Yamashiro Midori, 'Yoru no Onna to Konketsuji' (Women of the Night and Mixed-Blood Children), in *Kichi no ko*, p. 217.

20 Kōsei Iinkai Boshifukushi ni kansuru Kaigi Dai 1 go (Special Committee on Health and Welfare about Welfare of Mothers and Children, Meeting 1), December 6, 1952.

21 Kōseishō Jidōkyoku (ed.), *Jidō Fukushi Jūnen no Ayumi*, (The Course of Ten Years of Juvenile Social Welfare) (Tokyo: Nihon Jidō Mondai Chōsakai, 1959), 75.

22 Iihara Hisaya, 'Konketsuji no Fukushi ni tsuite' (About the Welfare of Mixed-Blood Children), in *Konketsuji Shidō II*, 165.

23 Monbushō Shotō Chūtō Kyōikukyoku (ed.), *Konketsuji Shidō Kiroku II* (Record of Guidance of Mixed-Blood Children II) (Tokyo: Monbushō, 1956), 3.

24 'Nyūgaku Tōsho no Sabetsushi o Kyōshi Kyōryoku de Kaiketsu shita ga, Kongo wa Katei Kankyō no Kaizen ga Nozomareu,' in *Konketsuji Shidō I*, 15.

25 Nyūgaku Tōsho no Sabetsushi, 23.

26 'Chinō wa Chūijō da ga, Riyu Naku Kasseki shi, Ranbō de, Katei no Kaizen ga Daiichi ni Hitsuyō de Aru,' in *Konketsuji Shidō Kiroku I*, 39.

27 Chinō wa Chūijō, 39.

28 'Zaitaku Konketsuji, Ippan kō e – Kanagawa Nyūgaku Taisaku ni Ketsuron' (Mixed-Blood Children Living at Home Will go to Regular Schools: Kanagawa decides its school entrance policy), *Mainichi Shinbun*, November 14, 1952;

58   *R.A. Fish*

'Konketsuji mo Futsū kō e,' (Mixed-Blood Children also to Regular School), *Mainichi Shinbun*, November 27, 1952.

29   15 Monbuiinkai 8 go, December 9, 1952.

30   Kōseishō Jidōkyokuchō, 'Konketsuji Mondai Taisaku ni Tsuite,' (About the Policy towards the Problem of Mixed-Blood Children), *Hakken* 398 gō, August 19, 1953. Reproduced in *Jidō Fukushi Jūnen no Ayumi*, Kōseishō Jidōkyoku (ed.) (Tokyo: Nihon Jidō Mondai Chōsakai, 1959), 281.

31   *Konketsuji Shidō Kiroku II*, 2.

32   15 Monbuiinkai – 12 go, February 28, 1953.

33   Monbusho Shotō Chūtō Kyōikukyoku Shōtō Kyōikuka, *Konketsuji Shūgaku ni tsuite: Shidōjō ryūisubeki ten* (About the School Attendance of Mixed-Blood Children: Points which should be paid heed to in their guidance) (Tokyo: Monbusho, 1953), preface.

34   *Konketsuji Shūgaku ni tsuite*, 5.

35   *Konketsuji Shūgaku ni tsuite*, 2.

36   Hirano Imao, 'Konketsuji' (Mixed-Blood Children), in *Gendai no Sabetsu to Henken: Mondai no honshitsu to jitsujō*, Suzuki Jirō, (ed.), 219.

37   Suzuki Jirō, 'Shiryō to Kaisestu to "Konektsuji" by Hirano Imao' (Documents and Commentary to 'Mixed-Blood Children' by Hirano Imao), in *Gendai no Sabetsu to Henken*, 233.

38   *Konketsuji Shidō Kiroku II*, 4.

39   *Konketsuji Shidō Kiroku III*, 4.

40   *Konketsuji Shidō Kiroku I*, passim, *Konketsuji Shidō Kiroku II*, passim, *Konketsuji Shidō Kiroku III*, passim.

41   *Konketsuji Shidō Kiroku II*, 4.

42   *Konketsuji Shidō Kiroku I*, passim, *Konketsuji Shidō Kiroku II*, passim, *Konketsuji Shidō Kiroku III*, passim. See also chapter six for a development of this argument in relation to the children in the Saunders Home.

43   'Mondai ga Okorisō ni Natteiru, Katei no Attatakai Ai to Shūi no Hitotachi no Omoiyari ga Hoshii,' in *Konketsuji Shidō Kiroku III*, 20.

44   'Jitsubo ga Kodomo o Tera ni Azukete Kekkonshiteshimau: Ima made mo ijimareru koto ga ookatta ga, kongo ga shinpai de aru,' in *Konketsuji Shidō Kiroku II*, 116.

45   'Yōgo Shisetsu ni Konketsuji o Toriatsukatta Baai' (The Case in which Mixed-Blood Children Have Been Placed in a Protective Institution), in *Konketsuji Shidō Kiroku I*, 114–27; 'Yōgo Shisetsu no Konketsuji no Rei (Kōritsu)' (Example of Mixed-Blood Children in Child Protective Institutions [Public School]), in *Konketsuji Shidō Kiroku II*, 119–35; 'Yōgo Shisetsu no Konketsuji no Rei (Kōritsu)' (Example of Mixed-Blood Children in Child Protective Institutions [Public School]), in *Konketsuji Shidō Kiroku III*, 36–45.

46   Fish, *The Heiress and the Love Children*, 31–69.

4 Burakumin in contemporary Japan

Ian J. Neary

> The Dowa problem is a major human rights problem specific to Japan in which a portion of the population, due to discrimination based on social status structures created during the process of Japan's historical development, were for a long period forced into conditions of economic, social and cultural disadvantage and suffer even now from obstacles in marriage, unfair treatment in employment and other forms of discrimination in their daily lives.
>
> (Ministry of Justice website, January 2007)

The 'Dowa problem' is the official euphemism used to refer to those Japanese usually called burakumin, who are believed to be descendants of the outcaste communities of the Tokugawa period (1600–1867). Although freed from formal restrictions in 1871, they have continued to be victims of stigma that has prevented their complete social integration. As we will discuss in greater length below, exactly how many Japanese are presently liable to such prejudices is a matter of debate, but it could be as many as three million people. Some Japanese people may genuinely be unaware of the extent of this problem, especially those who live in the area around Tokyo or places to the north, but most Japanese living in central and western Japan will be conscious of the problem, even if they are reluctant to admit it. There is some disagreement about the extent of the prejudice and discrimination that remains. Even the most radical of the burakumin activists would accept that the situation has improved over the last forty years. Discrimination is no longer as blatant as it was in the 1950s and before. Living conditions in the buraku communities are no longer as impoverished as they were. Such improvements lead some to argue that the 'problem' has been solved, although others suggest that discrimination is now taking on new, less obvious forms such that more subtle policies are required to deal with it and more sophisticated research is needed to enable us to accurately assess the current situation.

One important factor that enforced this change was that throughout the twentieth century burakumin organised themselves to resist and try to eliminate prejudice and discrimination. After a few false starts at the beginning of the century, a sustained movement, the Suiheisha, was launched in March 1922. This survived until 1942, when it was forced to close down amid the mobilisation for war. Leaders of the buraku community resumed activity critical of the government in 1945 and formed the Buraku Liberation League (BLL) in 1955. The main source of support for the BLL came from the parties of the left, the Japan Socialist Party (JSP) and the Japan Communist Party (JCP), both of which had also been formed in late 1945. There have been echoes of the ideological rivalries between these parties in the debates that have taken place within the BLL about the strategies appropriate to its aim of liberating burakumin. During the 1990s, as the political landscape was transformed, many of the certainties of what was known as the '1955 system' ended, and this included how the BLL fits in to political debates and policy making. This too has generated considerable discussion. We will consider some of these debates in the pages that follow.

During the first half of the century, the state's response to burakumin activity was a mixture of attempts to assert control over these marginal communities by rewarding those who agreed to work with the state while punishing those who insisted on making radical demands. But those who became involved in the Yuwa (Conciliation) movement were not simply trying to suppress dissent. There were among them liberals and conservatives who took the idea of equality before the emperor seriously and who therefore sought both to lobby for resources that would enable buraku communities to improve their living standards and to persuade mainstream society to abandon its old ideas.

Immediately before the outbreak of the war in the Pacific, the Yuwa movement was renamed the Dowa movement, and when the policy was revived in the 1950s the same name was used. In April 1969 Dowa projects enabled by the Special Measures Law (Tokubetsu Sochiho) were launched in the form of a Ten Year Plan that aimed at eliminating the conditions that supported discrimination. The policy was extended on a number of occasions before finally coming to an end in March 2002.

Thus the start of the twenty-first century was a major turning point both for those active in the liberation movement and those involved in the administration of improvement projects. Important questions had to be faced about what, if any, prejudice and discrimination remained, and what, if anything, could or should the state, or anyone else, do about it? Also, how did the specific problems of the buraku communities relate to other human rights issues both in Japan and elsewhere in the world?

In this necessarily brief introduction to the topic, we will begin with an outline of the origins of the social phenomenon of buraku discrimination. We will then turn to consider in more detail the developments within the liberation movement and government policy over the course of the twentieth century. Finally we will consider the evidence about the current situation in the buraku communities at the start of the twenty-first century and consider what is now being done and what else might be done.

ORIGINS

A simple view of social policies at the start of Tokugawa Japan would note how mainstream society was divided up into four groups: samurai, peasants, artisans and merchants. Marriage between these groups was not permitted, and many and various sumptuary regulations existed to control most aspects of their everyday lives. However, there were many who fell outside these main categories: the thousands of lesser clerics who staffed Buddhist temples and Shinto shrines and those who worked as servants for samurai or merchants, for example. While these occupations were regarded as belonging to the mainstream population, there were others, most of whom had some relationship to outcaste groups hereditary and non-hereditary, who were not regarded as part of mainstream society and who were subject to particularly severe regulations that were intended to keep them outside society. The hereditary group was called by a number of different names depending on area, but most often *eta* (filth abundant). They themselves preferred the name *kawata*, which referred to the leather industry that many of them were engaged in. The non-hereditary group, at least in the big cities, was known as *hinin* (non-people). Many of these were professional beggars or entertainers of some kind who gathered on the edge of entertainment areas such as Yoshiwara in Edo or Shimabara in Kyoto.

Over the course of the Tokugawa period, the neat four-level status system became frayed at the edges as the main determinant of the quality of life became wealth rather than status. Thus there were well-to-do samurai, merchants and village leaders who led comfortable lives, while poor samurai, shopkeepers, workmen and peasants suffered inadequate housing, poor nutrition and social uncertainty. Indeed, there were a small few among the outcaste groups, the leaders of the *kawata* communities for example, who led stable, even comfortable, lives. But most of those at the bottom, or indeed outside the status hierarchy, endured a miserable existence.

During the 1970s and after, the story of the origin of the buraku communities was told as if discrimination against them was something that was invented by the Tokugawa elite, such that the ruling class then, and their successors in the twentieth century, were in some sense 'to blame'. As Yamamoto (1999) has pointed out, this was a view based less on research than on the preconceptions of the early scholars of buraku history. An early theory of buraku history published in 1943 takes an emperor-centred view of history, seeing good things happen when the emperor had real political power and bad things happen when he was weak. Thus discrimination increased while the Shogunate wielded all real power, and only a few years after the emperor was restored to political prominence the outcastes were liberated. Post-war Marxists saw much of the injustice of the late nineteenth and early twentieth centuries as resulting from the undemocratic feudal practices originating in the pre-Meiji period, and tended to assume that discrimination was a product of the Tokugawa era. However, neither of these views was based on historical research. They lasted so long into the twentieth century first because they were easy to understand and second because they suited and supported the 'administrative struggles' (*gyosei toso*) strategy adopted by the BLL during the 1950s.

As research has accumulated quite rapidly since the 1970s, it is clear that the historical patterns that led to the modern buraku problem are complex. First, there was a great deal of variation across Japan. How local regimes dealt with their outcaste population was left largely to their discretion, even in the Tokugawa period. The names that were used for outcastes varied widely, as did the occupations that they followed. Many of the outcaste communities had at least some of their members involved in tanning, but there were some domains where the leather trade was considered an acceptable part-time activity for underemployed farmers. Second, it is clear that discrimination against certain communities and certain occupations can be traced back well before the start of the Tokugawa period. There is evidence that communities that supplied workers who were engaged in ritually polluting work in shrines and temples or in the slaughter of animals or the punishment or execution of prisoners can be found on the edges of settlements several hundred years before the prominence of the Tokugawa clan. At times when sumptuary laws were weakly enforced, it was possible to escape from the outcaste communities, so there was not necessarily a high degree of genealogical continuity across the centuries.

There is no doubt that the regulations introduced in the Tokugawa period resulted in outcaste communities becoming larger and more isolated from mainstream society than hitherto, but these regulations did not in themselves *create* the groups that were subject to them. As Yamamoto points out, just as the regulations of the 1590s depriving them of surnames, swords and servants may have defined the peasantry in the Tokugawa era without creating them, no more did the increased regulation of *kawata* and *hinin* communities *create* these outcaste groups. (Yamamoto 1999: 47) Nevertheless, over the subsequent 250 years of Tokugawa rule there was a change in the nature of the bottom end of the status hierarchy caused by the periodic redrawing of regulations. This was a response to changing social and economic circumstances and to the attempts by *kawata* communities to subvert or even challenge the rules they found irksome. The outcome of the process was that whereas in the seventeenth century outcaste communities were relatively small and few in number, subject to mainly socially endorsed prejudice, by the nineteenth century they were often large, numerous (at least in the west of Japan) and subject to formally endorsed discrimination.

Several social processes contributed to this change. First, in the period 1700–30 a series of edicts were issued by the central government that strengthened many aspects of the status system, including the definitions of outcaste status. Whereas previously some escape from marginal status was possible, now it became virtually impossible for even non-hereditary *hinin* to be absorbed into the mainstream. The stricter regulations enforced in the areas directly under Tokugawa control were emulated by many of the local regimes. Soon after this, in the 1730s, there was a major famine in the west of Japan that reduced the size of the farming population by about one-third.

At the start of the Tokugawa period, tanning and leather craft was a strategically important industry, since most of a samurai's armour was based on leather. Each castle town had its tanners and leather craftsmen, who were considered impure because of their contact with dead animals and were therefore avoided by other town dwellers. Under the conditions of peace provided by the Tokugawa Government, demand for these products dropped, and this resulted in underemployed urban outcaste communities. However, following the decimation of the peasantry in the famine of the 1730s, many of the local lords in western Japan urgently sought out labour so that their land could be farmed as productively as possible and their income restored. Moreover, as taxes were paid by the village as a unit, many village leaders were also eager to recruit outsiders to farm the now untilled land. So it was that soon after their outcaste status had been clearly defined, many *kawata* moved into rural areas to take up farming, often on the least productive land.

As *kawata* were not considered fully human, they were not included in the periodic censuses that were carried out from the 1720s, and their communities were not included on maps. The census data demonstrate that although the mainstream population increased hardly at all in the period 1720–1850, the total *kawata* population may have increased as much as 300 per cent, and there are examples of communities that grew more than sixfold. In part this was because bad luck or bad behaviour had forced some people to leave their homes, and these people would end up living in outcaste areas. Even those outcastes who had moved to work on the land in the early eighteenth century, becoming in some ways indistinguishable from the rest of the farming community, often maintained their connection to the leather industry or to some other handicraft industry that made them less vulnerable to crop failures. Their access to meat also made them better able to survive during times of poor harvests. Finally, some suggest that outcastes were less likely than the majority to restrict the size of their families by selective neonatal infanticide (*mabiki*).

Whatever the reason, the outcaste population, which had been scattered, fairly small and not looming large in the public mind, had by the mid-nineteenth century become large, visible communities. These communities were tightly regulated to segregate them from the mainstream and were regarded with contempt and fear by most. From the 1720s, increasingly detailed sets of regulations were imposed on most aspects of their lives. The precise content of these regulations varied from place to place, but usually *kawata* were only permitted certain types of clothing in order to ensure they were clearly visible. They were often not allowed to enter towns at night and were forbidden to enter religious sites at all. There were even rules controlling the size of their houses and forbidding them from having windows facing the road. Efforts by members of these communities to ignore or evade these rules were rewarded by ever-more-detailed sets of regulations. The result was that segregation and discrimination were at their peak shortly before the start of the Meiji era.

This account so far summarises a large and growing body of research on pre-modern *kawata* history. What is clear is that it rejects many of the previous popularly held views that *kawata* were somehow ethnically different to the mainstream Japanese; that they were descendants of Koreans captured in war at some stage of Japanese history or even, according to one of the wilder theories, that they were related to one of the lost tribes of Israel who somehow found their way to Japan. On the other hand, there is much that remains unclear. Not all of the trades that were regarded as *kawata* monopolies in the pre-Tokugawa era were defined as such after 1600, although it is not clear why. Similarly, whereas before 1600 the emphasis was on occupation, after 1600 it is on bloodline; but why this should be has not been fully explained. As debate develops about the future of the movement there remain many things to explain about the problem's past.

LIBERATION AND ORGANISATION

The process of dismantling the Tokugawa state included the abolition on 28 August 1871 of all the regulations that had restricted the daily lives of the *kawata* and *hinin*. However, although in Japanese society at large consciousness of one's former feudal status quickly became irrelevant, prejudice and discrimination against the former outcastes continued. They remained on the margins of society and were largely excluded from the development of the capitalist economy. Their attempts to take advantage of new possibilities to develop leather craft into modern shoe manufacture usually failed. Where they did become involved in the process of industrialisation, as in the development of the coal industry in northern Kyushu, they were usually to be found doing the dirtiest and most dangerous jobs in small mines with little modern machinery.

Until recently, it was the continuity with the Edo and Meiji periods that was emphasised, and the lack of positive effort by the Meiji regime to help former *kawata* to slough off the disadvantage accumulated over the previous centuries was the target for criticism. Now it is argued that the Liberation Edict of August 1871 should be regarded as a new phase in buraku history, much as the start of the Tokugawa era had been. While former *kawata* did not benefit much from the Meiji reforms, it is hard to argue that they were impoverished by the feudal restrictions and that the ending of these restrictions contributed to their further impoverishment. Rather it seems that the outcaste communities that grew up in the later nineteenth century were in urban areas in Osaka or Kyoto or in newly developing areas like the mining districts of north Kyushu. This suggests that there were different social processes now at work.

There was a clear difference between the institutionalised discrimination that existed in the Tokugawa era and the social discrimination of the Meiji period. Discrimination in marriage, education and employment that young burakumin encountered and objected to in the later nineteenth century simply had not been possible in the highly regulated feudal period. Their name changed too. *Eta*, *hinin* and *kawata* were still used, but the use of these names was resented. They still lived in small communities, called *buraku* (hamlets). The local governments referred to these in the early twentieth century as *tokushu buraku* (special hamlets) – later the liberation movement referred to *hisabetsu*, or *mikaiho buraku*, (discriminated or unliberated hamlets). In the English language literature about the issue, the convention has developed of referring to the buraku problem and to the residents as burakumin. We will stick with this for the rest of this article.

Burakumin were not passive participants in this process of social change. Once freed from the feudal regulations, they took part in the resistance to the creation of the emperor-centred Meiji state. Thus, for example, we find that as the liberal ideas of the Jiyuminken Undo (Freedom and Popular Rights Movement) percolated down to the educated peasantry in the 1870s, there were discussion groups also formed in buraku communities. After this brief blossoming, these groups faded away, only to revive as an active force at the local level in the 1890s as they began to consider ways in which discrimination could be overcome. One imagines that this was in part a response to the realisation of the discrepancy between the notions of the equality of the citizen's obligation to the emperor as expressed in the Meiji constitution and the reality of the special disadvantages being faced by younger educated burakumin. Groups were formed especially in western Japan, and they developed a realisation that there was a set of similar problems being faced by former outcaste communities across the country. This was the necessary precursor to the desire to create a national movement.

In 1903 a first national conference of burakumin, the Dainippon Doho Yuwakai (Greater Japan Fraternal Conciliation Society), was held in Osaka and was attended by 300 burakumin from all over the country, but it failed to develop into a sustained organisation. One characteristic weakness of the movement at this time was that most of its supporters accepted the idea that there was something wrong with them and their communities that they had to put right before they would be accepted by society at large. A document of 1918 described buraku discrimination as being based not on long-established custom but on the fact that they were unhygienic, unschooled and poor. In other words, they were unable to fulfil the duties of the citizen of the Japanese empire: to serve in the army, to be educated and to pay taxes. Thus a new rationalisation for discrimination had developed within the discourse of modernisation and the creation of the imperial state structure (Watanabe 1993: 10–12).

Autonomous political activity became difficult after 1905, as the Meiji Government created a network of government groups that aimed at restricting the influence of 'dangerous' liberal and socialist ideas. One aspect of this that affected the buraku communities was the formation within the buraku in several prefectures of Yuwa (Conciliation) discussion groups, which were always placed under the watchful eye of a trusted member of the community such as a school teacher or occasionally a policeman. There were even some places where local government bodies provided small amounts of money to relieve buraku poverty. As measures designed in inhibit buraku radicalism, they were partially successful. Surveys taken after the Rice Riots of 1918 found that the buraku communities where Yuwa groups existed had not become involved in violent activity. On the other hand, in the medium term the existence of these groups enabled the relatively rapid growth of the Suiheisha after it was launched in 1922. They did so in two ways. First, they encouraged younger burakumin to consider how their situation might be improved, so when the Suiheisha declaration was launched there was a ready audience for its ideas. Second, at an organisational level many of the discussion groups were in communication with others in their area, thus forming a network along which the Suiheisha's ideas could quickly flow. In some areas these groups changed virtually overnight from being Yuwa to Suiheisha groups, although at a later stage some would switch back again.

The Suiheisha was formed in the social context of the rapid increase in activity of the tenants' groups and labour unions and in the related ideological context of the rapid spread of socialist ideas that followed the revolution in

Russia. Intellectuals were taking an interest in social problems, including those of the burakumin. For example, Sano Manabu, soon to take a leading role in the creation of Japan's Communist Party, published *Tokushu Buraku Kaihoron* (On the Liberation of Special Buraku) in 1921. This was a great encouragement to the young burakumin of the Kyoto region to push ahead with their plans to create an independent movement for buraku emancipation. The Declaration of the Suiheisha is worth quoting in full, as it remains a point of reference for burakumin activists and indeed for the Japanese human rights movement.

Declaration of the Suiheisha

Tokushu Burakumin throughout the country: Unite!
Long-suffering brothers! Over the past half century, the movements on our behalf by so many people and in such varied ways have yielded no appreciable results. This failure is the punishment we have incurred for permitting ourselves as well as others to debase our own human dignity. Previous movements, though seemingly motivated by compassion, actually corrupted many of our brothers. Thus, it is imperative that we now organize a new collective movement to emancipate ourselves by promoting respect for human dignity.
Brothers! Our ancestors pursued and practiced freedom and equality. They were the victims of base, contemptible class policies and they were the manly martyrs of industry. As a reward for skinning animals, they were stripped of their own living flesh; in return for tearing out the hearts of animals, their own warm human hearts were ripped apart. They were even spat upon with ridicule. Yet, all through these cursed nightmares, their human pride ran deep in their blood. Now, the time has come when we human beings, pulsing with this blood, are soon to regain our divine dignity. The time has come for the victims to throw off their stigma. The time has come for the blessing of the martyrs' crown of thorns.
The time has come when we can be proud of being Eta.
We must never again shame our ancestors and profane humanity through servile words and cowardly deeds. We, who know just how cold human society can be, who know what it is to be pitied, do fervently seek and adore the warmth and light of human life from deep within our hearts.
Thus is the Suiheisha born.
Let there be warmth in human society, let there be light in all human beings.

March 3, 1922

As is often the case with mass movements, after the first few years of enthusiastic activity there was a lull, and debates erupted about the theory and tactics most appropriate for guiding the movement into the future. As with most social movements of the time, there were three possible alternative routes, as advocated by the anarchists, the Bolsheviks and the social democrats, each of whom had a different diagnosis of the movement's problems and a different set of solutions. Moreover, the government attempted to reassert its control over the buraku communities by coordinating the activities of the various Yuwa groups into a single national movement. This offered an alternative national leadership structure and a theory for the solution to the buraku problem that lay within the consolidation of the emperor-centred state system.

Despite the often-fierce internal debate and the threat from the Yuwa movement and the 'thought police', the Suiheisha outlived all of its contemporary social-movement organisations. It remained active until 1938, and only finally gave in to demands that it dissolve at the start of 1942. Two factors enabled it to stand out so long against the pressure to conform. First, buraku leaders were determined to emancipate themselves. Experience showed that they could not rely on the efforts of others, whether they were communists or government officials. They had rejected the idea that the problem was something to do with their inadequacy and instead argued that it was social attitudes that needed changing, not burakumin. Second, the development of the *kyudan toso* (denunciation struggle) became for the Suiheisha what the strike was to the labour unions and the rent-strike was for the tenants unions: their weapon in the class struggle, or at least in the battle against discrimination. At one level the aim was simply to encourage burakumin to protest about discrimination when they encountered it, rather than accepting it as an inevitable part of their lives. In the first few years of the movement's existence, this tactic was adopted enthusiastically, if indiscriminately, and activists would attack in word and deed all those who were regarded as discriminators. Fights broke out and sometimes developed into more extensive violence. However, as the movement matured the leadership was able to be more selective about which campaigns to pursue, and they tried to use the denunciation process so that it had an educative impact on both the discriminator and the wider society.

POST-WAR RECREATION OF THE MOVEMENT

Matsumoto Jiichiro emerged as leader of the Suiheisha in the late 1920s, and in the 1936 general election he was elected to the Diet, where he served as a member throughout the Pacific war. Only days after defeat, some of the former Suiheisha leaders met to consider how the buraku liberation activities might be resumed, and Matsumoto was not only a key member of this group but was also a central figure in the activity that established the JSP in November 1945. In 1946 the National Committee for Buraku Liberation (NCBL) was launched as a successor to the Suiheisha with the support of both the JSP and the JCP, which had become a legal political party for the first time in December 1945. Both parties included support for the NCBL in their first post-war manifestos, and nine burakumin were elected to the Diet in the first elections held under the new constitution in 1947, seven of them as members of the JSP. One of these was Matsumoto.

The buraku liberation movement developed into one of the most important human-rights-promoting NGOs in post-war Japan, but during the occupation it had a hard time arousing enthusiasm for its aims. This was in part due to the fact that living standards were so low across the country that there was a kind of equality of poverty, and most people had to spend all their time and effort eking out a bare existence, meaning that there was little time for political activity.

The reform of Japan instigated by the American occupiers included not only guarantees of human rights within the constitution, but also land reform and education reform that promised the thorough democratisation of Japan, including the elimination of buraku discrimination. The JCP endorsed this view. Their position pre-war had been that discrimination against buraku communities was an example of a remnant of the feudal structures that had not been completely swept away by the incomplete bourgeois revolution of the nineteenth century. They argued that the dismantling of the aristocracy, the dispossession of the large landowners and the infusion of democratic ideas across Japan was completing the historic task of the bourgeoisie, and in the course of time prejudice and discrimination would naturally disappear.

In October 1951, a pulp magazine called *All Romance* published a story entitled *Tokushu Buraku* whose author turned out to be an employee of the Kyoto city government. The story portrayed a community rife with illegal sake brewing, violence, crime and black-market activity. The local branch of the NBLC complained both to the publishers and to the Kyoto city council on the grounds that it gave a false picture of life in the buraku communities that was likely to sustain prejudices. As part of their campaign, the NBLC demanded that the city council mark on a map those sections of the city that lacked public water supplies, sewage disposal and fire hydrants, and also all areas with inadequate housing, high rates of tuberculosis, trachoma and other public health problems, high absenteeism in the schools and high concentrations of families on relief. The result was a vivid demonstration of burakumin problems, since the marked areas fell entirely within the eighteen buraku of Kyoto and its environs (DeVos and Wagatsuma 1973: 76). It was clear that although life was improving for the average Japanese citizen, members of the buraku community were falling behind once more.

Kyoto city accepted responsibility and immediately increased its budget for buraku improvements from nearly ¥6 million in 1950 to ¥45 million in 1952. These funds were used to improve water supply and sewage services and to build new housing and nursery schools. The effort that brought about these changes became a model for NBLC activists elsewhere, and many launched similar administrative struggles against councils, focusing on a specific instance of discrimination that they linked to institutional discrimination. During the 1950s this strategy successfully persuaded many local governments to allocate more money to improve the buraku living environment. The movement began to attract more support, and in 1955 it was relaunched as the Buraku Liberation League (BLL), a name that was thought to have more of a mass appeal.

Somewhat later, supporters of the JCP position would demonstrate that, despite its title, the story *Tokushu Buraku* was not about burakumin but about Koreans resident in Kyoto, who admittedly lived alongside burakumin in the impoverished communities. However, when more money became available from the Kyoto city authorities to build new houses in that community, it was used exclusively for benefit of the burakumin, and the zainichi Koreans were expelled (Ichinomiya 2003: 124–6).

In the late 1950s, the mainstream opposition parties began to take the buraku issue on board. In 1957 the JSP produced a report arguing that although complete liberation of the buraku communities would only be possible within a socialist society, even within the present structures it was important and necessary to improve their living conditions. They called for the creation of a special commission within the prime minister's office to devise a comprehensive policy (Neary 1986: 560–1, Morooka 1981–2 II: 383–7, 446–50). The JCP developed its own policy, which rejected the view that there was anything special about the problems faced by buraku workers. Buraku poverty was just one example of the contradictions within capitalist society, and the main target of the buraku working class should be the overthrow of the class system rather than the making of special demands on that system that would weaken their solidarity with the working class movement (Morooka 1981–2 II: 392–5).

The BLL wanted to build on the campaigns being conducted in the major cities to make the national government commit itself to a policy that would lead to major improvements. Pressure from the JSP led the then prime minister, Kishi Nobusuke, to agree that the continued existence of discrimination against burakumin was 'regrettable', and he undertook to introduce appropriate policies (Morooka 1981–2 III: 297–8 – speech made on 11 March 1958). In October of that year, the LDP set up a Dowa policy committee, which recommended that a number of 'model improvement projects' funded by central government be set up across the country. However, in 1959–60 the country was engulfed by a serious political crisis, the Ampo struggles, as mass protests tried to prevent Diet approval of the Security Treaty that had been renegotiated with the United States in late 1959. Diet approval occurred in May 1960, but the demonstrations continued into the summer months. The crisis was only defused by the resignation of Prime Minister Kishi and his replacement by Ikeda Hayato, who took a more conciliatory line. It was in the midst of this that the government abandoned its resistance to the creation of a commission of enquiry, and an act was passed to set one up in August 1960. However, two months later the government also announced its decision to cease to work directly with the BLL and instead give its support to the Nippon Dowakai, which had at its head Yamamoto Masao, who before 1945 had been a senior administrator of the Yuwa programme.

The Commission of Enquiry on Dowa Policy did include representatives of the BLL, and its report came very close to what the BLL wanted. It was divided into two parts. The first section gave a brief history of the problem, through which it established three points of principle. First was that there was no substance to the widely held view that burakumin are in some way racially or ethnically different from mainstream Japanese. This is something that was particularly important given the tidal wave of literature emphasising Japan's uniqueness that was to sweep across the country over the next thirty years. Second, it did not accept that the problem was simply a remnant of feudalism that would disappear with the development of advanced capitalism. And third, it rejected the view that the best solution is to ignore the buraku issue since discussion of it or special action only served to perpetuate awareness of a problem that if ignored would disappear. A solution to the problem, the report argued, must be based on knowledge, not rely on ignorance. The second section was a survey of the current state of buraku communities that used both existing data and some specially commissioned research. This portrayed ghetto-like communities located on land liable to flooding, where the quality of housing stock was poor and such public services as sewers, tap water, streetlights and fire protection were often lacking. Standards of educational achievement were well below the national average, few burakumin were employed in major companies or benefited from 'lifetime' employment and there was a high degree of dependence on social security. The report concluded that it was the duty of the state to take steps to eliminate some of these problems, beginning with the introduction of legislation that would enable government to address the social deprivation described in the report (Harada and Uesugi 1981: 252–9; Neary 1986: 563–4; Upham 1987: 84–6).

The JCP warned against the adoption of this policy, as it would privilege one section of the working class over another, thus dividing it. Even some leaders of the BLL, including Matsumoto Jiichiro, were uncomfortable with the idea of the provision of facilities exclusively for burakumin. It would, he feared, corrupt the movement and make the buraku communities over-dependent on state provision, contrary to the Suiheisha aim to 'emancipate ourselves'. Matsumoto died in 1966, and although the JCP continued to voice its concerns, the BLL enthusiastically engaged with the administration of the Dowa policy.

SPECIAL MEASURES 1969–2002

In 1969 the recommendations of the Dowa commission were put into action in the form of a 'Ten Year Plan to Resolve the Buraku Problem' whose framework was authorised by the Dowa Taisaku Tokubetsu Sochiho (Law on Special Measures for Dowa Projects – SML). This specified seven categories of policy: the physical environment; social welfare and public health; promotion of agriculture, forestry and fisheries; promotion of small and medium-sized enterprises; employment protection and social security; education; and human rights protection. The act was vague about who was to receive these benefits. It talked of the residents of the 'target areas', 'where the security and improvement of the living environment has been obstructed for historical and social reasons' (Upham 1980: 46). However, many buraku communities contained poor Japanese residents whose ancestors had not been outcastes. There were also, especially in the Kinki area, zainichi Koreans. Should these non-burakumin benefit from the new programmes? The JCP view was that they should, but the BLL argued strongly that as these programmes were the result of their long years of campaigning, only burakumin should be eligible. Moreover, the BLL was anxious to ensure that the various programmes were not used by central or local government to pacify buraku radicalism and put their communities under some kind of administrative control. There was a further fear that if the Dowa administration adopted a method to identify 'genuine' burakumin, this would create a set of records that at a later date could be used for the purpose of discrimination. Therefore, in many areas applicants for benefits from the programmes were screened by a committee that was composed of members of the local BLL branch and local officials. Rather than being co-option of the BLL into the state structure, this was regarded as being the only way of guaranteeing that burakumin were not co-opted.

There was some local variation, but broadly speaking there were three types of programmes. First, there were the projects that targeted the physical environment – improving streets, schools, clinics and community centres and constructing high-rise apartment blocks to replace the old housing stock. Second, there was a system of grants that were paid directly to buraku families. Upham describes the situation in the 1970s whereby a family in Osaka with two children could receive over ¥400,000 annually from a combination of grants rewarding school attendance and twice-yearly grants given to all families, not to mention one-off payments on marriage or the birth of a child (1980: 49). The third type of programmes related to education; these included programmes within the school classroom and also ones outside it that were aimed at changing attitudes among the general public. From the mid-1970s the BLL lobbied for the extension of these programmes, and they were renewed for periods of three to five years until March 2002, when the nationally funded programme came to a halt.

Between 1969 and 1993 the total amount spent on the SML projects was ¥13,880 billion. Most projects were carried out at the level of the municipal authorities (city, town or village), where the cost was split between the state, prefecture and municipality in the ratio 20:10:70. Around a quarter of the projects were implemented by the prefectures, with the costs shared 20:80 by the state and prefecture. Each time the programmes were carried forward, their scope was redefined and narrowed down. First to go were the generous grants. Later the scale of the construction programmes was curtailed. Whereas at the start of the implementation of the policy most of the expenditure was on capital projects, mainly housing schemes, gradually the proportion of the non-material projects increased. In the municipalities the change was from 67:33 in the first phase to 42:54 by the 1990s (Somucho 1995: 7).

While the state was taking measures to improve living standards in order to remove negative images of the buraku communities, it was clear that people were still discriminating against them, and the 1965 report had suggested taking legal steps to prevent this. Government was not enthusiastic about this, insisting that prejudice was a 'matter of heart' that is not amenable to legislative interference. However, it was persuaded to do something to make discrimination more difficult.

When the first family records (*koseki*) of the Meiji era were compiled in 1872, many local officials made sure that former outcastes continued to be identifiable by marking the new registration form in some way. In some areas they even insisted that all the 'new commoners' adopt the same name so that it would be easy to distinguish between them and the rest of the population. These and subsequent registration forms were open to public inspection, making it easy for a potential employer or parent-in-law to check out an individual's family background. In the later 1960s the BLL campaigned for access to the records to be restricted. First the 1872 *koseki* was placed out of bounds. Then in 1976 *koseki* were made inaccessible to all but professionals such as lawyers. This has not stopped determined private investigators getting access to the *koseki* using the services of lawyers and others, and there have been a number of reported incidents of them being accessed illegally (Teraki and Noguchi 2006: 73).

Nevertheless, it was now much more difficult to check a person's background, and so in the mid- to late-1970s some enterprising companies began to produce lists (*chimei sokan*) of the 5,300 or so areas reputed to be buraku. Armed with this list and knowledge of settlement patterns in a city, town or village, an investigator can make a fairly accurate assessment of whether an individual may be of 'buraku background'. This information alone may be sufficient to warrant cancelling a wedding or employment offer, or it may lead to further investigation. Eight editions of these lists are known to have been circulated, and as late as 2006 there were copies discovered still in use (Teraki and Noguchi 2006: 231).

The Osaka office of the Ministry of Justice condemned the purchase of the lists as 'an exceedingly pernicious violation of human rights', and the companies who purchased them were urged to achieve a 'fuller understanding of Dowa problems'. The response of the Ministry of Labour in 1977 was to create a system whereby all companies with more than 100 employees (and some with less) had to have key members of their workforce take training in 'fair employment practice', which included human rights education. These procedures were strengthened in 1987 and again in 1997 (Teraki and Noguchi 2006: 102–3). The implementation of these programmes is devolved to local government, which in some areas has adopted a proactive policy passing bylaws to make it illegal to employ investigators to research an individual's background for whatever reason. The first such ordinance was adopted in Osaka city in March 1985, but many of the more progressive local authorities have adopted similar laws since then (Kitaguchi 1999: 155–69).

RIVALRY IN THE LIBERATION MOVEMENT: TOWARDS A BROADER AGENDA?

As has already been mentioned, the JCP and its supporters held a different view of the origins of buraku discrimination from that of the BLL mainstream, and they also advocated a different solution. They were critical both of the theory and practice of the implementation of the SML on the basis that it would separate burakumin from the wider working-class movement, thereby weakening opposition to the LDP domination of the political system and the capitalist structure (Morooka 1981–2 III: 352–3). The tension between the two wings of the BLL was formalised by the creation in 1970 of a group within the organisation that aimed to change the movement's policy to make it closer to that of the JCP. Prejudice and discrimination were regarded as remnants of the feudal period that had continued to exist within the landlord–tenant relationship or the management relations of small and medium-sized enterprises. In the post-war period, monopoly capitalism had ignored human rights and used discrimination to divide the working class, but buraku discrimination was, they argued, no longer a necessary part of the system. There was no structural reason why it should continue into the twenty-first century.

The post-war movement continued to use the strategy of *kyudan toso*, and in the 1950s it was often linked to demands for provision of support by local governments. Use of the tactic was justified by BLL activists on the grounds that although human rights were guaranteed by the constitution, there was no legislation or system of redress that could be easily used by burakumin to insist on those rights when, for example, their right to equality of opportunity in education or employment was infringed. Denunciation was regarded as a way in which burakumin could assert their rights and thus maintain or regain their human dignity (Upham 1987: 105–10).

However, on two occasions what began as denunciation campaigns against discrimination in schools developed into violent confrontations between the mainstream BLL and JCP supporters. Following the Yata incident in April 1969, two BLL officials were tried for unlawful imprisonment of three junior high school teachers (Upham 1987: 87–103). Five years later, an incident at Yoka High School in Hyogo prefecture involved the confinement in the school for more than twelve hours of fifty-two teachers by members of the local BLL, and it led to the hospitalisation of forty-eight of them (Rohlen 1976: 682–99; Pharr 1990: 75–89). Court cases and appeals against court decisions concerning the Yata case continued into the 1980s, and in the Yoka case into the 1990s. The mainstream newspapers were unsure how to deal with these events and gave them little coverage. *Akahata*, the daily newspaper of the JCP, devoted many column inches to pictures and reports, and the two incidents were running sores in the relations between the two sections of the movement through to the end of the twentieth century. It was this series of violent disagreements between the groups within the BLL that precipitated the creation of a completely separate organisation in 1979, the Zenkoku Buraku Kaiho Rengokai (National Buraku Liberation Alliance – Zenkairen).

The Zenkairen complained that BLL control over the 'administrative window' gave it unfair access to the resources distributed under the SML. The BLL argued that they needed to control the programme's administration so that the Dowa policy did 'not become a means of conciliationism but one of liberation'. However, the Zenkairen charged that in practice this meant that if an applicant were an active member of the BLL there would be no problem in getting the resources in full, but if the applicant were not an activist or, worse, were a member of the Zenkairen, it would be difficult to get anything (Upham 1987: 91–3). Moreover, the Zenkairen started to allege that there was corruption in the system, meaning that at least some of the money was ending up in the hands of organised crime.

The 1965 report had suggested it was the duty of the state to deal with the issue of social deprivation and also that of redress for human rights infringements. As we have seen, the government was not inclined to address this issue, but from the 1980s it was part of the BLL strategy to demand the creation of a Basic Law on the Buraku Issue. Basic Laws have a special place within the Japanese legal framework, midway between the generalities of the Constitution and the nitty-gritty of ordinary legislation. In the words of one American legal scholar, 'they are symbols of permanent commitment to certain goals … [and they] establish a framework for government policy making in a particular area' (Upham 1991: 330). There are Basic Laws on such areas as education, pollution and the disabled.

The BLL sought the passage of a Basic Law with three aims:

- to institutionalise national commitment to the goals of the 1965 report and to establish a legal framework for a comprehensive approach to the buraku problem;
- to oblige the government to take action in a broad range of areas beyond urban renewal;
- to prohibit a wide range of discriminatory acts and provide the statutory basis for direct legal attacks on discrimination by individuals and groups.

Government would be obliged to submit an annual report to the Diet and conduct a survey on buraku conditions every five years. Moreover, a Buraku Deliberative Council would be created to investigate buraku discrimination-related problems (Buraku Liberation Research Institute 1994: 27).

In 1992 the then leader of the BLL, Uesugi Saichiro, announced that the movement would no longer demand the extension of the SML, then due to expire in 1997. Meanwhile, in the political background, there was the collapse of the Soviet Union and other European examples of 'actually existing socialism', plus the rapid and, as it turned out, terminal collapse of the JSP. This was accompanied by the increasing failure of the BLL to attract the support of the bright young people in the buraku communities. In fact many of them were moving out altogether.

Between 1995 and 1996 the movement engaged in an internal debate, in the course of which it set aside its previous set of principles based on a 'class-history perspective' in favour of one founded on the ideas of democracy and human rights. The new documents talk of realising a society without buraku discrimination and link this to a vision of supporting human rights internationally by creating a 'Suiheisha for the whole world' (Kaiho Shimbun, 8 May 1995, 9–10).

The BLL hoped that JSP membership of the Cabinet from June 1994 might enable it to get the Basic Law on Buraku Issues enacted. A 'project team' of members was created from the three governing parties – LDP, JSP and Shinto Sakigake – to devise a bill to be introduced to parliament in the summer of 1995. This did not happen, but in December that year a committee was established within the prime minister's office to create Japan's plan for the United Nations Decade of Human Rights Education. Then in January 1996 Japan finally ratified the Convention on the Elimination of All Forms of Racial Discrimination (CERD). In December 1996 a Law for the Promotion of Human Rights Protection was passed, effective in March the following year. This created a committee, nominally chaired by the prime minister, which produced a report on human rights education in 1998 and measures to address human rights violations in 2001.

The aim of this new policy is to 'resolve human rights problems, including the buraku problem'. In December 2000 a Law on the Promotion of Human Rights Education was passed, which requires central government to formulate a basic plan and report annually to parliament on its human rights promotion programme. There has also been a commitment by government to set up a National Human Rights Commission that would be able to deal effectively with a broad range of human rights issues, including dealing with instances of discrimination and similar infringements of human rights. Attempts in 2003 and 2005 to introduce the legislation failed, and at the time of writing there is no sign when this might happen. In December 2006 the BLL supported a fresh set of demands to establish a Basic Law on human rights and create a national human rights institution.

Meanwhile, the Zenkairen continued to oppose the plans for a Basic Law, arguing that there was not much more that the state could do and indeed suggesting that if it did more, there was a danger that rather than helping resolve the problem it would only serve to make it worse. Publications produced by the JCP and its supporters had consistently criticised the projects funded by the SML before 2002 and by local governments since then. While the mainstream media have been hesitant to comment on buraku-related issues, *Akahata* and related publications have no compunction in alleging waste of public money, corruption and involvement with organised crime syndicates (see, for example, Terazono and Ichinomiya 2002, Ichinomiya 2003).

The Zenkairen was formally dissolved in April 2004, to be replaced the following day by the Zenkoku Chiiki Jinken Undo Sorengo (National Regional Human Rights Movement General Alliance). While its central council consists of individuals with special responsibility for a range of human rights issues such as those relating to Ainu or Hansen's disease sufferers, it is clear that the organisation's main focus is the buraku issue and campaigning to challenge the aims and strategy of the BLL. It is strongly opposed to the proposed Basic Law on human rights.

In the late 1980s, as the BLL adopted a more international perspective following its campaign to persuade the government to ratify the CERD, it decided to sponsor the formation of the International Movement Against All Forms of Discrimination and Racism (IMADR). IMADR was granted formal NGO status by the United Nations in 1993, which entitles it to address United Nations organisations in its own right. It has links with groups in Latin America, Sri Lanka and Paris, and it has taken a sustained interest in the issues of trafficked people in Asia and Dalit women, as well human rights issues in Japan.

BURAKUMIN IN THE TWENTY-FIRST CENTURY

In the early 1990s, as the government was contemplating how to end the SML it carried out a major survey of the conditions in buraku communities and attitudes towards burakumin. The survey covered all of the 4,603 officially designated buraku communities and 60,000 buraku households, and surveyed the attitudes of 60,000 burakumin and 24,000 non-burakumin. The full report has sections on the situation in almost every prefecture, as well as a detailed breakdown of the country as a whole. It runs to over 2,000 pages, and there is only room here for a brief summary.

The report identifies a 'Dowa-related population' (*Dowa kankei jinko*) of 892,751 people, spread among 4,442 communities. The proportion of the 'Dowa-related population' to the overall population resident in these communities had fallen from a national average of 71.9 per cent in 1971 to 41.4 per cent in 1993. There are, however, very large differences between communities. At the extremes, the thirty-six relatively small buraku areas in Miyazaki Prefecture have only 2.7 per cent of their communities made up of burakumin, whereas the figure is 97.9 per cent in the six quite large buraku of Fukui. In Osaka the forty-eight buraku tend to be large (average size around 2,000 people) but full of burakumin (87.3 per cent), while the 606 smaller buraku found in Fukuoka (average size 500 people) only have about 36.6 per cent burakumin among their residents (Buraku Kaiho Jinken Kenkyosho 1999, 20–21).

These figures indicate why it is so difficult to accurately estimate the burakumin population. For the government, burakumin consist of the 'Dowa-related population' who are resident in the Dowa communities. It is an administrative definition. The BLL is speaking on behalf of all those who are living in these communities *and* those who do not but who might be subject to discrimination if their status were discovered. There is ample evidence that many people moved out of their native communities between the 1970s and 1990s, and many of these may be passing as non-burakumin, but this would not make them invulnerable to discrimination if someone were to investigate their background. Conversely, if you live in a buraku for too long you may become considered to be burakumin, even though this would not entitle you to any benefits.

Asked about their experiences of discrimination, one-third of the burakumin sample reported feeling that their rights had been infringed at some time in their lives, most frequently in incidents at work, in school or involving marriage (Somucho 1995:25). If marriage outside the buraku community can be regarded as showing the decreasing power of prejudice, there was some encouraging evidence. Around 80 per cent of those over the age of 80 had married fellow burakumin, but this had dropped to less than 25 per cent of those under 25. When asked a hypothetical question about the marriage of one of their children to a burakumin, 45 per cent of the mainstream respondents said they would respect their child's wishes, 41 per cent said that if the child felt strongly there was nothing they could do about it and only 5 per cent said they would completely oppose the marriage (Somucho 1995: 31). This latter figure is down from 7.6 per cent in 1985, but some suggest that it may reflect only the fact that most people now know that not to object is the 'right answer' to the question. In practice, a greater proportion may try to prevent such a marriage.

There was some evidence of improved income levels. Only 52 per cent of buraku households received 'livelihood security support' in 1993, compared to 76 per cent in 1975. However, this was almost twice as high as the non-buraku households in the same areas (28.2 per cent) and well above the national average of 7.1 per cent (Somucho 1995:4).

The evidence about educational performance showed a pattern of some improvement, but also showed remaining unresolved problems. Overall, the entry of burakumin children into senior high schools was close to that of the mainstream, 91.8 per cent compared to 96 per cent. However, the rate of persistent long-term absenteeism from primary and junior high schools among buraku children is almost twice the mainstream average: 1.6 per cent and 4.5 per cent, compared to 0.8 per cent and 2.4 per cent respectively. Access to higher education had improved: less that 2 per cent of burakumin over 55 had any experience of higher education, whereas at the start of the 1990s over 20 per cent of burakumin teenagers could expect to go to university (Somucho 1995: 10–11,15). This is a considerable improvement, but it still lagged behind the figure of nearly 40 per cent for the rest of the population. Probably linked to this difference in educational achievement was the fact that only 10.6 per cent of burakumin were reported to be employed in enterprises of over 300 employees, well below the national average of 23.3 per cent (Somucho 1995: 20). Since it is only the larger enterprises that can provide stable employment, higher salaries and better fringe benefits, these figures suggest that burakumin remain somewhat marginal to Japanese society.

The picture in 1993 was of some remarkable improvements, with plenty of room for more before the gap between burakumin communities and the rest is completely closed. The BLL has demanded that the survey be repeated. Just after 1993, the recession had a major economic and social impact. There is growing evidence that the 'gap between rich and poor' (commonly referred to as *kakusa*) has increased over the last ten years, and that even though the economy as a whole is recovering, the neo-liberal policies are benefiting those who are already better off more than the rest. In 2006 Japan overtook Turkey and Mexico to have the second-highest poverty rate in the OECD's statistics. How, one wonders, are burakumin faring? More than ten years after the previous national survey, all we have are a number of small-scale surveys of buraku conditions in certain prefectures. It would be very helpful to know more about the national picture so that we can assess what, if anything, now needs to be done.

CONCLUSION

Qualitative evidence from interviews (see, for example, McLauchlan 2003) plus survey data suggests that there continue to be many burakumin who have experience of discrimination or who feel that they or their children may be disadvantaged by discrimination at some stage of their lives. Many private investigators still earn a substantial living from looking into the background of young people for evidence of buraku or Korean ancestry.

The extent of institutional discrimination that may be contributing to this situation is difficult to ascertain. Certainly the 1993 surveys suggest, for example, that fewer buraku children go to university than in the population at large. However, we know that class background is closely related to access to higher education: lower ability children from middle-class backgrounds are more likely to go to university than children of similar ability from working-class backgrounds (Hashimoto 2003: 133). Does the relatively poor academic performance of buraku children simply reflect the class makeup of their communities? If so, is there anything that the state can do in its Dowa policy to change the situation?

The thirty-three years of the SML-funded projects generated a feeling among some Japanese that burakumin were benefiting from unfair positive discrimination. Indeed, this was part of the JCP argument opposing the SML. Nevertheless, these projects have eliminated the most obvious differences between buraku and non-buraku communities. It is no longer possible to spot where buraku communities start and end as you drive along a highway, as was possible thirty years ago. In terms of high-cost projects in the cities, there was probably not much more to do by the end of the 1990s. The JCP and some media have reported evidence of waste, corruption and links between Dowa projects and organised crime. No doubt these problems exist, as they do in the construction of highways, but that is not to say that no roads should have been built. While it is right that the JCP make public its evidence, one feels that its case has been sensationalised because it supports the negative image that still exists about burakumin. Some Dowa projects continue to be funded by local governments. Moreover, it is overall government policy to push tasks down from central to local governments and to reform the structures of local administrations. Buraku community leaders need to work out what role they want to play within these new structures.

Reber, among others, has criticised the lack of equal rights legislation that would make the constitutional commitment to human rights easier to enforce (Reber 1999). However, as Upham argues, the mainstream view is that 'Law ... should be limited to the affirmation of custom, and although it may unction to recognise or declare social change it should not lead cause or even contribute to such change' (1987: 208). We should not assume that even if there were evidence that civil rights legislation caused significant and positive change in the United States the adoption of similar laws would have the same impact in Japan. Government, for whatever reason, has been reluctant to create an independent human rights commission, despite pressure from international agencies and demands from the domestic human rights NGOs. The creation of such a body would contribute to the formation of a human-rights-respecting culture in Japan, and that might be more significant than legislation that might be seen as coercive.

Sections of the LDP are opposed to any further rights legislation. The BLL cut its links with the JSP in the mid-1990s, and has not sought to develop a similar relationship with any of the parties formed since. However, Matsumoto Ryu, grandson of Matsumoto Jiichiro, supports the Democratic Party of Japan (DPJ) in the Diet, having first been elected with JSP in 1990. He is a senior figure within the BLL and has at various times had responsibility for human rights policy within the DPJ. The DPJ supported the proposals for a human rights commission in August 2005, but this came to nothing when the Diet was dissolved prior to the 2005 general election. The JCP, while fading in political significance, has not disappeared from the political map as one might have expected in this post-Cold-War world. Its publications remain an important forum in which the activities of the BLL can be frankly discussed and alternative strategies can be proposed. It is hard to imagine circumstances in which it might gain greater political authority. If the BLL is going to make political headway in the foreseeable future, it will need the support of the DPJ.

A solution to the 'buraku problem' would be a situation where it would be possible for people to find out about my buraku background either from me or a third party and to react to that information with indifference or mild interest. It would not be information that I would want to hide from them or my children. This situation does not exist in Japan yet, but we are probably closer to it than we were fifty or even ten years ago. Progress towards that goal is patchy. It is closer in the rich metropolitan areas of eastern Japan than in the poor former mining towns of northern Kyushu. The role of organised burakumin in ensuring this target is reached has changed, and it will have to continue to change in the future. After all, the closer the BLL gets to that goal, the less important the movement will be, and there may come a stage when, as the JCP has argued for some years, the BLL's existence is an obstacle to reaching the final goal. I do not think we are at that point yet, but it is appropriate that over the last ten years it has entered in to close cooperation with the broader human rights movement, both in Japan and internationally. Even when the day comes that the BLL has fulfilled its historic mission of eliminating discrimination and prejudice against burakumin, there will no doubt still be a need to protect and promote human rights standards in Japan and elsewhere.

Useful websites

International Movement Against All Forms of Discrimination and Racism (IMADR), http://www.imadr.org.
Buraku Liberation and Human Rights Research Institute (BLHRRI), http://blhrri.org/.
Zenkoku Chiiki Jinkenundo Sorengo, http://homepage3.nifty.com/zjr/.

References

Buraku Kaiho Jinken Kenkyusho (1999) *Kyo no Buraku Sabetsu* (Buraku Discrimination Today) (Third edition), Osaka: Kaiho Shuppansha.
Buraku Liberation Research Institute (1994) *Suggestions for Human Rights Policies in Japan*, Osaka: BLRI.
DeVos, G. and Wagatsuma, H. (1973) *Japan's Invisible Race* (Second edition), Berkeley: University of California Press.
Harada, T. and Uesugi, S. (1981) *Long Suffering Brothers and Sisters Unite!* Osaka: Buraku Liberation Research Institute.
Hashimoto, K. (2003) *Class Structure in Contemporary Japan*, Melbourne: Trans Pacific Press.

Ichinomiya, Y. (2003) *Dowa Riken no Shinso 2* (Truth about Dowa Graft 2), Tokyo: Takarajimasha.

Kaiho Shimbun, (8 May 1995) No. 1718, Osaka: Kaiho Shuppansha

Kitaguchi, S. (1999) (trans. A. McLauchlan) *An Introduction to the Buraku Issue*, Richmond: Japan Library, 1999

McLauchlan, A. (2003) 'Solving Anti-Bukaumin Prejudice in the 21st Century: Suggestions from 21 buraku residents' (discussion paper), *Electronic Journal of Contemporary Japanese Studies*.

Morooka, S. (1981–2) *Sengo Buraku Kaiho Ronsoshi* (A History of the Post-War Buraku Liberation Theory Debate) (Three vols.), Tokyo: Tsuge Shobo.

Neary, I.J. (1986) 'Socialist and Communist Party Attitudes towards Discrimination against Japan's Burakumin', *Political Studies* 34, 556–74.

—— (1989) *Political Protest and Social Control in Pre-War Japan: The origins of buraku liberation*, Manchester: Manchester University Press.

Pharr, S. (1990) *Losing Face: Status politics in Japan*, Berkeley: University of California Press.

Reber, E. (1999) 'Burakumondai in Japan', *Harvard Human Rights Journal* 12, 297–59.

Rohlen, T.P. (1976) Violence at Yoka High School: The implications for Japanese coalition politics of the confrontation between the Communist Party and the Buraku Liberation League', *Asian Survey* 16, 7, 682–99.

Somucho (1995) *Heisei Gonendo Dowachiku Jittai Haakuto Chosakekka no Gaiyo* (Outline of the Results of the 1993 Surveys to Assess Conditions in the Dowa Areas), Tokyo: Somuchokan Kanbo Chiiki Kaizen Taisakushitsu.

Teraki, N. and Noguchi, M. (2006) *Buraku Mondairon e no Shotai* (Invitation to Buraku Issue Theory), Osaka: Kaihoshuppansha.

Terazono, A. and Ichinomiya, Y. (2002) *Dowa Riken no Shinso* (Truth about Dowa Graft), Tokyo: Takarajimasha.

Upham, F. (1980) 'Ten Years of Affirmative Action for Japanese Burakumin: A preliminary report on the Law on Special Measures for Dowa Projects', *Law in Japan: An Annual* 20, 30–87.

—— (1987) *Law and Social Change in Postwar Japan*, Cambridge, Mass.: Harvard University Press.

—— (1993) 'Unplaced Persons', in A. Gordon (ed.) *Postwar Japan as History*, Berkeley: University of California Press.

Watanabe, T. (1993) "Ima 'Buraku Rekishi" o Toinaosu' (Time to Review 'Buraku History') *Buraku Kaiho Kenkyu* 94, 1–28.

Yamamoto, N. (1999) 'Kinsei Mibunsei o Do Toraeruka' (How to Capture the Kinsei Status System), *Buraku Kaishoshi Fukuoka*, 95, September, 37–55.

5 The other other

The black presence in the Japanese experience

John G. Russell

Negroes don't exist in Japan.

(Anonymous blogger, 2006)[1]

INTRODUCTION

For many people awareness of the existence of blacks in the Japanese imagination first began to emerge in the mid- and late-1980s with reports in
the American media on the popularity of Helen Bannerman's *Little Black
Sambo*, on anti-black statements by a troika of conservative, right-wing
Japanese politicians, beginning with Prime Minister Nakasone Yasuhiro,
and on the questionable hiring practices of US-based Japanese companies.
On the whole, these Japanese attitudes toward blacks were discussed in
the context of external black, primarily African American, populations. That
Japan had its own, albeit small, black foreign population and stereotypes
about blacks, derived in large part from the West, went largely unremarked.
Nonetheless, by the late 1980s and early 1990s in the United States, Japanese
anti-black racism had become an expected characteristic of a society and
culture that was regularly depicted in the American media as insular,
xenophobic, and racist. Concurrently, this period also saw the emergence
of a growing discourse, both popular and scholarly, on the popularity of
'black culture,' particularly as embodied in hip hop and rap and other forms
of highly commercialized and commodifiable African American 'street
culture.'

In the intervening years, as trade relations between America and Japan
improved and the former turned its attention to new foreign 'threats,' the
image of Japanese as inveterate racists has largely been submerged, replaced
by perceptions of Japan as a loyal ally in the perpetual 'war on terror,' an
inspirational cornucopia of postmodern pop, and an ardent consumer of
things 'black.' Japan's younger generation is now often depicted as clueless

imitators of a people toward whom previous generations of Japanese are thought to have a particular disdain.

Discussion of the intersection of Japanese and black lives generally operates under the assumption that Japan's encounter with blacks is of relatively recent origin. 'Most Japanese born before 1935,' anthropologist Wagatsuma Hiroshi asserted, 'first discovered Negroes by singing 'Old Black Joe' and other Stephen Foster melodies at school' (Wagatsuma 1967: 433). Others, such as former Ambassador to Japan Edwin O. Reischauer, maintain that Japanese had 'almost no contact with blacks before the coming of the American army of Occupation' (Reischauer 1988: 397). Seldom has this discourse, particularly in its popular enunciations, acknowledged that the presence of black people and various forms of black culture – either directly or by proxy – has not been confined to the immediate pre-war and post-war periods. While Japanese contacts with Africans and later with African Americans were limited compared to their encounters with whites, their exposure to Western discourse about them was less limited, and shaped how Japanese would perceive blacks when they actually encountered them. These eventual encounters were transacted within a hierarchy of power relations wherein blacks occupied a subordinate position.

EARLY JAPANESE CONSTRUCTIONS OF BLACKNESS

Until recently, scholars on both sides of the Pacific have tended to view Japan's encounter with the West as almost exclusively between Japanese and Europeans, downplaying the presence of non-Western people. In addition to the presence of Malays, East Indians, Indonesians, and Southeast Asians, there was also an African presence, consisting of Africans who accompanied Europeans to Japanese shores as sailors, servants, interpreters, artisans, and slaves. Images of dark-skinned foreigners, some depicting Africans, can be found in sixteenth-century *namban* prints. While Japanese artists were not above producing demonized portraits of foreigners, the so-called southern barbarians – white *and* black – many of these prints are not dehumanizing caricatures, instead capturing in colorful detail the procession of Western power and the place of blacks within it.[2]

The mid-nineteenth-century artist Hashimoto Sadahide depicted the dignity and grace of black servants he encountered in Yokohama. His written impressions of the Africans stress the similarities between their customs and those of the Japanese and describe African women as 'rather charming' and as 'bear[ing] themselves with a sort of female dignity,' concluding that they are 'no different in human nature, being kindly and compassionate' (cited in Meech-Pekarik 1987: 44). By the late-nineteenth century and early-twentieth century, however, such sympathetic portraits would give way to broad caricature closely modeled on Western anti-black stereotypes. The written archive from this period does not ignore the African presence. Sporadic references to Africans do appear, although for the most part they are limited to their roles as servants and slaves, as objects of Japanese fascination and derision. Unfortunately, we know relatively little about how premodern Japanese viewed Africans and even less about how the Africans, in turn, regarded their Japanese hosts.[3] What records we do have come from Japanese who had contact with Europeans, and whose views of the Africans, consequently, were tainted by Western prejudices.

Historians trace Japan's first contact with blacks to the arrival of Portuguese and Dutch traders in the sixteenth and seventeenth centuries. However, some scholars contend there was an African presence in premodern Japan as a result of Chinese trade with Africa during the Tang (618–907) and Song (960–1279) dynasties.[4] According to Coupland, 'In 976 a great sensation was produced at the court of the Tang Emperor by the arrival of an Arab envoy with a 'negro slave' in his suite; and after that date Chinese books repeatedly refer to 'negro slaves' and ... to the Arab slave trade which produced them' (cited in Filesi 1962: 21). Duyvendak (1949: 23) asserts, 'thousands of them [Africans] are sold as foreign slaves.' Chinese scholars maintain China had already established trade relations with the African kingdoms of Kush and Axum during the Han dynasty (206 BC–AD 220), though 'African scholars tend to take a rather more skeptical view' (Snow 1988: 2). An intriguing reference to a 'black' man, presumably African, that suggests an African presence in Japan by way of Korea is found in a document produced in the 1670s:

> In the country of Inaba [Tottori Prefecture] there was a man of seven feet height. He was from the country of '*kuro*.' He had been captured in the Korean war [1592–8] and brought over to Japan. His color was that of soot and people called him *kurombō*.
>
> (cited in Wagatsuma 1967: 43)

Beginning in the sixteenth century, one obtains documented evidence of Japanese contact with Africans. In 1546 Portuguese captain Jorge Alvarez brought Africans to Japan. According to Alvarez, the initial Japanese reaction to them was primarily curiosity: 'They like seeing black people,' he wrote in 1547, 'especially Africans, and they will come 15 leagues just to see them and entertain them for three or four days' (Cooper 1965: 66). The most well-documented case is that of Yasuke, a Mozambican youth brought to Japan by the Italian Jesuit Alessandro Valignano (1537–1606), who was presented to *daimyō* Oda Nobunaga in 1581.[5] The first Japanese reference to Yasuke appears in Ota Gyūchi's (1527–161?) *Shinchō Kōki* (Chronicle of the Life of Oda Nobunaga) of 1600, wherein he is described as a healthy young man of 16 or 17, black as a bull, and possessed of a fine character (Fujita 1987a: 30). An account of Japanese reaction to Yasuke written in 1584 by the Portuguese Jesuit Luis Frois (1532–97), who accompanied Valignano to Kyoto, relates an incident in which the townspeople, clamoring for a glimpse of the African, broke down the doors of a Jesuit residence. The ensuing melee resulted in the death and injury of several participants. Upon seeing the African, Nobunaga had him stripped and bathed to determine for himself if his skin color was natural (Cooper 1965: 71). This aspect of Yasuke's life is frequently cited by scholars; less well-known – but no less remarkable – is the remainder of his life. Retained as an attendant by Nobunaga, he later accompanied him into battle against rival lord Akechi Mitsuhide (1528?–82), who, upon defeating Nobunaga at Horyuji, spared the African and subsequently released him.[6]

Fujita places the number of Africans temporarily residing in Japan during the sixteenth century at several hundred. Some came to Japan as slaves and servants, others as sailors, soldiers, and interpreters. Their roles were not limited to serving Europeans. Like Yasuke, a number of Africans were employed by *daimyō* in various capacities, as soldiers, gunners, drummers, and entertainers (Fujita 1987a: 30–3; and Leupp 1995: 2). During the Edo Period (1603–1867) a small number of black Africans lived in the Dutch settlement in Deshima. Despite the policy of national isolation, records show that Africans mingled freely among Japanese visitors and were allowed occasionally to leave the island, as were their European masters.[7]

Prior to the ban placed on Japanese slavery in the late sixteenth century by Toyotomi Hideyoshi (1536–98), privileged African and East Indian slaves in Japan kept Japanese slaves and mistresses, as did their European masters (Clemons 1990: 33–4). Significantly, the ban on the traffic in Japanese slaves applied to all foreigners, white and black alike. Equally significant is the fact that the Africans were allowed to have Japanese slaves at all; if Japanese considered blacks grossly inferior, it is unlikely they would have permitted them to own Japanese slaves. By the seventeenth century, however, restrictions were introduced that specifically prohibited Africans from consorting with courtesans, though doubt remains as to the degree this was enforced, for these restrictions did not prevent Japanese hosts from introducing Africans to the pleasure districts (Fujita 1987b: 253). Africans were also involved in criminal activities, mostly involving smuggling and the theft of animals and food, and, perhaps due to their mistreatment by the Dutch, were sometimes abetted by sympathetic Japanese who were charged as accomplices. Indeed, some Japanese expressed shock at how cheaply the Dutch valued the lives of their black slaves. Wrote Physician Hirokawa Kai:

The *kurobō* (blacks) ... perform backbreaking and dangerous tasks for their masters without complaint. They work hard, climbing the masts of ships without the least display of fear. The *kōmōjin* ["red-hairs"; i.e., the Dutch] have brought many of them here. I cannot fathom the ways of the red-hairs, who work and lash [their slaves] as if they were beasts and who kill the young and the strong who resist, throwing their bodies into the sea.

(cited in Fujita 1987b: 251–2)

Hirokawa goes on to note that sick blacks rarely received medical treatment and were poisoned by the Dutch if their condition deteriorated. Another writer reports that if the ailing blacks did not respond to treatment they were kicked to death (Fujita 1987b: 252).

With the importation of *Rangaku* (Dutch Learning) came not only knowledge of Western geography and science but also Western prejudices against Africans and other subjugated races. Geographic references to Africa based on conversations with the Dutch were, on the whole, unfavorable, depicting its inhabitants as salacious, savage, stupid, inferior, and cannibalistic. It is important to recall that few Japanese writing on Africa had ever visited the continent. Most of these accounts were filtered through information obtained second-hand from European merchants and missionaries. Even when Japanese set foot in Africa, their perceptions of the continent and its peoples were colored by their European mentors.

The general scholarly consensus has been that Japanese perceptions of blacks were monolithically negative (Miyoshi 1979; Wagatsuma 1967, 1978; Wagatsuma and Yoneyama 1980; Reischauer 1988). Citing the journals of Japanese envoys dispatched to the United States in the nineteenth century, Miyoshi (1979: 60) notes the revulsion they felt toward black skin. In his discussion of modern Japanese attitudes toward blacks, Wagatsuma writes, 'Although they are ambivalent toward Caucasian physical characteristics, the Japanese are *unequivocally and unanimously negative* toward the negroid features of black Americans and Africans' (Wagatsuma 1978: 121; emphasis mine). Wagatsuma and Yoneyama (1980) attribute this phenomenon to cultural values involving traditional Japanese aesthetic predispositions.

In fact, Japanese attitudes toward black people have been neither static nor universally negative. Rather it appears attitudes evolved in tandem with Japan's exposure to outside cultures, principally – but not exclusively – those of the West, whose own attitudes toward blacks and other dark-skinned peoples were decidedly negative when it encountered Japan in the sixteenth century. Cultural reductionist models that attribute Japanese anti-black attitudes to deeply embedded, remarkably static traditional aesthetics or to a visceral revulsion toward black skin tend toward an ahistoricism that retreats from interrogating power relations in the construction of color prejudice writ large and the role Western racial paradigms have played in the global invention of black alterity. Such models fail to explain why racially ascribed attributes such as laziness, stupidity, and hypersexuality – which Japanese had ascribed to outsiders regardless of skin color – came to be associated primarily with dark-skinned people. Nor do they explain why – unless one is prepared to posit a universal negrophobia – these traits are identical to those ascribed to blacks in the West. Conversely, Japanese predilection for whiteness does little to explain why whites – whom one might assume would have been privileged by virtue of their 'white' skin – were nonetheless despised during the early stages of Japanese–European contact as uncivilized, hirsute barbarians and feared and mocked as *tengu* (long-nosed demons). Only gradually did whites come to be regarded as the embodiment of civilization, sophistication and physical beauty.

While there exists a negative symbology surrounding the color black in Japan, the extent to which it informed premodern Japanese attitudes toward 'black' people is debatable. This is not to suggest that Japanese were colorblind. A variety of terms were used in premodern Japan to refer to dark-skinned outsiders, including *kurobō*, *kurobōshu*, and *kurosu*. The last was employed in the sixteenth century to identify black Africans, but by the Edo period (1615–1867) it had grown to include all dark-skinned people (Fujita 1987b: 240, 243). Another Japanese term, *konrondo* ("black slaves"), is derived from the Chinese ideograms for *kunlun-nu* (崑崙奴, 'slaves from Kunlun"), *Kunlun* originally referring to a fabled mountain range that was believed to span parts of Tibet and India. By the fourth century, the term was applied to frontier tribes and Khmers, and, in the eighth century, Malays and Africans.[8] Although *konrondo* originally referred to East Indians, like its Chinese cognate, it too later grew to include Arabs and Africans (Fujita 1987b: 244). The derivation of *kurombō*, a pejorative term for blacks and dark-skinned people that is often glossed in English as 'nigger,' is somewhat more obscure.[9] Citing an unidentified philologist, Wagatsuma contends that the term was derived from Colombo, Ceylon (Sri Lanka), since the dark-skinned servants aboard the Dutch ships were 'identified as people from Colombo' (Wagatsuma 1967: 432). Philologist Suzuki Tōzō (who presumably is Wagatsuma's unidentified source) makes essentially the same claim.[10] While these terms sometimes conflated Africans with Malays and other dark-skinned peoples, such was not always the case. A letter written in 1618 describes the *konrondo* on the Dutch ships as originally coming from Kaburi (Africa), adding that the Dutch called them *suwaruto yongozu* (*zwartze jongen*; black youth).[11]

The line separating Japanese discourse on people of African descent from Western discourse is a difficult one to draw given that Japanese-language accounts about Africans were written after contact with Europeans. Whatever the nature of Japanese premodern sensibilities, they do not appear to inform contemporary Japanese constructions of blackness. Rather, it is the lineage of Western-inspired imagery that survives. When asked what images come to mind when they hear the term *kokujin* (black person), most Japanese mention '*Chibi Kuro Sambo*' (Little Black Sambo), '*Kaze to Tomo ni Saranu no Mami*' (*Gone with the Wind's* Mammy), '*Tomu Oji-san*' (Uncle Tom), '*Tomu to Jeri no maido*' (*Tom and Jerry's* maid, Mammy-Two-Shoes), and any number of contemporary popular black entertainers and athletes. All of these figures are clearly not drawn from Japanese mythology, history, and literature.

Also problematic to the understanding of Japanese constructions of blackness and attitudes toward blacks is the fact that the historical conditions out of which Western images of blacks evolved did not exist in Japan, whose own colonial projects involved neither the systematic exploitation of Africa nor the barbarities of the slave trade. This is not to suggest that other mechanisms of 'othering' based on culturally meaningful categories of difference (including skin color) did not exist in Japan prior to European contact, or that contemporary manifestations of Japanese racialism are entirely Western derived. Japan's treatment of its internal and colonial subjects (Ainu, Ryūkyūans, Koreans, Chinese and South East Asians) as well as of burakumin, testifies to the prior existence of such systems.

One might object that this analysis neglects Chinese influence. Dikötter (1992) argues that premodern Chinese held Africans in contempt, viewing them as an inferior, ugly, and savage people, and notes their acquisition of African slaves prior to European contact. Given China's early encounters with Africans and historical ties with Japan, the possibility of a Chinese influence on Japan's images of blacks, predating Japan's exposure to European influence, cannot be easily dismissed, particularly in light of the fact that the preference for white skin in ancient Japan was itself rooted in Chinese aesthetics. The Japanese practice of *oshiroi* (cosmetic skin whitening) originated among the court elite of the Nara (710–94) and Heian Periods (794–1185) in imitation of the Chinese aristocracy, though among the elites of both societies, skin color served as a symbolic marker of class – not racial – difference. Indeed, the association of dark skin with low status predated Chinese contact with Africans, having its roots in the treatment of dark-skinned Chinese peasants who had acquired their 'black' skin toiling in the sun.

However, the question remains whether China's negative attitudes toward Africans derived from its own system of color symbolism or arose to justify its own, albeit limited, enslavement of Africans. Scholars disagree on the nature of premodern Chinese attitudes toward Africans. While Dikötter describes them as primarily negative, others suggest they were more ambivalent. Snow notes that Tang dynasty Chinese regarded the physical skills, discipline, and power of Africans with 'a mixture of admiration and awe' (1988: 18). Tang literature often depicted black Africans as resourceful, magical, heroic beings, though not the equals of Chinese (Harris 1987: 92; Filesi 1962: 19; Irwin 1977: 172). Song accounts reveal that they were impressed with the seafaring skills African displayed on Chinese ships (as, centuries later, Japanese commentators would be with the skills of *korosu* aboard Dutch vessels). Most scholars agree, however, that by the Song dynasty, with the growth of the African population in Canton composed, in part, of runaway slaves, Chinese images of Africans turned increasingly negative.

Significantly, many of the disparaging remarks made by Chinese about Africans that are cited by Dikötter as examples of pre-European-contact anti-African imagery are drawn from Song dynasty accounts, a period during which 'reports on the Arab slave trade became more common' (1992: 15). Chinese traders were dependent on Arab and Muslim middlemen for information about the African continent prior to actual contact, and they may have seen Africans through the eyes of these intermediaries (Dathorne 1996: 78, 85). Thus it is quite possible that these negative images of Africans were acquired from Arab and Persian slave traders. As Dikötter himself points out, 'The equation of 'black' with 'slave,' an important factor in the development of racial discrimination [in the West], was thus realized at a relatively early stage in China' (1992: 16). More intriguing, these second-hand accounts dovetailed with Chinese conceptions of primitive *kunlun* barbarians as the ultimate Other. Indeed, prior to contact with Africans, the concept of *kunlun* had lost its magical connotations and came to be associated with generic barbarian tribes without specific regard to skin color (1992: 76). Thus whether one is dealing with Persian, Arab, Muslim, Chinese or European accounts, negative perceptions of Africans were forged by conditions of slavery.

As in premodern China, there is evidence to suggest that attitudes toward dark-skinned people in premodern Japan were not uniformly negative and that changes in their depiction were – and continue to be – influenced by social and historical factors. For all its negative symbology, blackness had positive associations as well. *Nesshi*, the practice of cosmetically blackening the teeth, is believed to have entered Japan from Southeast Asia and, like *oshiroi*, it was practiced by the aristocracy and was central to Japan's aesthetic universe until it was outlawed in 1868. This was a time of tremendous social change, during which Japanese elites sought to eliminate customs and practices they believed the West considered uncivilized. Such considerations had a transformative effect on Japanese aesthetics. In 1683, an English visitor to Japan, Christopher Fryke, wrote that Japanese aesthetics were 'directly opposite to ours, taking Black to be the Livery of Mirth and Pleasantness, and White of Grief and Mourning.' Indeed, some Japanese representations portrayed the Buddha as both black and African. Describing the image of Sakyamuni Buddha in a letter to King James, merchant Richard Cocks wrote in 1616: '[I]n a littell Closet or Cubbard, was a negro or a blackamore's image, wch they tould me was the Idoll of Shacka [Shaka; the Buddha], the Cheefe god the[y] Adore ..."(cited in Leupp 1995: 4). This association of black Africans with the Buddha lasted well into the nineteenth century, though by then some Japanese had begun to doubt the wisdom of venerating the representative of an inferior people.

   The reification of skin color into a static hierarchy of racialized entities would not take shape until the arrival of Europeans on Japanese shores, and vice-versa, where exposure to racial inequality reinforced status symbolism. Had Chinese hegemony continued into the seventeenth century, a stronger case might be made for the Chinese origin of anti-black prejudice in Japan.

NINETEENTH- AND EARLY TWENTIETH-CENTURY FORMULATION

The process of seeing blacks through Western eyes is repeated in the nineteenth century with Japan's steady exposure to white American anti-black stereotypes. In 1854, Commodore Matthew Calbraith Perry, returning to Edo Bay to conclude a commercial treaty with Japan, treated Japanese negotiators to a blackface minstrel show – 'a serenade of pseudo-darkies,' as one witness to the performance put it (McCauley 1942: 77) – performed aboard the flagship *Powhatan*. Perry's 'Ethiopian minstrels,' as they were called, performed in several locations throughout Japan, including the ports of Hakodate and Shimoda, as well as in the Ryūkyūs, Macao, and Hong Kong. According to William Heine, acting master's mate and the principal artist of the expedition, Japanese were delighted by the comical, cavorting 'blacks.' In Hakodate, the minstrels performed 'songs and dances of plantation blacks of the South.' They were also a hit at a reception held for the commissioners of Matsumai and other high ranking Japanese officials. 'They applauded in every possible way and shouted again and again: 'Kussi! Kussi!' That word signifies the greatest degree of pleasure, mental and physical' (Heine 1990: 154–5).

   Real blacks did serve aboard the *Powhatan*, but, sadly, little is known about them.[12] When Perry officially presented himself to the Japanese on 14 July 1853, two ornate foot-long rosewood boxes containing his credentials and a letter from President Millard Fillmore to the Japanese emperor were 'guarded by a couple of tall, jet-black Negroes, completely armed' (Perry

1968: 98) who opened the boxes, removed their contents, and displayed their seals before the Japanese (Wiley 1990: 318–19). These stewards also served as Perry's personal bodyguard. Six armed blacks escorted him when he landed in Edo Bay in 1854. Blacks also held responsible positions as captains of the gun. How Japanese reacted to them and how they, in turn, regarded the Japanese are unknown. Their role may be dismissed as simply ornamental, yet the commodore's decision to use blacks in these roles is highly significant given his emphasis on their physicality and his use of their bodies as a twofold projection of American power: The blacks are imposing, yet not so powerful that they have escaped domestication, for they serve – and protect – a white master. Indeed, their dramatic display would appear to be intentional. According to William Heine, who was a witness to the event, Perry was intent upon out-pomping the Japanese. Unlike the Dutch and Russian emissaries before them, the Americans did not 'kneel and crawl, backward and forward, time after time' to their Japanese hosts. Perry would have none of that; the Americans would enter the reception pavilion standing erect, for 'the commodore has made up his mind; no disgraceful humiliation would be inflicted on *him*' (Heine: 73; original emphasis).

The impact of Western attitudes toward blacks in shaping Japanese attitudes is apparent in the journals of delegates of the 1860 Embassy to the United States and London and of the 1871 Iwakura Mission to the United States. Stopping in London on his return to Japan from America, a member of the 1860 mission wrote: 'The faces of these natives are black as if painted with ink and resemble those of monkeys ... According to the Americans, they are the incarnation of apes' (*Dojin wo miru ni kau-iro sumi wo nuru gotoku saru gotoshi ... Beijin no kata nite kono dojin wa saru no kesshin nari to zo*) (Wagatsuma and Yoneyama 1980: 64).[13] Miyoshi characterizes the attitude of the delegation toward the Africans they encountered in the Congo as monotonously contemptuous:

> All remarks about the Africans are more or less the same, sneering at their bare bodies and black skins, occasionally adding further details concerning their body odor and movement, their tattoos and ornaments. Some describe the chain gangs of slaves, but none expresses any sympathy for the captives; nor do they deplore the inhuman treatment of the Portuguese.
>
> (Miyoshi 1979: 60–1)

Yet such attitudes mark a significant departure from Japanese condemnations of Dutch slavery in the seventeenth century.

Beasley has described the disparaging Japanese discourse on Africans – and Asians – during this period as 'an account of the world as seen from the first-class cabins on the Far East run or from the salons of western capitals' (1995: 87). Beasley notes that this discourse relied less on first-hand Japanese observations than on hearsay that reflected not only the attitudes of their hosts, but also the degrading social conditions in which the non-whites they did encounter were forced to live in the Western-dominated world, and that it expressed the relief of Japanese travelers who, spared similar treatment, 'began to see themselves ... as "honorary whites"' (215–16).

However, Japanese could also be critical of their white hosts and show sympathy and even admiration toward blacks. In *Tokumei Zenken Taishi Bei-ō Kairan Jikki* (Journal of the Envoy Extraordinary Ambassador Plenipotentiary's Travels through America and Europe, 1878), Kume Kunitake (1839–1931), the private secretary to Iwakura Tomomi (1825–83), describes the African slave trade in critical terms, noting the harsh treatment of African slaves and commenting favorably on efforts by whites to establish schools for former slaves, who, he notes, received instruction not only in the three R's but also in Greek, Latin, and the sciences (213). After visiting one such Negro school in the South, Kume remarks that blacks had made considerable progress, noting their election to Congress and that some had amassed sizable fortunes (216). 'Skin color has no relation to intelligence' (*hifu no iro wa, chishiki ni kankei nai koto*), he writes, noting that 'The blacks also produce brilliant intellects against which uneducated whites stood no measure' (*kokujin ni mo eisai haishutsu shi, hakujin no fugaku naru mono wa, yaku wo taru ni itaran*) (216). Such enlightened sentiments may have been offered as a testament to the civilizing powers of Western learning; they may have also reflected the tutelage of progressive whites eager to share their egalitarian ideals. Whatever their source and motivation, they offered the assurance that if Africans in America had the potential to obtain equality with whites by mastering Western learning, then so too did Japanese.

The attitude of Japanese adventurers in Africa toward blacks during the Meiji Period is equally ambivalent. Although they were not averse to accepting the dehumanizing portraits of Africans painted by whites, their travel logs also depict oppressive, racially stratified white-dominated lands in which their own subordination to whites was a source of consternation and resentment. Wrote one Meiji traveler of South African apartheid:

> The oppressed blacks in this so-called civilized country are miserable. I would like to challenge these realities for the sake of humanity and ask the English who act as if this were normal is there any difference in the intrinsic worth of blacks and whites as human beings? If I could receive a clear answer, I would revise my opinion of them without hesitation. But if they could not answer, I am afraid my respect for

the Englishmen of South Africa would disappear. At any rate, even if it were impossible for blacks to have the same social status as whites, where is the cruel necessity for separate train cars? Should we not pity the weak? I would like to point this out to the wise Englishmen and I shall never cease to hope that they will strive to care for the blacks and to add to their welfare.

(cited in Aoki 1993: 75–6)

Most Meiji Japanese were in no position to witness the situation of blacks first hand; they would remain heavily dependent on Western sources. This was particularly true when it came to defining culture and civilization. As DeBarry puts it, 'In the mind of many in the rising generation [of Meiji intellectuals] the word of a western philosopher or sociologist would carry more weight than all the classics of the East' (1958: 131). This privileging of Western discourse is evident in the writings of europhile Fukuzawa Yukichi (1834–1901), whose discussion of cultural hierarchies in *Bunmei-ron no Gairyaku* (An Outline of a Theory of Civilization, 1875) reproduced Western racial hierarchies, privileging the West as the apotheosis of 'civilization' (*bunmei*), trailed by a 'semi-civilized' (*hankai*) Asia and 'barbaric' (*yaban*) Africa (Fukuzawa: 24). Although Fukuzawa's europhilia was qualified with the caveat that Japan acquire only the most useful elements of European culture, his hierarchical ranking of races and cultures leaves no doubt about the place of Africans and other non-Europeans on the ladder of cultural development.

With the importation of Western 'scientific' racism, Meiji intellectuals like Fukuzawa reconfigured evolutionist cultural hierarchies in which Japan's internal minorities occupied the barbarian category, but increasingly their Otherness was racialized, and their discrimination, marginalization, and forced assimilation justified on 'scientific' grounds. In Japanese attempts to prove themselves the equals of the West, to forge (in both meanings of the term) a national identity, to modernize, and to compete with the West, the Other was pushed further toward the periphery. The ascription of barbarity, backwardness and squalor to Japan's minorities served these ambitions well, since it not only confirmed the relative closeness of Japan to the West but also provided Japanese with a civilizing mission of their own, one that aimed both to elevate the primitive Other and themselves as well.

The introduction of Darwinist thought in the early Meiji period would see Japanese notions of Self and Other transformed by Western notions of 'race.' The American zoologist Edward Morse (1837–1925), a professor at Tokyo University, introduced Darwin to Japanese audiences in the 1870s. Several translations of Darwin's *Descent of Man* (trans. 1879) were published during the Meiji period. Even more widely translated were the works of Herbert

Spencer, of which around thirty translations appeared between 1877 and 1900 (Siddle 1996: 12).

Western scientific notions of race were not imposed on Japan from the outside but were employed by Japanese elites to support various, often conflicting, domestic agendas, ranging from nationalism and socialism to anti-Christian and anti-Buddhist ideologies (Shimao 1981: 94–5). For others it provided a means to account for – and reproduce – the conditions they presumed were responsible for the emergence of Western power. Nationalists had only to survey the condition of their Asian neighbors to surmise the fate that would befall those who were unable to compete in nature's struggle of the fittest. At the same time, social Darwinism offered a scientific basis for Japanese notions of hierarchy and proper place, as well as spurring a pre-occupation with the question of where Japan ranked in the social evolutionary scheme of things. Within Japan, the 'science of race' was employed to justify policies directed at the subjugation of its own internal minorities. The Ainu were not only racialized but became a 'dying race,' whose culture had to be 'preserved' – deposited in research laboratories, warehoused in museums, and exhibited – before their inevitable demise (Siebold 1996: 20). With the support of Heinrich von Siebold and other Westerners, Japanese scholars launched their own 'scientific' forays, inaugurating *Ainugaku* (Ainu Studies), which embraced the Ainu with the same kind of paternalistic, imperialist nostalgia that Westerners had displayed toward their own 'primitive' Others whose time on earth was numbered.[14]

If for the Japanese the Ainu represented the 'lowest rung' on the evolutionary ladder within Japan, social Darwinism left little doubt as to the positioning of Africans and their descendants in the global racial hierarchy. Racist caricatures of Africans as primitive exotics were not confined to scientific discourse; they were also to be found in Western popular culture imported to Japan. While Japanese intellectuals were extolling the virtues of Hegel and Spencer, the masses thrilled to such scientific romances as Jules Verne's *Five Weeks in a Balloon* (trans. 1880), Henry Morgan Stanley's *Through the Dark Continent* and *In Darkest Africa* (trans. 1890 and 1899, respectively), and other works that cultivated the image of Africa as a savage 'dark continent' (*ankoku tairiku*), imagery that would later serve as a template for Japan's own adventure-story writers, illustrators, and armchair explorers.

Through its encounter with the West, Japan's notions of race and place continued to evolve among its elites. Earlier expressions of revulsion toward whiteness were gradually subsumed, while perceptions of blackness grew increasingly negative, and other markers of racial difference were re-evaluated in the light of Western cultural capital and power. By the Taishō Period (1912–26), long, straight black hair, once so desirable as a marker of traditional beauty, had been replaced by the modern pageboy stylings and would, by the post-war period, be permed and dyed in imitation of white Hollywood stars. At the same time, the adoption of European aesthetic values produced self-doubts and insecurities, inviting a self-reflexive awareness through which Japanese began to adjust their own worldview to the realities of the West's encroaching cultural authority and power. Nowhere is this adjustment more apparent than in Japanese attitudes toward their own physical appearance, which they now began to regard as 'flawed,' an intolerable deviation from European standards of beauty. This recalibration of aesthetic sensibilities was facilitated, ironically, by invoking indigenous aesthetics as a rationale for its acceptance, as the following passage from Tanizaki Jun'ichirō's (1886–1965) *In'ei Raisan* (In Praise of Shadows, 1933) makes clear:

> From ancient times we have considered white skin more elegant, more beautiful than dark skin, and yet somehow this whiteness of ours differs from that of the white races. Taken individually there are Japanese who are whiter than Westerners and Westerners who are darker than Japanese, but their *whiteness and darkness is not the same* ... For the Japanese complexion, no matter how white is tinged by a slight cloudiness ... Thus it is that when one of us goes among a group of Westerners it is like a grimy strain on a white sheet of paper. The sight offends even our own eyes and leaves none too pleasant a feeling.
>
> (Tanizaki: 31, emphasis added)

In developing his argument, the power relation embodied in racial status relationships is not far from Tanizaki's mind, whites and blacks providing self-reflexive mirrors through which Tanizaki attempts to rationalize Japanese feelings of inferiority toward whiter-skinned Westerners, while commiserating with blacks as fellow objects of white racial contempt.

> We can appreciate, then, the psychology that in the past caused the white races to reject the colored races. A sensitive white person could not but be upset by the shadow that even one or two colored persons cast over a social gathering. What the situation is today I do not know, but at the time of the American Civil War, when persecution of Negroes was at its most intense, the hatred and scorn were directed not only at full-blooded Negroes, but at mulattos, the children of mulattos, and even the children of mulattos and whites. Those with the slightest taint of Negro blood, be it but half, a quarter, a sixteenth, or a thirty-second, had to be ferreted out and made to suffer. Not even those who at a glance were indistinguishable from pure-blooded whites, but among whose ancestors

two or three generations earlier there had been a Negro, escaped the searching gaze, no matter how faint the tinge that lay beneath their white skin.

And so we see how profound is the relationship between shadows and the yellow races. Because no one likes to show himself to bad advantage, it is natural that we should have chosen cloudy colors for our food and clothing and houses, and sunk ourselves back into the shadows. I am not saying that our ancestors were conscious of the cloudiness of their skins. They cannot have known that a whiter race existed. But one must conclude that something of their sense of color led them naturally to this preference.

(Tanizaki 1984: 32–3)

Having rhetorically adopted the perspective of whites, Tanizaki concludes that the preference for white skin is 'natural,' although, significantly, Japanese do not become aware of the 'cloudiness of their skins' until *after* their exposure to lighter-skinned Westerners, a point he finesses by positing some vague ancestral memory to account for this preference. His observations on the status of blacks in the United States, however, should chasten those who would decry Japan's blood chauvinism and preoccupation with racial purity as somehow uniquely Japanese. Tanizaki's narrative is explicit about the American racial hierarchy and the Japanese place within it. Having more or less accepted it, he is left with little recourse but to urge Japanese to resign themselves to their impurities and compensate for them by, as it were, praising shadows. Not only are 'white-skinned' Japanese unable to compete with the whiteness of Europeans, but, by the passage's end, they are no longer white but 'yellow' and are rejected by Caucasians as quite literally a 'colored' race.

Western views of race had a profound impact both on Japanese views of blacks and on their views of themselves, an impact not limited to scientific discourse on the subject. Much of their effect was provided though conspicuous displays of Western cultural capital, such as those Tanizaki describes at Ritsumeikan and other sites where proximity to and imitation of things Western served to enhance the social status and self-esteem of the performer. Their impact would increasingly manifest itself in the early pre-war and post-war years in American popular culture. In Tanizaki's era, Hollywood provided the template of fashion, behavior, and beauty for Japanese people, who, modeling themselves on Western movie stars, redefined themselves as *moga* (modern girls) and *mobo* (modern boys). Hollywood provided them with its version not only of modernity but of primitivism as well, reproducing in a more palpable form the racist hierarchies of the social sciences while providing an iconography upon which Japanese could elaborate their own

vision of ineffable black alterity. For if Hollywood offered Taishō Japanese
– and the world – images of privileged, affluent, sophisticated whiteness,
it juxtaposed them against those of black buffoonery and primitivism,
images whose impact on Japanese popular culture and perceptions of blacks
– and of themselves – would leave an indelible imprint on the Japanese
imagination.

THE PRE-WAR PERIOD

Pre-war Japanese interest in African and African American people was fueled
by a mixture of idealism, nationalism and imperialist ideology. For the most
part, Japanese elites were well informed about conditions in black America,
as well as being deeply and more directly concerned with anti-oriental
movements in California and Hawaii and discriminatory laws targeting
Japanese. Japan's interest in the question of racism had led it to introduce
an equality clause at the League of Nations in 1919, which was supported
by many black intellectuals who drew parallels between Japan's quest for
equality with the West and their own quest for racial equality in America
and who saw a need to internationalize the struggle against white privilege
and racial oppression in world affairs. Toward these ends, contacts between
African Americans and Japanese had taken shape: in mid-February of 1919,
a month after Japan's attempt to introduce the racial equality clause in the
Covenant of the League of Nations, the W.E.B. Du Bois-organized Pan-
African Congress met with Japanese in Paris. That same year, a delegation of
prominent African Americans leaders met with Japanese in New York prior
to the peace conference to seek Japanese support 'to remove prejudice and
race discrimination in all nations of the earth' (Kearney 1998: 87).
   Japanese attempts to ally themselves with black people in the United
States – and elsewhere – were both pragmatic and reasonable, given the
discrimination both groups faced. Nonetheless, the rhetoric of racial equality
left much to be desired, for not only did Japan's racial equality clause not
question the right of League members to possess colonies (at the time Japan
was also seeking a guarantee from the League of its rights to the Shantung
Peninsula in China, which had been seized from Germany during World War
One) but its demand for 'fair and equal treatment' applied only to 'civilized
nations' (*bunmei koku*) and League member states – not to their colonies
and subject peoples.[15]
   Japan's ruling elites were less interested in securing equality for non-
whites than in ensuring that Japan, as a sovereign nation and member of
the League, would be afforded the same privileges as Western nations,
including the right to overseas colonies. The equality clause would not have

prevented Japanese and other League members from discriminating against their own internal minorities. Nor did it dissuade Japan from supporting the Western powers' recarving of Africa following World War One and South Africa's annexation of Namibia in 1919, or from pursuing close diplomatic and economic ties with that racist state (Morikawa 1988: 44–8). Indeed, Japan's leaders were not averse to bending the principles of racial equality when it served the national interest. This was certainly the case in South Africa, where Japanese were exempt from the restrictions that applied to non-whites and enjoyed many of privileges held by its white minority. It might be argued that such treatment, while falling short of that desired of the racial equality clause, was in practice not inconsistent with the clause's main objective of guaranteeing Japanese equality with whites. Although the rhetoric of 'Africa for the Africans' expressed Japan's desire to remove whites from the affairs of the continent, Japan itself was exempt from the demand and had few qualms about affiliating itself with racist white regimes that allowed it access to African markets and resources. Between 1910 and 1920, Japan had become South Africa's second largest export market, and by 1933 Japan ranked among its six major suppliers of goods (Yap and Man 1996: 248). In the end, the Japanese countenanced discrimination so long as they themselves were exempt (albeit only partially and ambiguously), they could maintain national prestige, and they were elevated above other people of color.

African American responses to the Japanese were mixed. While not unreserved in his support of the Japanese, as editor of *The Crisis* and *Phylon*, W.E.B. Du Bois had persistently pointed out the hypocrisy of American criticism of Japan's aggression against China while America itself maintained a military presence in Haiti and remained silent on the English colonial presence in India. Another prominent voice, Langston Hughes, was more qualified in his assessment of the Japanese. In *I Wonder as I Wander* (1956), Hughes describes his two-week visit to Japan in 1933. Already a celebrity among the Japanese literati, Hughes meets with fellow writers, attends a play in Tuskiji, and meets backstage with its cast, who greet him 'with open arms,' and he is 'welcomed as the first Negro writer ever to visit their theater' (Hughes 1986: 241). Later he is invited to the Pan Pacific Club, where he makes a speech in which he informs his audience that in America 'it would hardly be possible for white and colored people to dine together at any of the leading clubs or hotels,' 'compliments the Japanese people on being the only noncolonial nation in the Far East, having their own sovereign government,' and expresses his hope that 'they would not make the old mistakes of the West and, like England, France and Germany, attempt to take over other people's lands or make colonials of others' (243). Although sympathetic to Japan, Hughes was no Japanophile. Unlike many of his contemporaries, including Du Bois, who were willing to overlook or downplay Japan's colonial abuses, Hughes sympathized with the Chinese and Koreans, who 'were in somewhat the same position as Negroes in the United States' (276). Suspected by Japanese police of being a communist spy and of expressing anti-Japanese sentiments, Hughes was deported.

Interest in Hughes and African American views of the Japanese was not confined to the Japanese police; it was shared by the FBI, which from 1942 to 1943 commissioned the Survey of Racial Conditions in the United States – code-named RACON (for 'racial conditions') – to gather intelligence on African American organizations in order to determine the impact of communist and Axis, primarily Japanese, propaganda on the African American community, whom the FBI suspected of constituting a potential fifth column.[16] Japanese agents had, in fact, attempted to propagandize American blacks by presenting Japan as an ally in the struggle against Western imperialism. The invasion of Ethiopia by Fascist Italy in 1935 brought blacks and Japanese together. Like Japan, black America held Ethiopia in high regard, since it had remained independent of European colonialism and had successfully defeated a previous attempt by the Italians to colonize it in 1896. Blacks around the world rallied in support of Ethiopia, raising money and sending medical supplies. In London, the International Friends of Ethiopia was formed, and in the United States, a group of black leaders, including Ralph Bunche, formed the Ethiopian Research Council. US blacks joined the Ethiopian army or volunteered their services as technicians, pilots, and teachers.

The Italo–Ethiopian War rekindled Japan's interest in Ethiopia. In the summer of 1935, a rally in Tokyo to protest the invasion, sponsored by the ultranationalist Kokuryū Kai (Black Dragon Society), was attended by 200 people. Japanese interest in Ethiopia was by no means new. In 1886 a translation of Samuel Johnson's (1709–84) Abyssinian novel *Rasselas* (1759) appeared under the title *Ōji Raserasu Den* (The Life of Prince Rasselas). In 1905 the preface of a new translation mentioned the defeat of the Italians by Emperor Menelik II during the first Italo–Ethiopian War. Menelik II and the Battle of Adowa were also the subject of Japanese short stories and adventure novels set in Abyssinia.[17] In the 1920s Japan developed relatively close diplomatic ties with Ethiopia. Haile Selassie met with Japanese at the League of Nations in 1920, the Ethiopian foreign minister was received in Japan in 1921, and economic missions were dispatched to Ethiopia to draw up commercial treaties. Japan's Ambassador to Turkey attended the coronation of Emperor Haile Selassie I in 1930. To Japanese, Italy's 1935 invasion of Ethiopia was a symbol of white domination. As another non-white people who had successfully escaped Western colonial domination, Japanese could easily identify with the Ethiopians. Both countries could boast of a history going back thousands of years into antiquity and of an equally long imperial line.

The attraction was mutual. Ethiopians felt an affinity with Japanese inspired by Japan's victory in the Russo–Japanese War and by Japan's successful modernization. The Ethiopian government adopted Japan as the model for its own modernization and modeled its constitution on the Meiji Constitution. In 1931 a diplomatic mission headed by Ethiopian Foreign Minister Walda-Sellase Heruy arrived in Japan. Later that year, Haile Selassie sent two lions to the Japanese emperor, and these were donated to Ueno Zoo. The following year, Sumioka Tomoyoshi, a Japanese diplomat, was awarded the Menelik II Medal, Ethiopia's highest honor, in recognition of his activities in promoting friendship between the two countries. Sumioka went so far as to postulate a linguistic link between Amharic and Japanese and suggested that Ethiopians and Japanese could trace their descent from a common ancestor who had emerged in Central Asia. Cultural and economic ties between Tokyo and Addis Ababa were to have been furthered through ties of blood as well. On 30 January 1934, the influential Tokyo *Nichi Nichi* newspaper reported that Kuroda Masako, the daughter of a Japanese aristocrat, had been chosen to wed Araya Ababa, a relative of Haile Selassie often described as a 'prince' in Japanese accounts. The event was widely reported in the Ethiopian, Japanese and African American press, where it was interpreted as indicting a lack of race prejudice among Japanese (Kearney 1998: 120–1; Okakura and Kitagawa 1993: 37–9). The marriage, alas, did not take place, allegedly because of Italian interference.

There seems little doubt that much of Japan's expressed solidarity with the Ethiopians was motivated by trade considerations and the rhetoric of race war. By 1927 half of Ethiopia's imports came from Japan, of which over 90 percent were cotton and artificial silk (Okakura and Kitagawa 1993: 31–2). The Japanese government, hard pressed to justify its own imperialist ambitions in China, including its invasion of Manchuria in 1931, refrained from criticizing the Italians. Eventually, Japan reached an understanding with the Italian Fascists, and in 1940 joined Germany and Italy in the Tripartite Pact; popular support for Ethiopia soon evaporated.

Several prominent African American intellectuals visited Japan during this period, including W.E.B. Du Bois, James Weldon Johnson, and Langston Hughes. Translations of the works of several African American writers had appeared in Japanese, including Booker T. Washington's *Up from Slavery* (trans. 1927), Jean Toomer's *Cane* (trans. 1930), Du Bois' *Dark Princess* (trans. 1930), Walter White's *The Fire in the Flint* (trans. 1930), and several works by Hughes. Japanese leftists introduced their readers to black revolutionary figures such as Nat Turner, Demark Vesey, and Toussaint-L'Ouverture, who served as powerful symbols of resistance to white power and privilege (Koshiro 2003: 193). The African American press carried reports by blacks who had visited Japan and had been impressed by the kindness and hospitality of their hosts. When the Philadelphia Royal Giants, a black baseball team composed of players from various Negro League teams, played several exhibition games against Japanese teams in Tokyo in 1927, they received a warm welcome.[18]

THE OCCUPATION AND POST-WAR PERIOD

With the end of World War Two came the greatest influx of blacks into Japan since the sixteenth century. To the panoply of images of black alterity introduced during earlier stages of their encounter – the slave, the savage, the buffoon – was added another: the black GI. As they did their white counterparts, Japanese viewed their black alien conquerors with a mixture of awe, envy, resentment, and hatred. In general, however, Japanese popular culture depicted the face of Occupation generosity as white. As Michael Molasky points out, 'While it seems likely that *nisei* [second generation Japanese Americans] and black GIs also availed themselves of the local PX (military base store) and tossed out their share of chocolate and chewing gum to eager Japanese children, non-white members of the occupation forces seldom appear in these canonical scenes of postwar life' (1999: 71). Indeed, the black GI would occupy a different role in the Japanese imagination, as predator and bestial curiosity on the one hand, and pure-hearted man-child and sympathetic victim of racial oppression on the other, and black GIs would come to embody a peculiar amalgam of white American power and black impotence (Russell 1991:8).

Democracy was not the only thing the Occupation imported to Japan. Ironically, the freedom that African American visitors to Japan experienced prior to the war soon vanished under the American Occupation. For the first time since Deshima, ordinary Japanese were once again directly exposed to large numbers of blacks. As before, there was little doubt as to their position vis-à-vis whites. While Occupation policy busied itself dismantling Japan's totalitarian apparatus, it exported its own system of social control, one aimed primarily at its own citizens. Despite the Occupation's progressive New Deal for Japan, GHQ continued to deal to blacks from a stacked deck. Social inequality remained a fact of life in America, and it was exported to Japan, where black GIs faced discrimination not only from whites but also from newly 'democratized' Japanese. Just how dearly white America clung to the ideology of racial inequality is suggested by the War Department, which justified segregation in the armed forces on the grounds that it 'cannot ignore the social relations between Negroes and whites which have been established by the American people through custom and habit' (cited in Polenberg 1980: 76).

Such customs and habits were exported wholesale to post-war Japan and were apparent to any Japanese who had to accommodate the racial peccadilloes of their conquerors. African American military personnel stationed in Japan bore the brunt of both American and Japanese racism. Segregation provided ample opportunity for white GIs to spread pernicious rumors about blacks. In the red-light districts, Japanese prostitutes were told to avoid black GIs because they were abusive, carried sexually transmitted diseases, were sexually insatiable, and had enormous penises. A common rumor was that blacks had tails. Japanese prostitutes had their own reasons for avoiding blacks: servicing them made them tainted goods who would not be able to attract white clientele (Inōe 1995: 75–6). While white GIs no longer regarded Japanese males as the sexual threat sometimes portrayed in American war propaganda, they cast themselves in the new role of valiant defenders of Japanese womanhood. Martin Bronfenbrenner, Kenan Professor of Economics at Duke University, describes such an encounter based on his experiences in Kyūshū during the Occupation:

> A burly quartet of colored troops reeled by with a scared Japanese girl half their average height and a bottle of the local sweet potato brandy. Fusako stared after them; such creatures she had never seen before. In school she had read of American Indians; were these, then, she asked Joe, the Indians she had read about? Joe translated the question.
>
> Sarge saw his chance for sociological experimentation. 'Tell her no. Tell her they're Niggers, dirty Niggers. They was born white, tell her, only they got syph and turned black. Tell her to keep away from them. Lay it on good.' Joe gulped slightly, but thought of C.I.C. and translating, laying it on – moderately good. Bob said nothing. Although no southern rebel, he agreed that the end justified the means. Nice girls like this Fu-something had to be protected from those black apes. Fusako's face registered disgust as her eyes followed the retreating stragglers, and Sarge was satisfied. 'These Jap babes, they all fall for that one. Air Force guy down from Tokyo was tellin' me ..."
>
> (Bronfenbrenner 1975: 30)

Post-war Japan served as a laboratory in which whites could not only test democratic ideals but also conduct experiments in racial demonology. Such 'sociological experimentation' did not end with the Occupation. African Americans who had been stationed in Japan during the Korean and Vietnam Wars relate identical stories of their encounters with white-spread racial slanders. An African American informant who had been stationed briefly in

Japan during the Vietnam War had been unable to fathom why an elderly Japanese man had reacted so bitterly toward him, until he learned that the man had been told by whites that blacks had piloted the plane that dropped the atomic bomb on Hiroshima.

The dehumanization of blacks was also cultivated through the infusion of American popular culture, which included not only a new generation of Tarzan films but also films, cartoons, novels, and other artifacts that reintroduced American stereotypes of blacks as savages and buffoons, objects of derision toward whom even Japanese in their long hour of national humiliation could feel superior. The production and reproduction of anti-black stereotypes in Japan were sanctioned by no less an authority than GHQ itself: There is no small irony in the fact that Japan's post-war economic recovery was in part financed by the manufacture and sale of stereotypical black figurines bearing 'Made in Occupied Japan' labels for overseas export.

The social division of races was particularly evident to shopkeepers and merchants whose livelihood depended on maintaining good and profitable relationships with their white clientele. Such considerations extended to brothel owners operating under Occupation supervision. Fearing that their American occupiers would go on a raping spree, the Japanese set up *iyanfujo* ('comfort stations,' a euphemism for military brothels) to service them, where the color line between black and white was preserved. The arrangement introduced new words into the Japanese lexicon. Japanese women who serviced American GIs were called *pan-pan* or *pan-suke,* of which two types were distinguished: *shiro-pan,* who serviced white GIs, and *kuro-pan,* who serviced blacks (Inōe 1995: 67, 85). Children born of interracial unions, called *konketsuji,* or 'mixed-bloods', were often abandoned. While some white-Japanese *konketsuji* were envied for their Caucasian features and went on to become models, actresses and singers, black-Japanese generally fared much worse.[19]

De facto social segregation of blacks stationed at home and abroad continued well into the 1970s. In Japan, separate white and black communities sprung up near military bases in Yokosuka, Yokota, and Okinawa. Tensions between the two communities were high, frequently igniting into violence that entangled local residents. As late as the 1970s, local residents in Okinawa found themselves caught precariously between these two polarized camps, merchants and shopkeepers often siding with whites, lest black patronage threaten to drive away better-paid white servicemen. Black GIs vented their frustration and anger on the Okinawans, which only exacerbated hostilities between the two communities.[20]

Given their presence, it is not surprising that the post-war period saw a proliferation of books featuring African American GIs, including Ōe Kenzaburō's *Shiiku (The Catch,* 1958) Matsumoto Seichō's *Kuro-ji no e*

(1965), Ariyoshi Sawako's *Hishoku* (1964), Morimura Sei'ichi's *Ningen no Shōmei* (Proof of the Man, 1977), and Murakami Ryū's *Kagirinaku Tōmei ni Chikai Burū* (Almost Transparent Blue, 1976).

The post-war period also saw a number of leftist Japanese intellectuals, scholars, and journalists visit the United States, where they described first-hand their encounters with American racial consciousness. In navigating the minefield of the color line, many of these observers were struck by their own liminal status, which situated them between two polarized worlds. Their narratives provide insights into the impact of power relations on not only the construction of blackness but also on the construction of Japaneseness, as the American color line, previously an abstraction encountered only in textbooks and newspaper articles, assumed tangible reality, prompting them to critically re-examine their identity as Japanese and to reassess their status as a 'white-skinned race' that, while enjoying some of the privileges of American whites, was not quite 'white' enough. Their narratives also reveal an emergent awareness of their identity as 'Japanese,' 'Asians,' and 'people of color,' as well as of Japanese racial prejudice toward blacks and other non-whites both abroad and at home.

In *Nan demo mita yarō* (Let's See Everything, 1961), Oda Makoto, a founder of Beiheiren (Citizen's Committee for Peace in Vietnam), lays out the practical and psychological benefits of racism for those positioned ambiguously between black and white worlds. As a Japanese visitor in the Jim Crow South, Oda is permitted the same privileges as whites: He is able to ride freely among them on buses, eat in their restaurants, and stay in their hotels. Like many of his compatriots, he initially believes that Japanese are somehow above American racism as third party neutrals whose intermediate position between black and white allows them to view the phenomenon dispassionately. In time, however, Oda abandons this view, expressing not only disillusionment with white America but also with Japanese racial alliances.

> Imagine a situation where there are three people: a Japanese, and two Americans, one white and the other black. Suppose there is a dispute – not a particularly serious one – which splits them into two camps. There are three possible combinations that might result: the two Americans allied against the Japanese; an alliance between the Japanese and the white against the black (excluding disputes of a political nature, such an alliance is probably more likely than the former); and finally, an alliance between the Japanese and the black against the white, which is probably the least likely of all. The black and the white form an alliance because they are both Americans; the Japanese and the white form one because of their mutual contempt for 'niggers' (*kurombō*). But while an

alliance between the black and the Japanese based on their awareness of being 'people of color' or to 'fight racism' sounds good, it is hardly likely. That is, in America, Japanese have unaccountably assumed the status of whites.

(1961: 129)

Despite ambivalence about their status, many Japanese travelers, while critical of Jim Crow, nonetheless complaisantly toed the color line, obtaining a sense of psychological satisfaction at their elevation above blacks. In *Amerika Kanjō Ryōkō* (Sentimental Journey in America, 1962), novelist Yasuoka Shōtarō, who visited America in 1960, writes that he had initially viewed the 'Negro' problem as 'a white problem ... from which Japanese, as neither black nor white were excluded,' but which itself prompts 'feelings of inferiority we have toward Negroes' (87). Noting that Japanese visiting the South often boasted of using the Negro toilets, Yasuoka suggests that Japanese attempts to ally themselves with blacks as fellow people of color 'work to overturn these feelings of inferiority with feelings of superiority.' Such actions, he writes, are 'meaningless as they constituted neither a threat to whites nor a meaningful display of sympathy toward blacks. Rather they merely reflect the fleeting sense of superiority and self-satisfaction [these Japanese] experienced when they have relieved themselves in toilets reserved for Negroes' (87). In America, race and place are inseparably intertwined, one's sense of self defined by where one sits – and shits – in the racial pecking order. Evoking the feelings of superiority experienced by Japanese men in the company of foreign prostitutes, Yasuoka observes a similar psychology at work in their associations with blacks, noting that while Japanese may find comfort among blacks, the encounters serve to ease their feelings of inferiority toward whites by indulging their feeling of relative superiority toward blacks (84–5).

The notion that Japanese occupy a liminal position between black and white fails, however, to recognize the three-dimensionality of American race relations. That is, Japanese are positioned not only between black and white, but also below whites and above blacks in the racial hierarchy. They may not be white, but at least they are not black. Wagatsuma and Yoneyama recount the recollections of a famous Japanese sociologist who, describing his travels through the American South, boasted he had entered a racially segregated restaurant and, defying the contemptuous gaze white patrons directed toward him, sat amongst them, an act the authors believed required little courage on the part of Japanese, but which left them wondering if the sociologist had ever considered the possibility of sitting with blacks (1980: 109).

Not all Japanese writers who visited America during this time saw anti-black racism as an essentially American phenomenon or devoted their narratives to their subjective experience of racial dislocation. Far more ambitious are a series of essays by *Asahi Shimbun* journalist Honda Katsu'ichi, who first visited America for a six-month period from 1969 to 1970. Published in book form as *Amerika Gasshūkoku* (The United States of America, 1981), the essays attempt to see America though the eyes of blacks.[21] Like others before him, Honda is appalled by American racism, but his critique does not end on American shores. Honda is one of the few Japanese writers who has critically probed Japanese racial attitudes, writing extensively on such controversial issues as the Rape of Nanking, school textbook censorship, and the treatment of Japan's Korean, Ainu and burakumin minorities. In *Korosareru Gawa no Ronri* (The Logic of Those Who Are Killed, 1971), another collection of his *Asahi Shimbun* essays, he returned to the theme of racial discrimination, focusing this time on Japan's treatment of blacks through interviews with black residents.

THE PRESENT

Koshiro has observed that 'Few people realize the extent to which Japanese people have interacted with and been influenced by African Americans and their history' (2003: 183). While there is some awareness of a black presence in Japan, it confines that presence to contexts and activities – the military, entertainment, and athletics in the case of African Americans, and civil war, disease, and famine in the case of Africans – that circumscribe the diversity and range of encounters between Japanese and people of the African diaspora. Contemporary discourse on 'black culture' almost invariably associates it with black, primarily African American, forms of musical culture, such as Negro spirituals, soul, jazz, reggae, and, most recently, gospel and hip hop, largely ignoring other areas of black achievement and arenas of historical interaction between blacks and Japanese that do not translate into expected stereotyped encounters *a la* Endō's *Kurombō* or the film-version of Tsutsui Yasutaka's *Jazz Daimyō* (1986). Indeed, for many Japanese young people today, black is now *kakkō ii* (cool), a boundless reservoir of style and play from which they may borrow to perform their own acts of social resistance. Like jazz before it, hip hop has become a synonym for black culture, the measure by which 'blackness' is gauged, providing a medium through which some Japanese attempt to give voice to their own sense of alienation and rebellion against the restrictive social norms of their society. At the same time, the ascendancy of hip-hop culture has abetted the synecdochization of black culture by means of which a fragment of that culture is used to stand in for the whole: thus 'blackness' comes to be globally identified with inner-city, heterosexual black male youth, 'the street,' and various stylized and ritualized forms of rebellious, largely antisocial acts, postures, and impostures.

At the same time, old stereotypes of blacks continue to circulate and be adapted and updated for new media and new audiences. Media images of blacks perpetuated by news programs and imported popular entertainment, when not portraying black people as inherently humorous and rhythmic, continue to stereotype them as dangerous, violent, and criminal. Black also emerges as a signifier of various forms of power and desire – creative, imaginative, transformative, athletic, sexual – and as a fetish to be consumed in sundry ways, including as masturbatory fodder.[22] Popular black *talento* (television celebrities) in Japan play to these stereotypes. Nigerian Bobby Ologun, voted in 2005 the most popular foreign celebrity in Japan, has become a ubiquitous presence on Japanese television, as has his American counterpart, former NFL athlete, K-1 kickboxer, and aspiring actor Bob ("the Beast") Sapp.[23] The personae of other black *talento*, such as Adgony Ayao and Zomahoun Rufin, have yet to break the template.[24] Through such characters (caricatures), Japan achieves, in its own mind, a virtual internationalization that confirms its view of itself as tolerant of foreign difference and of black alterity. In all of this, however, one is unable to spot the faces or hear the voices of those who would challenge this illusion. In January 2006, while Japanese television broadcasts and sports newspapers devoted considerable attention to an alleged violent confrontation between Ologun and his manager, the dismissal by an Osaka district court of Steve McGowan's groundbreaking anti-black-discrimination suit against an Osaka storeowner received only cursory coverage.[25] The same month, similar media indifference befell the release of United Nations Special Rapporteur of the Commission on Human Rights Doudou Diène's report on racism and discrimination in Japan.[26]

Embodiments of blackness are not confined to black celebrities or limited to human performances. The global expansion of hip-hop has spawned in Japan a burgeoning industry of products ranging from clubs and CDs, to hip-hop-themed fashion magazines, anime, and manga, to high-end Hong-Kong designer collectibles – complete with miniature bling and scaled-down, impeccably tailored 'street' fashions – that can be purchased in boutiques and on the Internet and that have partially supplanted once ubiquitous sambo, domestic, and jazzman effigies. Such black simulacra allow Japanese to realize, if only through proxy, Japan's internationalization, their proliferation giving shape to a multicultural, cosmopolitan Japan, albeit an illusionary one, in which real black people are an invisible or negligible minority. Such racial productions allow Japanese to savor 'blackness' without the bother of having to deal with real black people or to make a place for them within their society.

CONCLUSION

The Japanese encounter with black people has been older, more nuanced, and far more complex than has been generally recognized. Japanese regard of the black Other cannot be isolated from the social, political, and economic dimensions of its encounters with the West. The relationship between blacks and Japanese continues to be mediated by a confluence of the internal and external, the local and global.

In examining the presence of blacks in Japan and in the Japanese imagination, one becomes aware of the fact that the manner in which their presence is constructed involves not only Japanese preoccupations and concerns with race and place. It also involves the influence of Western discursive power and cultural capital, which define notions of race relations and racism by constructing them in terms of pairs of binary oppositions (white/black, white/yellow, black/yellow). As a consequence, in the Japanese imagination blacks have not simply constituted a polar, dark-skinned Other against which to compare and contrast themselves but also the Other of a White Other whose existence has provided a basis for the appraisal and reappraisal of Japanese identity since the sixteenth century.

Hegemony, Antonio Gramsci tells us, is not merely a matter of externally applied force. It is a process whereby people actively – and consensually – work toward their own subjugation. It is also most successful when it goes unnoticed. Brannen (1992) has argued a 'Japanese hegemony' is at work in the assimilation of Western cultural artifacts: rather than being dominated by Western ideologies, Japan recontexualizes and manipulates them in such a way as to reinforce their own sense of uniqueness and superiority. Since the nineteenth century, the boundaries of that 'unique,' 'superior' Self have been defined primarily in relation to a dominant, universal Western Other. Two crucial processes are involved, one reactive, the other creative. While Japan may invest Western cultural artifacts with new meanings, it does not necessarily obliterate the old. Indeed, one of the ironies of transplanted Western anti-black artifacts is that many Japanese refuse to recognize them as 'racist' *in Japan*, said items having lost whatever racist meanings attached to them in their previous lives by the virtue of the fact that Japan is believed to lack racial prejudice and discrimination. In this case, Japanese hegemony preserves not only the dichotomy between Japan, the West and the rest, but also the national myth of Japan as a racism-free society that always manages to retain uncorrupted its essentialistic character, despite cultural borrowings. It is the symbolic power, the cultural capital of these artifacts and their embedded ideologies, that ultimately serve to reinforce and sustain Japanese notions of difference.

Notes

1 A slightly different version of this essay appeared in the journal *Zinbun* (40), Kyoto University Institute for Research in the Humanities, August 2008. Japanese translations are the author's own, unless otherwise noted.
   Quote: 4-chan BBS black anime characters, http://www.world4ch.org/read.php/ anime 1127335674/140, 12 August 2006.
2 See Rubin 1967. The tendency of modern-day commentators to see only 'black devils' in these prints may betray a bias to seek historical confirmation of contemporary prejudices, a tendency classicist Frank Snowden (1983: 80) has detected in modern interpretations of black representation in Western classical art.
3 See Fujita Midori 1987a and 1987b for two pioneering studies of premodern Japanese views of blacks.
4 Duyvendak (1949: 23), citing Chinese sources, posits an African presence going back as far as the Ch'in dynasty (221 BC – 420 AD).
5 The historical Yasuke serves as the model for the titular protagonist of Endō Shusaku's comic novel *Kurombō* (*Nigger*, 1973), although the novel portrays him as a cowardly and buffoonish man-child (see Russell 1991).
6 See Fujita 1987a: 28–32.
7 Mansell Upham, a South African historian and former diplomat at the South African Embassy in Tokyo who has researched the genealogy of European families in South Africa, has discovered a property inventory documenting the sale of one 'Anthony Moor from Japan,' registered as the son of a Japanese mother and a 'Moor' father, to a European settler in Capetown in 1701 (*Japan Times*, 16 December 1993: 3, and personal conversation 1993). Although the term 'Moor' is racially inconclusive and the inventory does not confirm that he was in fact a black African, the finding does raise the question of the extent of miscegenation between Japanese and black Africans in premodern times.
8 Duyvendak notes that 'the Chinese applied the term … to peoples, mostly of the Malay race, whom they found at the ends of the earth. At first chiefly confined to the races of the South-West, later, as the geographic knowledge of the Chinese expanded, the same term was applied to the native races of the countries around the Indian Ocean, including the negroes' (1949: 23). Given the ambiguity of the term as a racial marker, Irwin cautions that those 'described as *kunlun* in medieval Chinese accounts cannot be assumed to be African unless other evidence supports that conclusion' (1977: 170), and notes that the term was also used as a sobriquet for a fourth-century priest and a Chinese consort, perhaps owing to their dark complexions. Still, it is noteworthy that despite their dark complexions these individuals enjoyed positions of power and privilege in premodern China. By the tenth century, accounts of *kunlun* with 'frizzy' or 'wooly' hair would suggest an African origin.
9 Unlike the neutral *kokujin* (black person), *kurombō* (black one) is pejorative and belittling. In Japanese the suffix '-*mbō*' connotes childishness, immaturity, and disreputable character, as can be seen in such terms as *okorimbō* (hothead), *amaembō* (pampered one), *chorimbō* (a derogatory term for burakumin), and *shirombō* (white one, whitey), an appellation once applied to albinos and Caucasians. This suffix is also used to express endearment, as in *akambō* (baby). *Kurombō* is also applied to naturally dark-skinned and tanned Japanese.

10 Suzuki Tōzō 1992: 102; the book is a reprint of *Kotoba Monogatari* (The Story of Words), *Nishi Nihon Shimbun*, 1961.

11 *Tsūkō Ichiran* (Transit Summary), Vol. 239, Osaka: Aobundō shuppan, 1914: 717.

12 In fact, a former black slave turned whaler, Pyrrhus Concer (1814–97), arrived in Japan in 1845, almost a decade before Perry and his black honor guard (Koshiro 2003: 183); see also Bill Bleyer (2006), 'Legacy: Pyrrhus Concer' http://www.newsday.com/community/guide/lihistory/ny-history-hs509b0.7157701.story.

Bleyer incorrectly states that Concer 'was the first black man Japanese had ever seen,' ignoring over 200 years of interactions between Japanese and blacks.

13 Oddly, Wagatsuma's English translation in *Daedalus* omits 'the Americans' (*Beijin*); cf. Wagatsuma 1967: 415.

14 See Oguma (1995: 2–86) on the impact of social Darwinism on Ainu studies.

15 For a critique of the racial equality clause, see Morikawa 1988: 35–60 and Kearney 1998. Kearney notes that had Japan's proposal been adopted, 'Japanese nationals residing in the United States could demand that no distinctions be made against them on account of race and nationality. In addition, Liberia and Haiti, as members of the League would become able to make demands on the United States which native-born Americans could not. For black Americans to receive equal democratic treatment accorded other nonwhite members of the League, they would have to leave their country and reside abroad' (90).

16 See Hill 1995: 507–49.

17 For a discussion of the Japanese image of Ethiopia during the Meiji and early-Shōwa periods, see Aoki 1994: 3–18; Shirasi Kenji 1983: 171–97; and Okakura and Kitagawa, 1993: 29–61.

18 Sayama 1990: 83, and 1993. Sayama argues that the Negro League played a major role in the emergence of Japanese baseball, describing it as 'the mother of Japanese professional baseball.'

19 See Wagatsuma 1978; Burkhardt 1978; and Thompson 1967.

20 See Ikemiyagi 1971: 4; and Takamine 1984: 214–16.

21 Honda's essays were serialized under the title '*Kuroi Sekai*' (Black World) in the *Asahi Shimbun* from August 1969 to February 1970.

22 See Russell 1998 for a discussion of the commodification of black sexuality in Japan.

In 2008, a search of the word *kokujin* in the DVD section of the Amazon.co.jp website produced 280 titles, almost all domestically produced pornography involving black men and Japanese women.

23 'Kono Jinbutsu no Omote to Ura: Bobi Orogun,' *Nikkan Gendai*, 11 August 2005: 23. According to a survey of 8,000 Japanese, out of 30 foreign celebrities, respondents ranked Ologun the most popular rising foreign personality and the second most favorably viewed (TVmania, http://tvmania.livedoor.biz/archives/29627421.html). Sapp's success in Japan has allowed him to secure roles in Hollywood films, including small parts in *Electra* (2005) and *The Longest Yard* (2005).

24 Despite their public personae, both Zomahoun and Adgony hold advanced degrees. Zomahoun, who as a regular on Kitano 'Beat' Takeshi's *Koko ga Hen Da Yo, Nihonjin* (This is Strange, Japanese), a popular television program featuring sparring panels of Japanese and resident foreigners who debate topical issues, parlayed his colorful, volatile persona into public celebrity, received his doctorate in sociology from Japan's Sophia University. Adgony, who, along with Ologun, got his start on the popular 'Funniest Japanese' segment of *Sanma's*

Karakuri TV, where he appeared as one of a trio of black Japanese-language 'students' who are instructed by a fluent white *talento* constantly exasperated by their comic antics and exaggerated linguistic incompetence, holds a doctorate in acting and directing from the Beijing Drama Academy (*Hiragana Times*, August 2002: 6–7).

25 In his suit, McGowan, a black designer and an 11-year resident of Kyoto, claimed that in 2004 he was denied entry to an eyewear shop by the owner because he was black. McGowan appealed the verdict, and on 18 October 2006 the Osaka High Court reversed the district court ruling and ordered the storeowner to pay damages. Reportedly, McGowan's initial suit was dismissed because it failed to demonstrate that he was refused entry specifically *because* he was black. Similarly, although the High Court ruling compensates McGowan for the 'emotional pain' caused by the discrimination he experienced, it still does not recognize that his skin color was the reason behind the shop-owner's behavior. (For a discussion of the court rulings, see 'Reporter Eric Johnson on McGowan Victorious Appeal,' *Debito.org Newsletter*, 24 October 2006, http://www.debito. org/index.php/?p=52, posted October 19, 2006.)

26 It has been suggested that the Japanese media ignored the report because it was backed by IMADR (International Movement Against All Forms of Discrimination and Racism), an NGO formed by the Buraku Liberation League (BLL) in 1988, the media being generally reluctant to cover burakumin issues – unless they involve scandals by BLL members.

References

Aoki, S. (1993) *Afurika ni watatta Nihonjin* (Japanese in Africa). Tokyo: Jiji Tsūshinsha.

—— (1994) 'Meiji Jidai no Afurika-zō: Bungaku sakuhin ni arawareta Afurika to Nihonjin' (The Image of African in the Meiji Period: Africa and Japanese as seen in literature), in Kawabata Masahisa (ed.), *Afurika to Nihon*, Tokyo: Keisō Shobō, 3–18.

Beasley, W.G. (1995) *Japan Encounters the Barbarian*, New Haven: Yale University Press.

Bleyer, B. (2006) 'Legacy: Pyrrhus Concer,' http://www.newsday.com/community/ guide/lihistory/ny-history-hs509b0.7157701.story.

Brannen, M.Y. (1992) 'Bwana Mickey: Constructing cultural consumption at Tokyo Disneyland,' in Joseph J. Tobin (ed.), *Re-Made in Japan*, New Haven: Yale University Press, 216–234.

Bronfenbrenner, M. (1975) *Tomioka Stories of the Occupation*, Hicksville, New York: Exposition Press.

Burkhardt, W.R. (1978) 'Institutional Barriers, Marginality, and Adaptation Among the American-Japanese Mixed Bloods in Japan,' *Journal of Asian Studies* 42(3): 519–44.

Clemons, E.W. (1990) 'The History of Blacks in Japan: The Japanese response to the African diaspora from premodern times to the twentieth century,' undergraduate thesis, Amherst College.

Cooper, M. (1965) *They Came to Japan: An anthology of European reports on Japan, 1543–1640*, Berkeley: University of California Press.

Dathorne, O.R. (1996) *Asian Voyages: Two thousand years of constructing the other*, Westport, Connecticut: Bergin and Garvey.

DeBarry, T. (ed.) (1958) *Sources of Japanese Tradition Vol. II*, New York: Columbia University Press.

Dikötter, F. (1992) *The Discourse of Race in Modern China*, Stanford: Stanford University Press.

Duyvendak, J.J.L. (1949) *China's Discovery of Africa*, London: Probsthain.

Endō, S. (1973) *Kurombō* (Nigger), Tokyo: Kadokawa Bunko.

Filesi, T. (1962) *China and Africa in the Middle Ages*, California: University of California Press.

Fujita M. (1987a) 'Nihon-shi ni Okeru "Kurobō" no Tōjo: Afurika ōrai kotohajime' (Early History of Afro-Japanese Relations: People called kurobō in the sixteenth century), *Hikaku Bungaku Kenkyū* 51, 28–51.

—— (1987b) 'Edo Jidai ni Okeru Nihonjin no Afurika-kan' (Japanese Images of Africans in the Edo Period), *Chūtō Gakkai Nenpō* No. 2, April, 239–90.

Fukuzawa, Y. (1962 [1875]) *Bunmei-ron no gairyaku* (An Outline of a Theory of Civilization), Tokyo: Iwanami Shoten.

Harris, J.E. (1987) *Africans and Their History*, New York: Penguin.

Heine, W. (1990) *With Perry to Japan*, Honolulu: University of Hawaii Press.

Hughes, L. (1986 [1956]) *I Wonder as I Wander*, New York: Thunder's Mouth Press.

Hill, R.A. (ed.) (1995) *The FBI's RACON: Racial conditions in the United States during World War II*, Boston: Northeastern University Press.

Ikemiyagi, S. (1971) *Okinawa no Amerikajin* (Americans in Okinawa), Tokyo: Simul.

Inōe, S. (1995) *Senryō-gun Iyanfujo: Kokka ni yoru baishun shisetsu* (Comfort Stations for Occupation Troops: State-managed brothels), Tokyo: Shinhyōron.

Irwin, G. (1977) *Africans Abroad*, New York: Columbia University Press.

Kearney, R. (1998) *African American Views of Japanese: Solidarity or sedition?*, Albany: State University of New York Press.

Koshiro, Y. (2003) 'Beyond an Alliance of Color: The African American impact on modern Japan,' *Positions: East Asia Cultures Critique* 11(1), Spring, 183–215.

Leupp, G.P. (1995) 'Images of Black People in Late Mediaeval and Early Modern Japan: 1543–1900,' *Japan Forum* 7(1), April, 1–13.

McCauley, E.Y. (1942) *With Perry in Japan: The diary of Edward Yorke McCauley*, Allan B. Cole (ed.), Princeton: Princeton University Press.

Meech-Pekarik, J. (1987) *The World of the Meiji Print: Impressions of a new civilization*, New York and Tokyo: Weatherhill.

Miyoshi, M. (1979) *As We Saw Them: The first Japanese Embassy to the United States*, Tokyo: Kodansha International.

Molasky, M. (1999) *The American Occupation of Japan and Okinawa: Literature and memory*, London and New York: Routledge.

Morikawa, J. (1988) *Minami Afurika to Nihon: Kankei no rekishi, kōzō, kadai* (South Africa and Japan: The anatomy and history of a relationship), Tokyo: Dōbunkan.

Oda, M. (1979 [1961]) *Nan demo mite yarō* (Let's See Everything), Tokyo: Kadokawa Shoten.

Oguma, E. (1995) *Tan-itsu Minzoku Shinwa no Kigen* (The Myth of the Homogeneous Nation), Tokyo: Shindosha.

Okakura, T. and Kitagawa, K. (1993) *Nihon-Afurika Kōryū-shi* (A History of Japan-Africa Exchange), Tokyo: Dōbunkan.

Perry, M.C. (1968 [1856]) *The Personal Journal of Commodore Matthew C. Perry*, Washington, DC: Smithsonian Institution Press.

Polenberg, R. (1980) *One Nation Divisible: Class, race and ethnicity in the United States since 1938*, New York: Penguin.

Reischauer, E.O. (1988) *The Japanese Today*, Tokyo: Charles Tuttle.

Rubin, A. (1967) *Black Nanban: Africans in Japan during the 16th century*, Bloomington: Indiana University Press.

Russell, J. (1991) 'Race and Reflexivity: The black other in contemporary Japanese mass culture,' *Cultural Anthropology* 6(1), February, 3–25.

—— (1998) 'Consuming Passions: Spectacle, self-transformation and the commodification of blackness in Japan,' *Positions: East Asia Cultures Critique* 6:1, Spring, 113–77.

Sayama, K. (1990) 'Yasashii Bōru: Kokujin rīgu wa Nihon puro yakyū no "haha" datta' (Gentle Ball: The Negro leagues were the mother of Japanese professional baseball), *Number*, February.

—— (1993) 'Densetsu no Niguro Rīgu: Nihon puro yakyū tanjo mitsushi' (A History of the Legendary Negro Leagues and Its Relationship to the Development of Japanese Professional Baseball), in *Kokujingaku Nyūmon* (An Introduction to Black Studies), Tokyo: Takarajimasha, 43–52.

Shimao, E. (1981) 'Darwinism in Japan: 1877–1927,' *Annals of Science* 38, 93–102.

Siddle, R. (1996) *Race, Resistance and the Ainu of Japan*, London and New York: Routledge.

Siebold, H. von. (1996) *Sho Shîboruto Ezo Kenkanki* (Siebold's Study of the Ezo, Abridged), Japanese trans. of *Ethnologiesche Studien über die Aino auf Insel Yesso* (1881), Harada Nobuo, trans., Tokyo: Heibonsha.

Snow, P. (1988) *The Star Raft*, New York: Weidenfield and Nicolson.

Snowden, F.M. (1983) *Before Color Prejudice: The ancient view of blacks*, Cambridge, Massachussetts: Harvard University Press.

Suzuki, T. (1992) *Nichijō-go Gogen Jitten* (An Etymological Dictionary of Everyday Words), Tokyo: Tokyodō Shuppan.

Takamine, T. (1984) *Shirarezaru Okinawa no Bei-hei* (The Unknown American GIs of Okinawa), Tokyo: Kobunken.

Tanizaki, J. (1984) *In'ei Raisan* (In Praise of Shadows), Thomas J. Harper and Edward G. Seidensticker, trans., Tokyo: Charles Tuttle.

Thompson, E.B. (1967) 'Japanese Rejected,' *Ebony* 22, September.

Wagatsuma, H. (1967) 'The Social Perception of Skin Color in Japan,' *Daedalus*, Spring, 407–43.

—— (1978) 'Identity Problems of Black-Japanese Youth,' in Robert L. Rotberg (ed.) *The Mixing of Peoples: Problems of identity and ethnicity*, Stamford, Connecticut: Greylock, 117–129.

Wagatsuma, H. and Yoneyama, T. (1980) *Henken no Kōzō* (The Anatomy of Prejudice), Tokyo; NHK Books.

Wiley, P.B. (1990) *Yankees in the Land of the Gods*, New York: Viking.

Yap, M. and Man, D.L. (1996) *Color, Confusion and Concessions: The history of the Chinese in South Africa*, Hong Kong: Hong Kong University Press.

Yasuoka S. (1962) *Amerika Kanjō Ryōkō* (Sentimental Journey in America), Tokyo: Iwanami Bunko.

6 Creating a transnational community

Chinese newcomers in Japan

Gracia Liu-Farrer

Rooted in American experiences, immigration studies traditionally inves-
tigated how immigrants fare in the new society, with the expectation that
they eventually shed their old cultural practices and political loyalties to
become assimilated into the host society's sociocultural and economic
systems (Warner and Srole 1945; Gordon 1964; Alba and Nee 1997). With
the expanding scope of international migration in every part of the globe,
advancing modern communication and transportation technologies, and
the intensified global capitalist process, immigrants' adaptation practices
increasingly cut across national boundaries. Their cultural and social
identities become rooted in both home and host societies (Glick Schiller
1999). Diaspora voting and dual citizenship ensure immigrants' political
representation in the home country (Basch *et al.* 1994; Laguerre 1999;
Guarnizo 1998; Guarnizo *et al.* 2003; Kearney 1991, 1995; Kyle 2000).
Transnational entrepreneurship has become an alternative means of economic
adaptation (Portes *et al.* 2002). Frequent travels between the host and home
societies help immigrants maintain a closely-knit transnational social field
and preserve their social and cultural roots in the home country (Glick
Schiller and Fouron 1999; Goldring 1998).

Transnational practices and outlooks characterize the Chinese newcomer
community in Japan. In a country reluctant to become an immigrant country,
despite surging immigration and a society widely (even if falsely) perceived
as racially homogeneous, maintaining economic and social ties with the
home country and making transnational living arrangements have become
strategies Chinese immigrants have adopted, both to circumvent their marginal
social positions and to gain socioeconomic mobility in Japan. Beginning with
a brief history of the Chinese in Japan, this chapter introduces the patterns of
contemporary migration and the characteristics of the Chinese newcomers.
It categorizes their transnational modes of social and economic adaptation
as well as their living arrangements, and it describes the construction of the
identity of 'new overseas Chinese' (*shin hua qiao*).

The data used in this chapter mostly came from my independent fieldwork among Chinese immigrants in Japan between 2001 and 2007. Three years of participant observation in Chinese social dance parties (2002) and Chinese religious congregations (2003 and 2004), over 150 in-depth interviews with a wide variety of Chinese newcomers in Japan, an independent survey of 218 individuals, and Chinese immigrant media in Japan provide the basis for sociological insights into this diverse and vibrant ethnic community.

MERCHANTS, ARTISANS, LABORERS AND STUDENTS: CHINESE IMMIGRANTS IN HISTORY

The Chinese have a long history in Japan. Until Japan annexed Korea in 1910, the Chinese were the biggest foreign community in Japan. Merchants, skilled workers, and artisans pioneered the Chinese migration into Japan. Despite Ming China's ban on trade with Japan in 1547 and Tokugawa Japan's national isolation policy instituted in 1639, Chinese merchants, particularly those from Fujian, were active in Japan's southern coastal city of Nagasaki, which remained open to traders (Vasishth 1997). In the late seventeenth century, several thousand Chinese resided in Nagasaki's Chinese residential quarter and surrounding areas (Uchida 1949). After the mid-nineteenth century, Chinese nationals were restricted from independent trading activities. Instead, Chinese business people showed up in Japanese port cities as compradors brought in from Chinese treaty ports by Western traders. Although formally intermediaries between Western and Japanese firms, these Chinese compradors, allied with Chinese merchants in Japan, in fact monopolized the trade between China and Japan (Vasishth 1997).

Besides trading, the Chinese concentrated in several service businesses: restaurants, barber shops, and the clothing industry. As a result, the popular image of the older generations of Chinese in Japan was the 'three-blades' (*san ba dao*) – the chef's knife, tailor's scissors, and barber's razor (Jiang 1998). Some historians point out that skilled Chinese workers and artisans brought in traditional Chinese skills that became indispensable components of the Japanese lifestyle, such as making tea and combs. With the skills learned in Chinese treaty ports, they also contributed to the Westernization of Japanese life in the mid to late nineteenth century. They brought in Western tailoring and hairstyles, and they installed the first gas lights in the streets of Nagasaki (Kamachi 1980, Vasishth 1997). Chinese household servants from Shanghai contributed to the development of Western-style cooking in Japan (Cwiertka 2007).

Chinese laborers' migration into Japan until the end of nineteenth century mostly took place through kinship networks, and therefore Chinese settled in several Chinese residential quarters in Yokohama, Kobe, and Nagasaki according to the regions that they were from. Usually working for Chinese businesses, these Chinese laborers were less welcomed by Japanese society. Their increase in the late nineteenth century, with their alleged lack of personal hygiene and opium addiction, fueled anti-Chinese sentiments. In 1899, an Imperial Ordinance was issued to restrict Chinese laborers from being employed outside of the foreign concessions, which in turn reduced Chinese labor migration into Japan. As a result, by the end of the nineteenth century the Chinese immigrant community was largely composed of merchants, artisans, skilled workers, and their families and employees (Vasishth 1997).

A distinct group of migrants from mainland China were the Chinese forced laborers who came during World War Two. Strictly speaking, they were not immigrants but conscripted laborers. Some were abducted by the Manchukuo Government for Japan's war industries. Between April 1943 and May 1945, 38,935 Chinese laborers arrived in Japan, toiling in 135 mines, ports, and factories, from Kyushu to Hokkaido. These Chinese men were put into wired camps, given below-subsistence-level provisions, and treated as slaves. In a two-year period, 6,830 people, or 17 percent, died from malnutrition, diseases, injuries, or armed crackdowns during incidences of rebellions (Nishinarita 2002). The harsh treatments of these Chinese laborers – who were mostly repatriated by the end of World War Two – and Japanese governments' evasive attitudes toward their compensation cast a lasting shadow on the Sino–Japanese diplomatic relationship.

Of all types of Chinese migrants into Japan, the most numerous were Chinese students. Between 1896, when the Chinese government started to send out students, and 1945, when World War Two ended, tens of thousands of Chinese students arrived in Japan to study. Japan was the most popular destination for Chinese students because of linguistic, cultural, and geographic proximity. Starting with thirteen government-sponsored students in 1896, the number of Chinese students increased to thousands within a decade. In 1905 and 1906, in the wake of Japan's victory over Russia and China's abolition of the 1,300-year-old Imperial Examination (*ke ju*), the Chinese student body in Japan swelled to 8,000.[1] At one point in 1906, 12,000 students were found in various educational institutions in Japan (Saneto 1960: 530). In any given year between 1903 and 1945, thousands of Chinese students studied in Japan. A fraction of these students were selected and funded by the government – either the Qing Imperial Government or later the Nationalist Government – to learn modern scientific knowledge, military technology, and social scientific and cultural skills (Shen 1997). The majority were self-financed.

Many influential political and military leaders of both the Nationalist

Party and the Communist Party, such as Zhou Enlai and Chiang Kai-shek, and leftist writers and artists in China, such as Lu Xun, Chen Duxiu, Guo Moruo, Tian Han, and Nie Er (the composer of People's Republic of China's national anthem), were once students in Japan. Before Japan invaded China in the early 1930s, Chinese students freely crossed the Chinese and Japanese borders. Many ended up living in Japan on and off for many years, depending on the political and social environment in China. Most Chinese students who arrived in Japan from 1896 to 1945 eventually returned to China.

CHINESE NEWCOMERS IN JAPAN

In 1951, Japan and the United States signed the San Francisco Peace Treaty, stripping all former colonial subjects of Japanese citizenship. The majority of Koreans and Chinese were repatriated. Those who stayed became resident aliens. In 1952, about 44,000 Chinese people, mostly from former colonial Taiwan, remained in Japan (Vasishth 1997). With no diplomatic relations and with China experiencing drastic social and political changes under the Communist Party, migration from mainland China to Japan was virtually halted until 1972, when these two countries re-established diplomatic relationship. In 1978, China signed a peace agreement with Japan, and formalized the diplomatic relationship between the two countries. The re-establishment of diplomatic relations ensured the resumption of migration from China to Japan.

In 2006, over 700,000 Chinese-born people resided in Japan.[2] The majority of them, called 'newcomers' (Tajima 2003), came after the mid-1980s. Despite the economic downturns in Japan and the booms in China, the eventful diplomatic relationship between the two countries, and changing immigration-control policies in Japan, the Chinese population has been rapidly growing since the mid-1980s, showing no sign of slowing down.

Contemporary migration to Japan

Students pioneered the contemporary migration from China to Japan. Between 1972 and 1978, the Chinese government sent several dozen Chinese students to Japan to study Japanese. In 1979, the two countries started official educational exchange programs (Wang 2006). Between 1980 and 1984, the Chinese government passed a series of policies that allowed Chinese students to pursue education abroad at their own cost. In 1984, Chinese citizens were permitted to go abroad to study if they could secure financial sponsorship or scholarships, and by 1986, the Chinese government further relaxed the restrictions on Chinese citizens' emigration. In the meantime, China's higher educational institutions were nearly destroyed in the decade-long Cultural Revolution from 1966 to 1976. When the college entrance examinations were reinstituted in 1977, only a small fraction of the hundreds of thousands of high school graduates could enter college. Post-graduate education was even rarer. Chinese youth hungry for knowledge and desiring higher academic credentials turned to Western countries and Japan for educational opportunities (Shao 1995).

On the other side of the East China Sea, Japan entered the 1980s with a strong economy and an ambition to become a political superpower. In order to internationalize the country, Prime Minister Yasuhiro Nakasone proposed the 'Plan to Accept 100,000 Foreign Students before the Beginning of the 21st Century.' In 1984, responding to this policy initiative, the Japanese government simplified the application procedures for student visas, including those for pre-university language education (Wakabayashi 1990). There was no language proficiency requirement or age limit for student visas. As a response, numerous language academies opened overnight in order to make a profit on international education. Immediately, large numbers of Chinese people with various motivations and academic backgrounds arrived. From 1984 to 2004, over a quarter million Chinese citizens entered Japan with either university or pre-university language-student visas.[3] Currently, except for trainees, language and university students combined form the largest group entering the Japanese border every year. Registered students

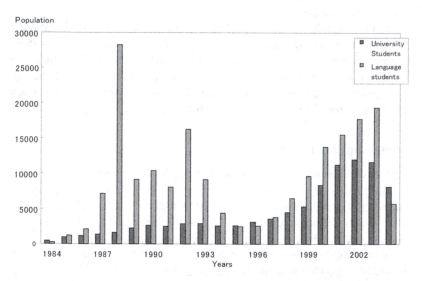

Figure 6.1 Yearly trends of student migration from China to Japan between 1984 and 2004 (Data source: Ministry of Justice)

accounted for one-fifth to one-third of the total registered Chinese population in Japan, comprising two-thirds of the foreign student population on Japanese university campuses.

Students are possibly the most visible Chinese immigrants in Japan, but in recent years the biggest entrant group has been trainees. In 1981, the Industrial Training Program for Non-Japanese was established. Although the program was established for the purposes of contributing to the development of human resources in the economic improvement of developing countries, trainees have been used as low-wage unskilled or semi-skilled labor by Japanese manufacturing industries (Ohmi 2006). The acceptance requirements for trainees were relaxed in the latter half of the 1980s, when labor was in short supply. In 1990, when the Immigration Control Act was revised, the number of trainees increased dramatically. In 1993, the Technical Intern Program was established to allow trainees to stay up to three years after completing their trainee program. In 2003, the maximum period of stay was extended to five years. Over three-quarters of technical interns are from China, toiling in the textile and clothing industry, in machine manufacturing, and in the food industry. Although numerous, trainees are largely invisible to the Japanese public. Moreover, bound by contracts, they have designated tasks, limited mobility, and no legal possibility of settling in Japan.

Besides students and trainees, thousands of Chinese, particularly women, enter Japan every year as spouses of Japanese nationals. It is reported that in the two decades between the early 1980s and early 2000s, 39.6 percent of Chinese people who married a foreign spouse in Shanghai married a Japanese citizen.[4] Dependants, the family members of the primary migrants, also enter Japan in large numbers. In 2005, over 50,000 Chinese residents in Japan held spouse visas and over 35,000 held dependant visas. In addition, though reluctant to admit unskilled labor, the Japanese government has been more welcoming of engineers and high-tech professionals. Thousands of skilled workers in the categories of 'engineers' and 'intra-firm transferees' are recruited from China.

Characteristics of Chinese newcomers

Because of the varied means of entry, the Chinese community in Japan is the most diverse among the major immigrant communities in terms of legal resident status. In 2004, over 70 percent of Koreans were 'special permanent residents' who were born in Japan or came to Japan before World War Two.[5] Brazilians, the third largest immigrant community, entered mostly as descendants of overseas Japanese and their family members. Filipinos, the fourth largest immigrant population, came as entertainers and spouses. In comparison, the Chinese community in Japan is evenly composed of students, workers (engineers/professionals/skilled laborers), trainees/technical interns, and permanent residents, as well as undocumented immigrants (Figure 6.2).[6]

In terms of region of origin, the Chinese population in Japan has undergone significant change during the past two decades. Shanghai and Fujian migrants dominated the Chinese community in the late 1980s and early 1990s. In the 1990s, with increasingly diverse means of migration, such as the return of descendants of Japanese war orphans and international marriages, Chinese immigrants from other regions started showing up in Japan. The largest increase was among those from the northeastern provinces, areas that hosted the majority of Japanese left behind at the end of the Pacific War. In fact, since 2001 Liaoning and Heilongjiang have surpassed Shanghai as the number one and two regions of origin for Japan-bound migrants. However, the increase of northeastern migrants does not mean that they dominate the current Chinese community in terms of population. Recent statistics show that numbers of immigrants are increasing from all regions of China, particularly from coastal areas with heavy Japanese investments and transnational economic exchanges. Eight provinces and cities, Liaoning, Heilongjiang, Jilin, Beijing, Shanghai, Jiangsu, Shandong and Fujian, almost all on the east coast, accounted for over 70 percent of mainland Chinese immigrants in Japan in 2005.

Demographically, the typical Chinese immigrant in Japan is young and female. While the Korean community resembles the native Japanese in age composition, with just under 14 percent of its population over the age of 65 in 2003, the Chinese are much younger, with only 2 percent older than 65. Among the Chinese in Japan there were 36 percent more

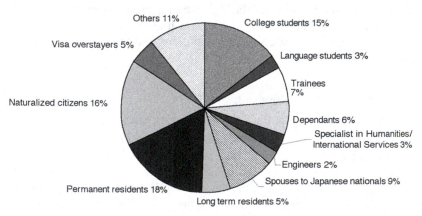

Figure 6.2 Resident visa statuses of Chinese immigrants in Japan in 2005 (Data source: Ministry of Justice)

women than men (Japan Immigration Association 2004). This reflects the demographic consequence of the major patterns of migration. According to visa status, the biggest categories are students, spouses of Japanese nationals, dependants, and trainees and technical interns. While the student population is mostly gender-equal, the spouses of Japanese nationals and dependants are predominantly women. So it is not surprising that there are more Chinese women living and working in Japan than there are men.

The Chinese newcomers have in recent years started settling down in Japan. In a recent survey of 141 Chinese living in a housing compound in Saitama Prefecture, north of Tokyo, Tajima (2005) reported that, independent of their desires to stay on in Japan or go back to China, 80 percent of respondents either had already obtained permanent residency or planned to apply for permanent residency. More than 25 percent of those surveyed already held Japanese citizenship or were planning to naturalize. Figure 6.2 shows that in 2005 naturalized Chinese immigrants and permanent residents accounted for one-third of the total Chinese immigrant population in Japan. From 1990 to 2005, 58,879 Chinese immigrants chose to become Japanese citizens. Among them, 46,012 naturalized in the decade after 1996, with an average of 4,600 people naturalizing every year. The rate of obtaining permanent residency has also increased more rapidly in recent years. In 2005, one-fifth of the total Chinese population, or 106,269 individuals, were permanent residents. Between 2000 and 2005, an average of 11,384 individuals obtained permanent residency every year. This means that two-thirds of Chinese permanent residents in Japan obtained such status in the last six years. This rapid increase in the number of naturalized citizens and permanent residents among the Chinese in Japan indicates the maturation and stabilization of the Chinese community in Japan.

THE TRANSNATIONAL COMMUNITY

Though settling down in Japan, the Chinese by no means sever their ties with their homes in China, nor do they consider themselves 'immigrants' in Japan. Being geographically proximate, embedded in the transnational economy with China, and on the margins of Japanese society, Chinese people's career practices, living arrangements, and self-identification all indicate a transnational orientation.

Transnational economic practices

Chinese people's transnationality is most saliently shown in their economic practices in Japan. The era of employing 'three blades' as a means of living has become a distant memory. The flourishing transnational economy allows newcomers to find their economic niches within economic globalization processes. Chinese immigrants in Japan, especially Chinese students, see their opportunities for socioeconomic mobility in the transnational economy between Japan and China. They tend to follow two types of careers – corporate employment in transnational business or transnational entrepreneurship.

Transnational employees

China has recently become the most important production site and one of the largest consumer markets for Japanese businesses. It is not only large conglomerates such as NEC and Mazda that maintain large production and sales operations; numerous small and medium-sized Japanese firms are also active, and to some degree desperate, players in the transnational economy between Japan and China. In 2007, Shanghai alone had 4,828 Japanese corporate branches (Sasatani 2007). Chinese immigrants are frequently employed by Japanese firms to manage transnational sales and marketing deals with China or to actualize the firms' plans to enter the Chinese market.

A common title for Chinese employees in Japanese firms is that of 'representative' (*tantou*) in an overseas marketing department, or 'overseas representative' (*kaigai tantou*) in the sales department in a smaller firm. Japan-educated Chinese student migrants are the most likely to hold these positions. Among the Chinese students who obtained employment visas in 2005, over two-thirds were in the visa category of 'specialist in humanities/ international services.' These visas are mostly granted to those who are employed by Japanese companies that are engaged in transnational business with China. Employees of this type use their linguistic and cultural skills, as well as their social networks in China, to help expand the firms' transnational business. Zhang Tian, a sales representative who worked for a Japanese steel company, explained that his Chinese connections helped him and his firm to survive an economic downturn.

> There were a couple of years when global steel prices became so low that we lost many clients. You see, the reason why the company has a good evaluation of me is that when other people do their sales through their local branches, I am running around China searching for potential clients. For example, a Japanese Hong Kong sales rep goes through the Hong Kong office for clients, while I have clients directly in contact with me. A friend's mother in a Chinese iron and steel research institute helped introduce me to some manufacturers. I personally developed these clients.

Zhang Tian proudly claimed, 'Without me, the company would lose these clients.' As a result of his indispensability, he was offered the status of permanent employee (*seishain*) a year after he was first employed. When I interviewed him in 2003, he had the title of section manager (*kacho*). In 2007, when I interviewed him again, he was working in Shanghai as the manager of a branch office that he had created under a special contract with the company.

Many Chinese engineers in Japanese firms, despite their specific technical skills, also aspire to work in the transnational economy, and they see business with China as providing the greatest opportunities for career advancement into managerial positions. Some even leave technical positions to join the marketing teams. With the recent and rapid expansion of offshore production, many engineers, especially software professionals, have acquired the title of 'bridge engineer' (BE) or 'bridge software engineer' (BSE), and serve as liaisons between the clients, the development teams in Japan, and the production teams in China. A qualified BSE typically requires three types of skills – software development skills, language and communication skills in both Chinese and Japanese, and management skills. Therefore, only Chinese employees who have mastered the Japanese language and have been working in Japanese firms for an extended period are able to do the job. As a result, being a BSE is considered a milestone in a technical workers' career path, and they are increasingly in demand.

Both Chinese men and women are active in transnational businesses. Although Japanese women are frequently assigned to corporate positions with little responsibility or potential for promotion, the value of Chinese women as bilingual and bicultural human resources helps them to overcome some of the gender barriers in Japanese corporations. Few Chinese women work in Japanese firms as the typical 'office ladies' ("OLs") in pink, beige, or cream-colored uniforms. Instead of providing general office support to male workers, they work as sales and marketing representatives. Almost all of the thirty-eight Chinese women employees in my interview sample worked in departments that already did business with China or were planning to do so. Their jobs entailed frequent overseas travel – a practice conventionally restricted to men. One informant said she was the only woman in her company who didn't have to wear a uniform, and she was also the only woman in the marketing department of her company.

Transnational entrepreneurs

Becoming a transnational entrepreneur is a common aspiration of Chinese migrants in Japan (Liu-Farrer 2007). In 2004, 1,268 Chinese migrants registered in Japan as investors, ranking first among all foreign investors (Ministry of Justice 2005).[7] But this number does not adequately describe the scale or scope of business ownership among Chinese migrants. In fact, most Chinese business owners are long-term residents, permanent residents, and naturalized immigrants.

Transnational entrepreneurship is often a career extension from corporate employment. The majority of Chinese transnational entrepreneurs I have encountered in my fieldwork had once worked for Japanese corporations. The career choice of becoming independent is partly a result of their unsatisfactory corporate experiences in Japan, but it also is supported by the human and social capital accumulated through their economic practices in corporate Japan. Although the transnational economy provides Chinese immigrants with niches and mobility channels within Japanese corporations, host labor-market constraints are still important reasons for Chinese immigrants' decisions to become independent. Such constraints include job insecurity, unfair treatment, and blocked career-mobility paths. In addition, negative reactions to the corporate culture in Japan drive many Chinese employees to become independent. One reason many of my entrepreneurial interviewees gave for their decision to leave is their own 'character' or 'personality.' Statements such as 'I am not the kind that works for others' are frequently given as explanations. Although describing their choices in personal terms, they complain about the strict hierarchical management and the lack of room for creativity and personal development in a rule-based Japanese society. Some describe the culture within Japanese firms as depressing. Although Chinese employees recognize that these are standard conditions in corporate Japan and that Japanese colleagues are following these rules even more closely than is expected of Chinese, they nonetheless feel unhappy in such an environment. In many instances, they exit the company to enjoy the freedom of being the boss.

In working for Japanese companies, Chinese immigrants 'learn the ropes.' Through their corporate experiences, they learn the Japanese business culture and specific trade knowledge and skills, and they establish social networks they can deploy in their own businesses. As An Jianxing wrote:

> I often hear Chinese friends say, 'I want to have my own business, but I don't have the (economic) capital (zi jin).' In fact, the capital is not the most important factor for doing business. I think the most important conditions are: first, whether you are familiar with the business you want to be in (Working for a Japanese company is no doubt the best learning experience.); and the second, a trusting relationship with your business partners.
>
> (An 1998, p. 6)

As a consequence, Chinese entrepreneurs often continue in the same business after they leave their corporate employers. An Jianxing spent three years working for a trading company in the construction material business, preparing import and export documents for sales and marketing. He realized that he, on his own, could do the work done by 120 people in that company. The only difference was scope. He left the company and set up his own business importing construction materials. In order to show gratitude to his former boss, he did not sell to his former clients. Instead, he cultivated new clients. Several other entrepreneurs I interviewed found a market related to the business they were engaged in when working for a Japanese institution. For example, Shen Chao, after working for several years for a research firm that specialized in intellectual property rights, started a company that specialized in technology transfers between Japan and China.

Some pioneering transnational entrepreneurial efforts among Chinese immigrants in Japan were in educational, hospitality, and consulting services, all of which facilitated business between Japan and China. They published periodicals introducing Chinese economic behavior, organized Japanese company owners to tour China, and introduced Chinese government investment delegations to the Japanese business world. One such company, while publishing a bi-weekly publication called China–Japan News (*Zhong-Ri Xin Bao*), from 1992 to 1997 organized 117 Japanese delegations to China to seek business opportunities. Among them, thirty-seven Japanese companies made successful investments in China (Liu 1998).

With expanding offshore production and trade, as well as the prolonged economic recession at home, Japanese people have become more accepting of commodities made in other Asian countries, especially if they are cheaper. As a result, 'one-coin' (100 yen) shops have flourished. Most of the goods sold in these shops are made in Asian countries with cheaper labor costs (Pacific Asia Resource Center 2004). China is the primary supplier. Many Chinese entrepreneurs therefore find their businesses in the complementary markets in China and Japan. Some entrepreneurs in my sample invested in Chinese factories in order to produce commodities for the Japanese market. Su Qiming and his Japanese partner owned a company that helped Japanese families install and repair air-conditioners. He opened a factory in China to manufacture air-conditioner parts.

Some entrepreneurs are active as middlemen. When I went to interview Ogawa, an entrepreneur, he was having a business meeting with a Chinese business associate. Ogawa asked his associate to produce some small commodities, such as socks, underpants, and accessories. He carefully drew pictures to show how each item should look. He later explained to me that a Japanese company wanted to put out vending machines that sold those commodities. They wanted the products to be of very low cost, cheaper than 100 yen. Ogawa was helping them find Chinese factories that could manufacture such commodities for extremely low prices.

The discrepancy in labor costs between Japan and China is also what energizes the Chinese transnational information technology industry in Japan. Chinese 'Soft Houses' utilize the low-cost labor reserve in China by outsourcing the actual software programming to China, and they also recruit talent directly from Chinese university campuses, dispatching people to projects in Japan. According to one such entrepreneur, who had companies in both Japan and China, the market price in Shanghai in 2003 for a newly graduated computer science major was about 2,000 RMB (about 30,000 yen or 250 US dollars), a small fraction of what their Japanese counterparts made in Japan.

Because of the cultural affinity between Japan and China, Chinese entrepreneurs sometimes trade in exotic Chinese goods such as dieting foods or nutrition supplements. China and Japan have also become attractive tourist destinations for each other. Since September 2003, Japanese citizens who plan to visit China for less than fifteen days can obtain a visa upon entry. Japan is the first foreign country to enjoy visa exemption in China. In return, Japan relaxed the restrictions on tourist visas for Chinese citizens, particularly those from coastal provinces. Responding to the increased opportunities these have provided, Chinese travel agencies have multiplied in Japan.

Although newcomer economic practices apparently respond to economic opportunities, these transnational career practices also represent Chinese immigrants' conscious efforts to overcome their marginal socioeconomic positions in Japan. My informants frequently reported that their employers recruited them because of existing business with China or because of interest in developing business with China. A Chinese woman, a former student, commented, 'If it is a position dealing with the domestic market, why would they need you? A native Japanese speaker can do such things better than you do.'

For the transnational entrepreneurs, the dynamic Chinese economy provides opportunities to turn their Chinese background into an asset. By working in the transnational economy, they avoid becoming fully assimilated into Japanese society. Chang Lili said,

> I don't think it is necessary for us to assimilate (*rong yu*) into Japanese society. We can't be really assimilated, and neither do we want to. Chinese are Chinese. We have different ways of life. We just participate in their society and work with them. Besides, the economy has become global. I'm in the health business. Health has no national boundary. Everybody in the world cares about it. I am working in the global economy, not a particular Japanese one.

Transnational living

It is generally considered easier to be naturalized than to be granted permanent residency; the former requires five years of continuous residency, while the latter requires ten years. Nonetheless, eligible Chinese immigrants increasingly choose permanent residency over naturalization. During the past five years, three times as many Chinese immigrants obtained permanent residence than obtained Japanese citizenship. According to an article in the biggest Chinese immigrant newspaper, Chinese Review Weekly (*Zhong Wen Dao Bao*), Chinese people preferred permanent residencies over citizenships because,

> In the long run, (with a permanent residency), (you) can get the benefits of both (societies), e.g. buying houses, children's schooling, life after retirement ... Later (you) can judge which side is better and lean in that direction. (Moreover, you) don't have to struggle with psychological barriers; don't have to give up the conveniences available in your home country; don't need to go to the immigration office to get a visa; won't be accused of 'selling out the ancestors for prosperity (*mai zu qiu rong*)' ... Permanent residency, in the eyes of the majority of Chinese, is almost a golden choice. Besides, people with permanent residencies can apply for naturalization, while naturalized people cannot regain their Chinese citizenships.[8]

The practice of 'getting the benefits of both societies' involves transnational living arrangements, which are most evident in child rearing. Chinese newcomers frequently leave small children with their grandparents so that both parents can work full-time in Japan. Although apparent among both documented and undocumented Chinese immigrants, this practice is more common among the undocumented migrants. Undocumented migrants work in the low-wage irregular labor market. Having a child live with his or her parents entails extra expense, as well as loss of the mother's income. Moreover, some young undocumented immigrants live together without registering their marriage, and may each have a family to support back home. Many mothers reluctantly part with their nursing babies only weeks after their birth.[9] Documented Chinese often visit their children a couple of times a year and bring them back to Japan when they are old enough to enter kindergarten. Most undocumented parents, however, do not see their children again for years.

Chinese parents in Japan, especially those who have migrated as students and skilled professionals, generally have high academic aspirations for their children. Many share the concern that Japanese public education is mass education teaching to the average child, while the Chinese schools train the elites. Though some families pay the expenses for cram schools and private Japanese schools, many use the economic resources accumulated in Japan to send their children to private elite schools in China. These children either stay with their relatives in China or are accompanied by their mothers. Some Chinese immigrants intend for their children to become transnational actors in their own right. Chang Huijun, an engineer, spent most of his time in Japan alone. Chang's son, accompanied by the son's mother, was at a prestigious middle school in Shanghai. Chang was proud of his son's spoken English, and explained, 'It is better to learn English first, and then study Japanese. If he studied Japanese first, he would have trouble pronouncing English properly.' He planned for his son to attend college in China, because he realized that 'If the Japanese wants to use a Chinese, what he really wants is to use his Chinese language ability. He would probably use you as a bridge to communicate with China and to manage his Chinese side business.'

Transnational living arrangements often take a toll on family life. Prolonged separation creates difficult family relations. I have heard parents lament the emotional estrangement of their children. Chang Huijun's role was that of providing financial support and fancy toys for his son, but he lacked parental authority: 'He is not afraid of me. Sometimes when he does something naughty, and I try to stop him, he doesn't listen to me.' Some Chinese rely on technology, especially the Internet, to tie the family together. Zheng Hailin, a software engineer and a permanent resident, tried to maintain a 'normal' relationship with his son, who was in elementary school in China, by speaking through video cam and playing computer games together every day. On weekends, these lone parents and spouses go to social clubs and religious congregations where Chinese immigrants gather, looking for companionship and emotional support (Liu-Farrer 2004, 2006).

Many Chinese immigrants' transnational living arrangements involve having homes in both countries. While settling in Japan, they also purchase houses in China. For many, residence in Japan resembles living under someone else's roof. By contrast, their home is a place in China where they can relax and recuperate. Among naturalized Japanese citizens, transnational living is a life-course design, most commonly reflected in their retirement plans. Most aspire to retire in China; some are entertaining the option of a third country. Australia seems attractive to quite a number of Chinese newcomers in Japan. It is also worth noting that the idea of returning to China after retirement is popular among Chinese who have Japanese spouses. I met a Chinese woman in her late forties at a sushi-train restaurant. She married a Japanese man in his sixties who lived on a pension. He had no children of his own, so she entertained the idea of taking him to China to live with her family for half a year and then living in Tokyo for half a year. This was in part driven by economic necessity, since his pension of 300,000 yen a month would stretch much farther in China than in Japan. Another woman with a Japanese husband, Lin Li, bought an apartment in Shanghai because, despite her Japanese citizenship, she did not want to die in a foreign country. She and her husband planned to live in China after retirement.

Becoming the new overseas Chinese

Chinese newcomers' transnational outlooks are equally evident in their self-identification. Despite their Japanese citizenship or permanent residency, Chinese who I interviewed or spoke with frequently objected to my using 'immigrants' (*yi min*) to describe them and to my applying the concept of 'immigration' to their migration activities. The preferred identification was that of 'overseas Chinese' (*hua qiao*). In order to distinguish themselves from the Chinese who arrived in Japan before World War Two, they label themselves 'new overseas Chinese' (*xin hua qiao*). Only in Japan are there media publications that include 'New overseas Chinese' in their titles. One popular bi-weekly newspaper called Japan New Overseas Chinese News (*Riben Xinhuaqiao Bao*) started in 1999, and a bi-monthly journal called New Overseas Chinese started in 1997. Along with the term 'new overseas Chinese,' people also employ the expression 'new ethnic Chinese' (*xin hua ren*) to refer to those who have become Japanese citizens. The 'New Overseas Chinese and Ethnic Chinese Association in Japan' (Xin Huaqiao Huaren Hui) was founded on September 21, 2003, after the emergence of several regional 'new overseas Chinese' and ethnic Chinese associations.

Chinese people prefer the label 'new overseas Chinese' to 'Chinese immigrants' for two reasons: (a) because of the strong association of the concept of immigration with the United States; and (b) because of popular perceptions of which countries are immigrant countries and which are not. In the minds of most Chinese, immigration happens in 'immigrant countries' such as the United States, Canada, Australia, and New Zealand. Therefore, one can 'immigrate' to Canada, but one comes to study or work in Japan. This idea persists despite the reality that many Chinese have become Japanese citizens. In addition, the preference for identifying oneself as 'overseas Chinese' rather than as an 'immigrant in Japan' shows how Chinese newcomers perceive Japanese society and their relationship to both countries. Chinese in Japan share an ambivalent attitude toward Japan and an uncertainty toward China. When asked about their impression of Japan, the majority of interviewees used such phrases as 'island country' and 'single race' – typical Japanese cultural nationalist discourses – to describe the country. Many reported frustrating experiences dealing with Japanese at certain junctures in their lives, and attributed these to ingrained 'narrow-mindedness' (*xia ai*) and 'exclusiveness' (*pai wai*) on the part of the Japanese. Mo Bangfu, the prominent Chinese journalist active in Japanese media who coined the term 'new overseas Chinese' in the early 1990s, laments that while many metropolises now publicize a globalized and multicultural image by referring to immigrant residents as 'new Singaporean,' 'new Hong Kong people,' or 'new Shanghaiese,' the 'new Tokyoites' are yet to be born. Tokyo, a global city, still maintains the 'closed door' Japanese legacy (Mo 2007). With these social and cultural assumptions about the nature of Japanese society, Chinese perceive Japan as incapable of opening itself to immigrants, and consequently refuse to regard themselves as immigrants.

However, many Chinese in Japan do not see themselves returning to China either. Although entertaining the concept of returning home, not all dare to take this action. They are encouraged by the developments in China in recent years, but also complain about the chaos and noise in urban China, as well as the lack of efficiency and professionalism when they need services during their homecoming trips. The lack of employment opportunities for some and the relatively low wages provided by local employment for others also deter Chinese migrants in Japan from returning to China on a permanent basis. Hu Mei described such a dilemma:

> Here, life is not going to improve much. I will still have an exhausting lifestyle. Our income will not increase much, while the rent is rising and the child's education is taking up a bigger and bigger share. We cannot afford illness, let alone getting old. Sometimes I feel I have been on the Japan train for too long. I might be missing the speeding China Express. Other times I am afraid if I got off the (Japan) train carelessly, I would not find my destination on a noisy and chaotic (China) platform.
>
> (Hu 1998, p.180)

Among those who are lured home, the illusion of home is sometimes shattered upon return. The aforementioned Zhang Tian took his family back to China when his son was three years old.

> I have never felt discriminated against in Japan. But when I had a rough time at work and was under huge pressures, I felt I was living under other people's roof and the idea would emerge – I have a road to retreat (*tui lu*), going home. This idea became stronger and stronger. ... I waited a couple of years, hoping to be sent back by the company as an expat. That did not work out ... I decided to leave the company and come back. I thought I would come back sooner or later. Why not do it when I was still young?

But when he returned to China and settled down in Shanghai, he began to regret his decision.

> It is totally different between staying at hotels and living in an apartment, or going around in taxis and taking public transportation … When I was in Japan, I visited Shanghai frequently. I thought Shanghai streets looked a lot like Tokyo's. Now I discover that they are totally different. I have only negative feelings now.

Since the entire family possessed permanent resident rights in Japan, moving back to Tokyo was only a matter of logistics. When I interviewed Zhang in 2007, he was making plans to return to Tokyo first by himself, and then to fetch the whole family.

Chinese people's interpretation of their migration behavior and their self-identification as 'new overseas Chinese' has direct impacts on their practices. The term itself implies a strong China-orientation. Although the Chinese-born population in Japan in 2005 was only half of that in the United States in 2000, there were many more Chinese-language publications in Japan than in the United States. Since the onset of large-scale student migration in the mid-1980s, over 120 types of Chinese-language publications have emerged in Japan, ranging from daily newspapers and periodicals to annuals (Duan 2000). Many are short-lived. Walking into any Chinese supermarket in Tokyo, one can collect over a dozen Chinese-language newspapers published by Chinese in Japan.

In recent years, the 'new overseas Chinese' have begun to interact with older, well-established global Chinese networks. In 1999, the Chinese Chamber of Commerce in Japan (CCCJ) was established. Its members include both old and new overseas Chinese businesses in Japan. Since its birth, CCCJ has sent delegates to participate in the World Chinese Entrepreneurs Convention, and in 2007 it took charge of organizing the Ninth World Chinese Entrepreneurs Convention in Kobe. Over three thousand overseas Chinese business people attended this event. Several entrepreneurs I interviewed emphasized their connections with the old overseas Chinese community, and considered these conventions great opportunities to develop global business networks.

CONCLUSION

Since the late-1970s, millions of Chinese have arrived in Japan as students, workers, family members, long-term residents, and undocumented laborers. Hundreds of thousands of them have chosen to settle in Japan. One hundred years ago, the Chinese comprised the largest foreign community in Japan, and the current population is well on the way to repeating that achievement. One characteristic of the Chinese newcomers in Japan is their strong ties with China and the prevalence of transnational practices. They make careers in the transnational businesses between Japan and China, and accommodate transnational lives. Although transnational political, economic, and social processes are manifested among all immigrant communities around the world, the Chinese in Japan are distinct in that their socioeconomic wellbeing hinges upon the transnational economy between the home and host societies.

Such strong transnational tendencies among Chinese in Japan represent, first of all, their responses to the macroeconomic opportunity structure. The rising economic power of China and the increasing interdependence of the Japanese and Chinese economies have brought unprecedented opportunities for the Chinese community in Japan. Ease of communication and travel has further narrowed the geographical distance between these two neighboring countries. By situating themselves in the transnational economy, Chinese gain access to both the corporate labor market and entrepreneurial niches in Japan. A transnational living arrangement also allows them to maximize the utility of their economic resources and enjoy the benefits of both societies.

These transnational practices also represent immigrants' strategies to overcome their marginality in a society they perceive as resistant to immigration and closed to outsiders. Institutionally, at least, Japan is ill-prepared to become an immigrant society. Although an illusion in some respects, America presents itself as a melting pot that turns every newcomer into an American. Japan, on the other hand, often represents itself as a racially homogeneous nation. The Chinese arrive in Japan fully conscious of the clear distinctions made between Japanese and foreigners. In a corporate culture in which permanent employment remains the holy grail, foreign employees are often placed in peripheral and dispensable positions and are hired for their immediate utilities. Occupying positions in transnational business is simply Chinese employees' best chance for career advancement. Meanwhile, though appearing orderly and civil, with many desirable social amenities, Japanese society remains unwelcoming and exclusive in the eyes of many Chinese. Despite Japanese citizenships or permanent residence, Chinese newcomers are fully aware that a 'wall' (*kabe*) stands between themselves and mainstream society.

Identities are derived from the role or position an individual occupies in the social structure (Burke 1980). As a consequence of strengthened economic relations with China, and employment opportunities that draw upon their linguistic and cultural abilities in the marketplace, the Chinese in Japan embrace the identity of 'new overseas Chinese,' a label invented and popularized by the Chinese in Japan. Although the Chinese in Japan are inclined to identify themselves primarily as Chinese, and see themselves as part of the overseas Chinese community, they are becoming an integral part of Japanese society, helping to construct a multicultural and multiethnic Japan.

Notes

1 Here I used Saneto's (1960) account. Some historians estimated the number to be over 10,000.
2 This number includes 560,741 registered foreign residents, 100,000 who had naturalized as Japanese citizens, 34,045 immigrants who had overstayed visas, and an indefinite number who entered the border without visas.
3 From 1984 to 2004, 81,403 Chinese entered as university-degree students and 135,050 as pre-university students – mostly students in Japanese-language programs. The data is compiled from Japan's Ministry of Justice's annual reports on population entry and exit statistics.
4 National Population and Family Planning Commission of China. URL: http://www.chinapop.gov.cn/rkxx/gdkx/t20040326_7719.htm, accessed on May 26, 2008.
5 The status of 'special permanent resident' grants legal status of permanent residence to foreign nationals whose Japanese nationality was taken away as the result of the San Francisco Peace Treaty between the United States and Japan, and also to those who lived in Japan before the end of the war, as well as to the descendants of such foreign nationals (Article Two of the Special Law on the Immigration Control of Inter Alia, Those Who Have Lost Japanese Nationality on the Basis of the Treaty of Peace with Japan).
6 The number of Chinese visa overstayers ranked second after Koreans. However, 80 percent of the arrested clandestine entrants were Chinese (http://www.kaiho.mlit.go.jp/info/ kouhoushi/kouhoushi3.htm). In my own survey, a third of currently undocumented Chinese immigrants came without visas. Combining the clandestine entrants and visa overstayers, Chinese are easily the largest undocumented migrant population in Japan.
7 Among them, only thirty-five Chinese immigrants entered Japan as investors/business managers (Ministry of Justice 2006).
8 'Chinese in Japan Pondering over Permanent Residency and Naturalization,' by Du Hailing, December, 2007, available online at http://www.chubun.com/modules/article/view.article.php/58802/c43, accessed on March 26, 2008.
9 Having a baby in Japan could easily cost an undocumented couple over a million yen. The common practice is to borrow a legal resident's insurance card and pay a fee. The cardholder sometimes registers the child as his or her own at the Chinese Consulate in Japan, and then takes the baby back to China.

References

Alba, Richard and Victor Nee. 1997. 'Rethinking Assimilation Theory for a New Era of Immigration,' *International Migration Review*, 31(4): 826–74.
An, Jianxing. 1998. 'Yecao de zhongzi' The Seeds of Grass, in *Fuji Dongying Xie*

Chunqiu (*Writing History in Japan*), ed. Duan Yaozhong. Shanghai: Shanghai Education Press. 1–8.

Basch, Linda, Nina Glick Schiller, and Cristina Szanton Blanc. 1994. *Nations Unbound: Transnational projects, postcolonial predicaments, and deterritorialized nation-states*. Amsterdam: Gordon and Breach.

Belson, Ken. 2004. 'Japanese Capital and Jobs Flowing to China,' *New York Times*, February 17.

Burke, Peter J. 1980. 'The Self: Measurement requirements from an interactionist perspective,' Social Psychology Quarterly, 43: 18–29.

Cwiertka, Katarzyna. 2007. *Modern Japanese Cuisine: Food, power and national identity*. London: Reaktion Books.

Duan, Yaozhong. 2000. *Zai Ri Zhongguoren Meiti Zonglan* (*An Overview of Chinese Media in Japan*). Kawaguchi, Saitama: Japan Overseas Chinese Press.

Glick Schiller, Nina. 1999. 'Transmigrants and Nation-States: Something old and something new in the U.S. immigrant experience,' in *Handbook of International Migration: The American experience*, eds. C. Hirschman, P. Kasinitz and J. DeWind. New York: Russell Sage. 94–119.

Glick Schiller, Nina and George E. Fouron. 1999. 'Terrains of Blood and Nation: Haitian transnational social fields,' *Ethnic and Racial Studies*, 22(2): 340–66.

Godley, Andrew. 1994. 'Enterprise and Culture: Jewish immigrants in London and New York, 1880–1914,' *The Journal of Economic History*, 54(2): Papers Presented at the Fifty-Third Annual Meeting of the Economic History Association: 430–2.

Goldring, Luin. 1998. 'The Power of Status in Transnational Social Fields.' in *Transnationalism from Below*, vol. 6: *Comparative urban and community research*, eds. Michael Peter Smith and Luis Eduardo Guarnizo. New Brunswick, NJ: Transaction. 165–95.

—— 2002. 'The Mexican State and Transmigrant Organizations: Negotiating the boundaries of membership and participation,' *Latin American Research Review*, 37(3): 55–99.

Gordon, Milton M. 1964. *Assimilation in American Life: the role of race, religion and national origin*. Oxford: Oxford University Press.

Guarnizo, Luis Eduardo. 1998. 'The Rise of Transnational Social Formations: Mexican and Dominican state responses to transnational migration,' *Political Power and Social Theory*, 12: 45–94.

Guarnizo, Luis Eduardo, Alejandro Portes and William Haller. 2003. 'Assimilation and Transnationalism: Determinants of transnational political action among contemporary migrants,' *American Journal of Sociology*, 108(6): 1211–48.

Haller, William and Patricia Landolt. 2005. 'The Transnational Dimensions of Identity Formation: Adult children of immigrants in Miami,' *Ethnic & Racial Studies*, 28(6): 1182–214.

Hu, Mei. 1998. 'Gan mobanche de luren' ('The Traveler Catching the Last Train'), in *Fuji Dongying Xie Chunqiu* (*Writing History in Japan*), ed. Duan Yaozhong. Shanghai: Shanghai Education Press. 175–81.

Japan Immigration Association. 2004–2006. *Statistics on the Foreigners Registered in Japan*. Tokyo: Japan Immigration Association.

Japan Ministry of Justice. 2005. *Immigration Control*. Available online at http://www.moj.go.jp/NYUKAN/nyukan46-1.pdf, accessed on July 7, 2006.

—— 'About the Employment of Foreign Students Who Entered Japanese Companies in 2005,' available online at http://www.moj.jp/, accessed on July 7, 2006.

Jiang, Yichao. 1998. 'Tansuo rensheng,' in *Fuji Dongying Xie Chunqiu* (*Writing History in Japan*), ed. Duan Yaozhong. Shanghai: Shanghai Education Press. 312–18.

Kamachi, N. 1980. 'The Chinese in Meiji Japan,' in *The Chinese and the Japanese: Essays in political and cultural interactions*, ed. A Iriye. Princeton: Princeton University Press.

Kearney, Michael. 1991. 'Borders and Boundaries of State and Self at the End of Empire,' *Journal of Historical Sociology*, 4: 52–73.

—— 1995 'The Local and the Global: The anthropology of globalization and transnationalism,' *Annual Review of Anthropology*, 24(2): 547–65.

Kyle, David. 2000. *Transnational Peasants: Migrations, networks, and ethnicity in Andean Ecuador*. Baltimore: Johns Hopkins University Press.

Laguerre, Michael S. 1999 'State, Diaspora and Transnational Politics: Haiti reconceptualized.' *Millennium: Journal of International Studies*, 28(3): 633–651.

Liu, Cheng. 1998. 'Mai xiang 21 shiji, wancheng xin shiming' ('Forward into the 21st Century, accomplishing new missions'). In Fuji Dongying Xie Chunqiu (Writing History in Japan), ed. Duan Yaozhong. Shanghai: Shanghai Education Press, 629–33

Liu-Farrer, Gracia. 2004. 'The Chinese Social Dance Party in Tokyo: Identity and status in an immigrant leisure subculture,' *Journal of Contemporary Ethnography*, 33(6): 651–74.

—— 2006. 'Chinese Catholic Center in Tokyo: Institutional characteristics in contexts,' in *Religious Pluralism in Diaspora*, ed. Pratap Kumar. Amsterdam: Brill. 13–31.

—— 2007. 'Producing Global Economies from Below: Chinese immigrant transnational entrepreneurship in Japan,' in *Deciphering the Global: Its spaces, scales, and subjects*, ed. Saskia Sassen. New York: Routledge. 177–98.

Mo, Bangfu. 2007. ''Shin Tokyojin'' itu Tanjo? (When will the 'New Tokyoites' be born?) *Asahi Shinbun*, February 2, 2008: B3.

Nishinarita, Yutaka. 2002. *Chūgokujin Kyōseirenko* (*Chinese Labor Conscription*). Tokyo: University of Tokyo Press.

Ohmi, Naoto. 2006. 'Problems of Foreign Worker Policy in Japan – From the Trade Union Viewpoint,' available online at http://www.jil.go.jp/english/documents/JLR08_oumi.pdf, accessed on December 12, 2006. 110–11.

Pacific Asia Resource Center. 2004. *A Complete Anatomy of 100-Yen Shop: Globalization in daily life* (*Tettei Kaibo 100-yen Shoppu: Nichijouka suru Guroubarizeishon*). Tokyo: Commons.

Portes, Alejandro. 1996. 'Transnational Communities: Their emergence and significance in the contemporary world system,' in *Latin America in the World Economy*, eds. Roberto Patricio Korzeniewics and William C. Smith. Westport, CT: Greenwood Press. 151–68.

—— 1999. 'Conclusion: Towards a New World – The Origins and Effects of Transnational Activities,' *Ethnic and Racial Studies*, 22(2): 463–75.

Portes, A, Louise E. Guarnizo, and William J. Haller. 2002. 'Transnational Entrepreneurs: An alternative form of immigrant adaptation,' *American Sociological Review*, 67: 278–98.

Saneto, Keishu. 1960. *Chūgokujin Nihon Ryūgakushi* (*A History of Chinese Studying in Japan*). Tokyo: Kuroshio Shuppan.

Sasatani Hiroyuki. 2007. 'Kanan de no Nihonjin Genchisaiyou no Tokushou' ('The Characteristics of Local Employments of Japanese Nationals in Southern China'), Whenever Shanghai, July 2007: 124.

Shao, Chunfen. 1995. 'Ryugaku Senryaku no Kettei Yoyin – Zainichi Chugokujin Ryugakusei, Shugakusei no Baai' ('Determining Factors of Studying Abroad – Situations among the Chinese University Students and Language Students in Japan'), Tokyo Toritsu Daigaku Shakaigaku Kenkyukai 'Shakaigaku Ronko' (Tokyo Metropolitan University, Sociological Research Society 'Sociological Inquiries'), No. 16: 86–105.

Shen Diancheng. 1997. *Zhongguoren Liuxue Riben Bainian Shi* (*A History of a Hundred Years of Chinese Studying in Japan*). Liaoning: Liaoning Educational Press.

Tajima, Junko. 2003. 'Chinese Newcomers in the Global City of Tokyo: Social Networks and Settlement Tendencies,' *International Journal of Japanese Sociology*, 12: 68–78.

—— 2005. 'Daitoshi ni Okeru Chūgokukei Ijyūsha Chōsa' ('A Survey of Chinese Migrants in the Metropolis'), in *Chugokukei Ijyusha kara Mita Nihonshakai no Shomondai* (*Japanese Social Problems in the Eyes of Chinese Migrants*), ed. Tajima Junko. Tokyo: Research Foundation for Safe Society. 7–37.

Uchida, N. 1949. *Nihon Kakyō Shakai no Kenkyū* (*Research on Overseas Chinese in Japan*). Tokyo: Dobunkan.

Vasishth, Andrea. 1997. 'A Model Minority: the Chinese community in Japan,' in *Japan's Minorities: The illusion of homogeneity*, ed. Michael Weiner. London: Routledge. 108–39.

Wakabayashi, Keiko. 1990. '"Blind Movement" of Chinese Population: Background for the recent influx of Chinese working students and disguised refugees into Japan,' *Jinkou Mondai Kenkyuu* (*Research on Population Problems*), 46(1): 35–50.

Wang Xiaoqiu. 2006. 'Zhongguoren liuxue riben 110 nian lishi de huigu yu qishi' ('Retrospect and Revelation of the 110-Year History of Chinese Returned Students in Japan'), *Journal of Xuzhou Normal University* (Philosophy and Social Sciences Edition), 2006(4).

Warner, W. Lloyd and Leo Srole. 1945. *The Social Systems of American Ethnic Groups*. New Haven: Yale University Press.

7 Multiethnic Japan and Nihonjin

Looking through two exhibitions in 2004 Osaka

Eika Tai

INTRODUCTION: MULTIETHNIC JAPAN AND SOCIAL ACTIVISM

The recent increase of foreign residents in Japan (up to two million or 1.57 percent of the total population in 2005), which began in the late 1980s in response to labour shortages, has diversified the ethnic composition of the country, and has stimulated the spread of multiculturalism in a society that has been dominated by the ideology of ethnic homogeneity. In the mid-1990s, grassroots activists and school teachers started to empower newcomer foreigners, adopting the idea of multiculturalism introduced from Canada, the United States, and Australia. In the process of the dispersion of the idea, it was combined with '*kyōsei*' (living together), which had been used as a guiding principle in the civil rights movements for people with disabilities and for women, and which was formulated as '*tabunka kyōsei*' (multicultural co-living). By the beginning of the twenty-first century, this idiom has spread among various kinds of people, ranging from activists and educators to local administrators and business leaders, and even to officials in the central government. As I discuss below, different people employ the idiom with different meanings.

The dispersion of the idiom of *tabunka kyōsei* has not brought about the decline of the ideology of monoethnicity, which has been espoused by political leaders in post-war Japan. Even in the 2000s, many influential politicians, including Asō Tarō, Suzuki Muneo, and Omi Kōji, have articulated the ideology in their public statements. It is also still widely shared among common Japanese. Xenophobic reactions to the increase of foreigners as frequently reported by the media indicate that many Japanese believe, in line with the ideology of monoethnicity, that there should be only Nihonjin (Japanese) in Japan. At the intersection of the discourses of monoethnicity and multiethnicity, this category is being defended, modified, and reconstructed.

In this article, I want to examine social activism for resident foreigners and ethnic minorities, focusing on two 2004 exhibitions held at two major museums in Osaka, a place known for its high social concern about the marginalized. I aim to shed light on the political and educational intentions of the curators, mostly activists and progressive researchers, delving into the specific messages they tried to convey to the public about the multiethnicity of Japanese society. I am particularly interested in examining how they tackled the category of 'Nihonjin', which I believe stands at the heart of the question of what it means to speak of a multiethnic Japan. As we will see, the curators posed a serious challenge to the conventional understanding of the category.

The exhibition 'Taminzoku Nihon: Zainichi Gaikokujin no Kurashi' (Multiethnic Japan: The Life of Resident Foreigners),[1] held at the National Museum of Ethnology (hereafter Minpaku[2]) from March 25 through June 15, presented the cultural lives of foreigners in Japan. It demonstrated ambiguity in classifying gaikokujin (foreigners) and Nihonjin. It did not deal with the question of how Japanese and foreign nationals differ in citizenship rights. This is the central theme at the exhibition held at Osaka Human Rights Museum (hereafter Liberty Osaka, its official nickname) from April 13 through June 13. Situating the theme in the historical context of the multiethnic Japanese empire, 'Tsukurareru Nihon Kokumin: Kokuseki, Sensō, Sabetsu' (The Japanese Nation as Constructed: Nationality, War, Discrimination) illuminated how entitlement to nationality and citizenship rights shifted according to changing political circumstances.

According to the curators, it was by coincidence that the two exhibitions were held almost simultaneously. However, the timing of the exhibitions was far from accidental. The nationalistic social climate at the beginning of the 2000s pushed those concerned about ethnic minorities and foreigners to take action. This social climate was marked by the National Anthem and Flag Law of 1999, the government's approval of revisionist history textbooks, moves to legalize the use of military force, and politicians' visits to Yasukuni Shrine, laden with the glory of imperialism. The media's reports on the 2002 confirmation of North Korea's abduction of Japanese nationals played a significant role in spreading nationalistic sentiments to common people. The population decrease reinforced such protectionist sentiments. Against this backdrop, Koizumi Jun'ichirō's neo-liberal reform took place, making many Japanese suffer from the restructuring of the labour market and the reduction of social welfare, and turning them into xenophobic nationalists. They were susceptible to xenophobic propaganda made by right-wing politicians such as Tokyo Governor Ishihara Shintarō. Government officials proposed 'reforms' to the Education Law[3] and tried to reconstruct Nihonjin as patriotic subjects loyal to the state, while ignoring the history of the multiethnic Japanese empire, through which this category was established. The penalization of non-compliance with the administration's order to respect the national flag and anthem inhibited teachers from educating their students about that history, even when they resisted the adoption of revisionist textbooks. The two exhibitions informed, and were informed by, this social climate. The effect of the multicultural co-living movement was limited, and the expression of cultural difference was suppressed. Old-comer Koreans had a renewed sense of deprivation of freedom to express their Korean-ness.[4] Following the path of old-comers, newcomer children hid their ethnicities in public schools. The curators sought to change such a social atmosphere.

I choose to discuss the two exhibitions as sites for examining social activism precisely because museums as educational institutions play an important role in social activism in Japan. As Tony Bennett (1995, 2004) discusses, museums have been deployed as instruments of education, often for social control, since the end of the nineteenth century. Following this line of argument, other authors look into the political nature of contemporary museums. Timothy W. Luke (2002: xiii), for example, sees the museum as the contested ground of politics, arguing that museums 'possess a power to shape collective values and social understanding in a decisively important fashion'. In the United States, museums came to integrate the idea of multicultural education in the 1980s (American Association of Museums 1984), and became important sites for the politics of cultural identity, or, in the words of Steven C. Dubin (1999: 4), 'hotly contested battlegrounds' for cultural war. As racial and social inequalities played out in established museums have come under critical scrutiny (Mesa-Bains 2004), multiculturalism has become a key concept in museum displays.

In Japan, museums have also been playing educational and political functions. Museums and exhibitions were first created as the country began nation building and colonial expansion. As Yoshida Kenji (1999: 74–96) discusses, the oldest museum in Japan, Tokyo National Museum, was designed to propagate the idea of the supremacy of the Japanese national culture. Yoshimi Shunya (1992) has unveiled how exhibitions on Japan's colonies were held to demonstrate the legitimacy of the empire's civilizing mission. In post-war Japan, museums were created to dispatch antiwar messages, as exemplified in Hiroshima Peace Memorial Museum and Nagasaki Atomic Bomb Museum. In the 1980s, museums became important strategic sites for social activism. A peace movement brought about an increase in the number of antiwar exhibitions and peace museums, and the liberation movement of burakumin (former outcastes) contributed to the creation of Liberty Osaka and the rise of human rights museums. Initially focusing on burakumin issues, human rights museums soon came to include other kinds of marginalized groups, such as Koreans and people with disabilities.

Today, human rights and peace museums, numbering a couple of hundred among Japan's five thousand museums, play a significant role in social activism and liberal school education (Asaji 1999; Kojima 2005). However, multiculturalism has yet to gain importance in Japanese museums, except in museums for the Ainu. Human rights museums provide opportunities for minority groups to express their voices, but largely in relation to social discrimination. The Multiethnic Japan Exhibition was the first major exhibition that focused on the idea of multiculturalism and displayed the cultures of various ethnic groups.

I see the two exhibitions as suitable sites for examining the treatment of the 'Nihonjin' category in social activism, because I think that, as Paula Young Lee (1997: 11) says, 'museums offer spaces where ideas about classification can be made visible, debatable, revisable, projectible'. Just like other modern institutions such as courts and schools, museums perform 'the functions of collection, classification, and categorization', but they differ from the others in that 'their primary purpose is to *represent* this very process'. The two exhibitions showed how ethnic and national classification was created, modified, and undermined. Without close attention to such a process, social activism for ethnic minorities can be co-opted by the very force it challenges, i.e., the ideology of monoethnicity and nationalism. When left unexamined, the category of 'Nihonjin' may be reinvigorated and reinvested with privilege, as conservatives want it to be in their assertion of multicultural co-living.

Much of the following discussion is based on my fieldwork in Osaka between 2001 and 2006. I have made a dozen trips to this prefecture and studied the multiculturalism movement. I visited the two exhibitions and attended a few preparatory meetings for the Multiethnic Japan Exhibition. I had numerous in-depth interviews with several key curators.

GAIKOKUJIN AND NIHONJIN IN THE MAKING OF THE MULTIETHNIC JAPAN EXHIBITION

The Multiethnic Japan Exhibition marked a new page in the history of Minpaku, which had never held an exhibition on foreigners. This national research institution, specializing in ethnic cultures, recognized the existence of foreigners in Japan as bearers of ethnic cultures worth being displayed to the public. Closely associated from its inception in the 1970s with the national policy of internationalization, Minpaku displayed ethnic cultures found in other countries along with additional exhibits on Ainu and Okinawa cultures and Japanese regional cultures. It paid little attention to '*uchi naru kokusaika*' (internal internationalization), the idea raised in the mid-1980s to criticize political and intellectual leaders for upholding internationalization without due attention to foreigners within Japan (Hatsuse 1985). At the beginning of the 2000s, most Minpaku faculty were still hesitant to see Japan as multiethnic. Concerned about the political nature of the multiethnic view, which challenged the dominant ideology of monoethnicity, they were not supportive of the curators of the exhibition, who were mostly recruited from outside Minpaku. The exhibition came into being as a result of the curators' efforts.

The curators of the exhibition, who made up the project team, were grass-roots activists and concerned researchers, and many of them were resident foreigners themselves.[5] The team was led by Shōji Hiroshi, a Minpaku professor specializing in Finno-Ugric languages, whom Nelson Graburn (2007) rightly calls a 'social scientist in action'. To avoid conflict with his colleagues, Shōji chose for the exhibition's official goal a politically innocuous one: to spread the value of tolerance for cultural diversity necessary for creating a society of co-living. Yet the curators were politically motivated. To begin with, they chose to focus on foreigners from Asia and South America, who are discriminated against, rather than those from Europe and the United States, who are given a privileged status in Japan.[6] The team selected as the subjects of the exhibition not only 'newcomer' foreigners, whose arrivals triggered the rise of multiculturalism, but also 'old-comer' foreigners, formerly colonized people from Korea and Taiwan and their offspring, whose presence is a reminder of Japanese imperialism. Endorsing the liberal view that minority populations should be given 'a chance to exert control over the way they are presented in museums' (Lavine and Karp 1991: 6), the team encouraged foreigners, especially those they selected as representative foreigners – Chinese, Filipinos, Brazilians, Vietnamese, and Koreans – to participate in the making of the exhibition. Through lending personal belongings, making suggestions, and putting on cultural performances, local ethnic communities turned the exhibition into a site for playing out *their* politics of recognition. The exhibition was considered a success, not simply because it attracted over 37,000 visitors and received positive feedback from those visitors and the media, but more importantly because it served the needs of Asian foreigners to demonstrate their cultural existence in a society still dominated by the ideology of monoethnicity.

The exhibition was held in a two-storey, well-hole-style building. The team arranged the first floor according to themes. They used much of the wall for a historical account of modern Japan, illuminating the fact that Japan was once a multiethnic empire. Along with culture-oriented sections such as 'Ethnic Festivals Square', 'Ethnic Shopping Street', and 'Ethnic Media', they created sections on social discrimination, immigration procedures, and NGO activities. 'Panda Classroom' was set up to expose schoolchildren to toys, games, foods, and clothes of several countries. The team divided the donut-shaped second floor into five sections for the representative groups, displaying various kinds of personal belongings such as family photos, clothes, musical instruments, legal documents, kitchen utensils, and furniture.

Shōji first conceived the idea of the exhibition in 2000, when he began a research project on multilingual phenomena in Japan.[7] Witnessing the multicultural nature of society, he thought it important to make the public aware of this reality and of the existence of foreigners generating it. He saw them as bearers of ethnic cultures, going against the media-led social tendency to categorize them into one group, gaikokujin, and treat them as labourers, potential criminals, or targets of xenophobia. The classification of gaikokujin helped to sustain the boundaries of Nihonjin. Shōji was critical of the dichotomy and essentialism underlying it. While primarily seeking to demonstrate the cultural presence of foreigners, he hoped to contribute to debunking the dichotomy. Thus the exhibition was not only about foreigners' ethnicities, but also about the categories of gaikokujin and Nihonjin.

In designing the exhibition, the project team seriously discussed whether to include the Ainu and Okinawans, who are both Japanese nationals. Their inclusion would be politically charged because it would indicate the definition of the Japanese nation as multiethnic, the definition conservatives could hardly accept. While the Ainu were acknowledged as an ethnic group by the 1997 law, and this recognition has been widely shared among not just activists but also non-activist Ainu, the status of Okinawans as an ethnic group has been kept ambiguous in public discourse, despite efforts made by activists to establish it (see Siddle 2003). To avoid confronting this political controversy, the team decided to stick to Shōji's original idea of focusing on foreigners.[8]

By eliminating the Ainu and Okinawans, the project team seemed to have excluded Japanese from 'multiethnic Japan'. One may argue that the myth of homogeneous Japanese nationals was unchallenged in the exhibition, where 'multiethnic Japan' meant the presence of multiethnic foreigners. Yet at the exhibit hall, Japanese-ness appeared, albeit implicitly, in many displays that were supposed to represent the lives of gaikokujin. How did that happen? In participating in the making of displays, ethnic communities chose to emphasize their cultural distinctiveness from mainstream Japanese. However, they could not eliminate Japanese elements from their self-representations. Brazilians of Japanese descent insisted on presenting themselves as Brazilian rather than as Japanese, but the history section indicated the Japanese origin of most Brazilians in Japan. The section on old-comer Chinese was full of Chinese cultural materials, but it had a note stating that third-generation Chinese were culturally almost the same as Nihonjin. In the Korean section, a wall full of photos of celebrities in sports and entertainments revealed that they were of Korean descent but were projected as Nihonjin in the media. There were displays on school lives of children with foreign roots, most of whom were partly of Japanese descent. Thus, many displays suggested ambiguity in distinguishing Nihonjin and gaikokujin. This reflected the reality of the hybridized lived experiences of gaikokujin, which the project team wanted to demonstrate.

Those people were all labelled as gaikokujin in the exhibition. This labelling was accepted by participating ethnic community members, and was endorsed by the project team. Here we need to look at how gaikokujin was defined. Shōji's definition, which he made from public discourse on gaikokujin, was displayed at the entrance of the exhibition:

> The term '*gaikokujin*' in the Exhibition refers to people who have roots (*rūtsu*) in foreign countries, and does not exclusively refer to foreign nationals in a legal sense or 'those without Japanese nationality'. It is applied to those who have naturalized to Japanese nationality, those whose parents are *gaikokujin*, and those who have lived in foreign countries as immigrants. It is also used to refer to those who have strong attachments to foreign countries and cultures.[9]

As he elaborates on the definition in the exhibition catalogue, Shōji (2004: 6) summarizes the meaning of gaikokujin as 'so-called those who tend to be excluded from the category of "Nihonjin"'.

Shōji was surely aware that in public discourse the word gaikokujin symbolized otherness and exclusion. Yet he was not interested in condemning the act of calling people gaikokujin. Rather, by exhibiting the rich cultural lives of those called gaikokujin, he intended to change the hitherto derogatory meaning of the word to a neutral or positive one. As he told me, his aim was to promote the acceptance of those people called gaikokujin as culturally different local residents. What he wanted visitors to think about was not the question of who should or should not be called gaikokujin, but the question of how to create a society of co-living that would respect people designated as gaikokujin for whatever reason. In his approach to gaikokujin, Shōji is in line with progressives in the multiculturalism movement, opposing the conservative position that seeks the integration (*tekiō*) of foreigners into Japanese society with only a minimum recognition of cultural diversity. The progressive position goes squarely against cultural assimilation.

However, in praising the difference of gaikokujin from Nihonjin and in broadening the boundaries of gaikokujin, the progressive position may inadvertently contribute to deepening the divide between the two categories and fortifying the category of Nihonjin as 'pure Japanese', i.e. Japanese without any foreign element. One can argue that when practised based on the dichotomous view, tolerance, as set up as the goal of the exhibition, 'effectively further marginalizes minority cultures by locating them as something to be tolerated' (Lee 2003: 109). As Laura Maritano (2002: 64) notes in her study on multiculturalism in Italy, the term 'foreigners' is crucial 'in order to identify common national elements and to distinguish themselves from "the rest" '. As for Japan, Iwabuchi Kōichi (2004: 324) delineates how the representation of gaikokujin in the media or in immigration policy is used to reconstruct 'Nihonjin'. He points out the image of gaikokujin has become based on Asians and Africans, instead of Whites, as it used to be in the 1980s (2004: 327).[10] Shōji's approach to gaikokujin could contribute to strengthening the boundaries of 'pure Japanese' in an exhibit hall full of Asian foreigners. It might help buttress, not debunk, the ideology of monoethnicity.

There is thus an inherent paradox in playing out the politics of difference. Foreigners want to express their cultural distinctiveness and challenge the ideology of monoethnicity. Yet in doing so, they risk being marginalized. In stressing the cultural difference of foreigners, often in essentialist terms, many Japanese multiculturalists end up contributing to the marginalization of foreigners, and they re-establish Japanese identity, albeit unconsciously. Shōji and other curators tried to avoid this pitfall by paying particular attention to the problem of essentialism and by taking advantage of the effect of museum displays to make ideas about classification visible. The project team tried to demonstrate that 'Japanese nationals' included those discursively categorized as gaikokujin, and encouraged foreigners to reveal ambiguity in their self-representations.

What should not be forgotten in demonstrating ambiguity in classification is that the marginalization of gaikokujin takes place not merely in discursively constructed cultural identifications but also in legal rights. In Japan, as in other countries, nationality matters, as it monopolizes full citizenship rights. This is the central theme at the Japanese Nation Exhibition, which situated it in the history of Japanese imperialism. For now, let us stay at the Multiethnic Japan Exhibition, which prioritized cultural rights over civil rights,[11] and turn to the exhibit on Chūgoku kikokusha (returnees from China). The curator actively tackled the theme of ambiguity.

THE POLITICS OF AMBIGUITY: RETURNEES FROM CHINA

The lives of returnees from China were displayed in the Chinese section along with the exhibits on old-comer and newcomer Chinese. Let us look at the definition of 'Chūgoku kikokusha' posted at the exhibit hall:

'*Chūgoku Kikokusha*' refers to *Chūgoku zanryū Nihonjin* and their families, who have returned to Japan as a result of the opening of Japan's diplomatic relations with the People's Republic of China in 1972 or the start of a systematic investigation in 1981. '*Chūgoku zanryū Nihonjin*' refers to those Japanese who moved to Northeast China before or during the war, became integrated into Chinese families in that region in the chaotic aftermath of Japan's defeat, and were made to remain in China because of the Japanese government's discontinuation of its repatriation effort in 1958.[12]

The historical background of Japanese in Northeast China was found in the history section of the exhibition. Under the headline 'Japan, Multiethnic Empire', there were brief notes on the 1931 Manchurian Incident, the 1932 creation of Manchukuo in Northeast China, and the immigration of a total of 320,000 Nihonjin to Manchuria before 1945. The exhibition catalogue states that the number of people designated as Chūgoku kikokusha is about 100,000.

The cultural lives and identifications of the returnees are complex. Minami Makoto, a returnee who took charge of the exhibit on the returnees, wanted to demonstrate this complexity.[13] To begin with, social institutions, most importantly the Japanese government, the media, and support groups, have produced various category names, drawing group boundaries accordingly. Two frequently used names, *Chūgoku zanryū fujin* (women remaining in China) and *Chūgoku zanryū koji* (orphans remaining in China), which refer to the two major groups of 30,000 Japanese left behind in China, make subdivisions among the returnees. Minami considers 'Chūgoku kikokusha' acceptable because this label is inclusive. The social institutions have also created various discourses about the returnees, which have been spread to the public by the media. The discourse of '*sensō no higaisha*' (war victims) has become hegemonic. In it, the returnees are seen as Nihonjin, i.e. as the same as those Japanese war victims who stayed in Japan proper or repatriated soon after the end of the war. Yet, they are perceived as Chūgokujin (Chinese) by those who contact them in everyday life because of their Chinese cultural life styles. This points to the fact that Japanese returnees lived in China for several decades and came back with their spouses who were mostly Chinese, and their children and grandchildren, many of whom were born in China.

Self-identifications are just as complex as others' identifications. Minami observed that the returnees identify themselves in various ways: as Nihonjin, as Chūgokujin, as both, or as neither. They also situationally changed their identity positions. Importantly, they were asserting their being Nihonjin in the political movement they initiated in 2001. This self-organized movement evolved around the fifteen class lawsuits filed by 2,100 first-generation returnees against the Japanese state. It involved the majority of the returnees and created a tight network and a strong sense of community across generations. The plaintiffs demanded compensations from the state, accusing it of neglecting its duty to bring them, Japanese nationals, back to Japan much earlier and to take care of them after their arrival in Japan. Instead of continuing its repatriation effort, the government issued death declaration notices for 13,600 Japanese left behind in China, treating them as dead without much investigation. It did not provide enough material assistance or language training for the returnees, causing more than 60 percent of elderly returnees to be on welfare.[14] Minami argued that the government was trying to integrate the returnees back into the Japanese nation, but only as 'others', on the margins. Thus the returnees used the term 'Nihonjin' to gain access to civil rights, and the government used the term to turn them into second-class nationals.

When Minami was invited to join the project team in 2003, Chūgoku kikokusha had already been included in the Chinese section. He was bewildered (*tomadotta*) by this classification because of their public assertion in their legal battles that they were Nihonjin. Yet he accepted the invitation, hoping that the exhibition would be a good opportunity to play out the politics of recognition for the returnees, who were made invisible in society after the initial media fervour in the 1980s. While fully supporting their legal battles, Minami decided to focus on their cultural lives and to represent their complex identifications to museum visitors as *aimai* (ambiguous). To reflect the inclusion of those with 'ambiguous' ethnic backgrounds, the title of the Chinese section was changed from 'Zainichi Chūgokujin' (Resident Chinese in Japan) to 'Zainichi Chūgoku-kei' (Residents in Japan of Chinese Heritage). The suffix *kei* usually refers to 'of descent' when attached to an ethnic group, as in the case of the widely used word *nikkei* (of Japanese descent), but 'Chūgoku-kei' here means both cultural and genealogical heritage.

Minami's strategy in making the exhibit was to juxtapose Japanese and Chinese aspects of returnees' lives. In an introductory note, he described the returnees as both Chūgoku-kei and *nikkei*. With photos, he contrasted their current lives in Japan and their previous lives in China. In the education corner, he showed elderly returnees learning Japanese and younger generations studying Chinese to communicate with their parents and grandparents. In the food corner, he demonstrated how different generations of returnees had different mixtures of Japanese and Chinese foods. He placed a pair of Chinese and Japanese passports with a caption stating that many returnees had two nationalities. He juxtaposed a returnee's college diploma from China and his license for practising law in Japan. Minami included a display on the returnees' political movement, showing relevant documents, such as a death declaration notice, and newspapers with front-page headlines on their lawsuits. To demonstrate returnees' connections with Japanese society, he included a graphic list of non-governmental organizations working with them.

In this way, Minami tried to show ambiguity in the lives of the returnees. He also focused on the concept of ambiguity in his essay in the exhibition catalogue (Minami 2004). By using this concept, he aimed to problematize the tendency among people in Japan (and in China) to take conventional national classification for granted and to avoid looking at anything 'anomalous'. Referring to Fukuoka Yasunori's (2000: xxix–xxx) typology of 'Japanese' and 'non-Japanese' based on nationality, lineage, and culture, Minami argues that returnees from China are diverse with respect to each of these three elements. They have various kinds of cultural and genealogical backgrounds. They can receive Japanese nationality relatively easily, but many of them, especially second and third generations, prefer to maintain Chinese nationality and obtain permanent residency. Indeed, they cannot be classified according to Fukuoka's typology,[15] let alone according to the conventional classification system that simply categorizes people into national groups. Their identifications and lives point to the impossibility of drawing neat boundaries between Nihonjin and gaikokujin. Minami believed people should learn to accept such impossibility, i.e. ambiguity, as inherent in national classification, if they wanted to create a society of co-living. He sought to teach visitors about tolerance for such ambiguity.

Most importantly, by using the term *aimaisa*, Minami wanted to point to the richness (*yutakasa*) of the returnees' lived experiences. He sought to illuminate the richness hidden behind the hegemonic discourse that represented the returnees merely as war victims. In tackling this problem theoretically, he used the concept of 'transposition' as offered by Ōta Yoshinobu (1998: 246), i.e. 'linking of enunciation positions'. The government, the media, and support groups articulated their views on the returnees, generating their enunciation positions. Constrained by those enunciation positions and the hegemonic discourse based on them, the returnees themselves tried to articulate their own positions. By linking and relating various enunciation positions (transposition), Minami sought to reveal the constructed nature of the public image of the returnees on the one hand and to reveal the richness of their border culture on the other. He wanted to show this dynamic at the exhibit.

Not all returnees from China supported Minami's effort. While collecting data, he confronted a returnee who refused to talk to him as soon as she noticed the word 'gaikokujin' in the exhibition title. She asserted: 'I am not a foreigner'. Another returnee tried to downplay the fact that she once held Chinese nationality. Minami respected their personal views, but he suspected that they were pressured by society to suppress their Chinese cultural heritage. Similarly, in her study of Japanese repatriates and returnees from China, Tamanoi Mariko (2006: 233) observes pressure on returnees to identify as Japanese. She correctly points out that they 'have a right not to be constrained within an exclusionary Japanese cultural identity'. Referring to Sharon Stephens's (1995: 4) discussion of children growing up in a multi-cultural setting and the 'cultural battles' fought upon their bodies and minds, Tamanoi criticizes cultural battles imposed upon returnees from China by various parties such as the media and the government. She points out that 'there is a serious danger that they will be consumed in these cultural battles, their voices left unheard' (Tamanoi 2006: 233).[16] Minami wanted to make their voices heard, and to encourage them to fight their own cultural battles, which would inevitably challenge conventional national classification.

Minami could have dealt with the role of war and colonization in creating ambiguous national boundaries. He did not, following the direction of the Multiethnic Japan Exhibition. Intended to contribute to creating a society of multiethnic co-living in the future, this exhibition provided the history of the Japanese empire only in a compartmentalized fashion, separately from culture-centred displays. It is the Japanese Nation Exhibition that illuminated the role of that history in national classification. Let us now turn to this exhibition, where we will see that many of those treated as gaikokujin at the Multiethnic Japan Exhibition were once Japanese nationals.

DECONSTRUCTING NATIONAL CLASSIFICATION AT THE JAPANESE NATION EXHIBITION

Liberty Osaka is the oldest and most established human rights museum in Japan. It was created in 1985 through the liberation movement of burakumin as a reference centre for preserving historical documents on the movement.[17] At its 1995 renewal, it included thematic displays on gender, disability, and ethnicity, turning into a comprehensive museum. The Japanese Nation Exhibition took place as the curators prepared for the 2005 renewal.[18]

As they began to discuss the second renewal in 2000, the curators suspected most visitors to the current exhibits merely felt sympathy for the marginalized without relating themselves to discrimination. The curators wanted to solve this problem. By 2003, when they submitted a blueprint for the renewal, they had conceived the idea of creating a corner in which visitors would examine their own values over a dozen themes, such as education, occupation, and gender. The objective of the corner was to learn a relativistic point of view, i.e. to learn that a person would discriminate against other people in respect to some themes, but would be discriminated against in respect to others. To implement this new approach effectively, the curators decided to hold experimental exhibitions on some of the themes before the renewal. The Japanese Nation Exhibition was one such exhibition, focusing on the theme of *kokuseki* (nationality, formal membership in a state). Its official objective was to examine the notion of the Japanese nation in relation to nationality, war, and discrimination.

Moon Kong Hwi, an old-comer Korean curator active in the civil rights movement for foreigners, was selected to take responsibility for the exhibition.[19] Given the current move to reconstruct 'Nihonjin' in ultra-nationalistic terms, he thought it important to look into the process of national classification in the past. To situate the issue of nationality in a relativistic framework as dictated by the renewal plan, he drew from the literature on nation building, colonialism, and total war. At research meetings for the renewal, he met prominent scholars on these topics, learning from Komori Yōichi how elite Japanese colonized the masses in Japan; from Makihara Norio how masses became national subjects; and from Narita Ryūichi how total war solidified the nationalizing project.[20] Moon decided to show how Japanese and non-Japanese were both subject to political forces and how access to nationality and citizenship rights shifted according to changing political situations. With this exhibit design, he aimed to make Japanese visitors understand the plight of foreigners as their own problem.

Moon created five sections in the exhibit hall, a rectangular room. He set up the first section, 'Are Japanese Nationals Happy?', as a place for visitors to think about what it meant to be Japanese. The next four sections covered Japanese history from the 1870s to the 1980s. In the second section, 'The Birth of the Japanese Nation', Moon showed how the concepts of nation and civilization were co-constituted, by exhibiting books written by the leading Meiji scholar, Fukuzawa Yukichi. To demonstrate how the processes of nation-building and imperialist invasion took place simultaneously, Moon juxtaposed two sets of coloured woodblock prints: one set was on the 1889 creation of the Meiji Constitution and rebellions against the new government, and the other was on uprisings in Korea caused by Japanese capitalism and Japanese military victories in Taiwan. He placed the coloured prints of the Meiji emperor's glorious parades to suggest that the masses were turned into national subjects under his sovereign power.

Moon demonstrated how Japan boasted of its colonial power in the section 'Colonies and the Japanese Nation'. One poster was for the 1912 Colonization Exhibition held in Tokyo, which listed the names of Japanese colonies under the headline 'Beautiful Japan'. Moon displayed travel guides for Okinawa, Taiwan, and Korea with postcards that featured women from those colonies. By presenting books by the pioneer in Japanese anthropology, Tsuboi Shōgorō, Moon indicated how the colonized were constructed as uncivilized. To reveal the empire's contradictory treatment of Koreans, he juxtaposed documents on the household registry system, which defined them as the colonized, with a book on the theory of their common ethnic origin with Japanese. He included flyers that depicted how leaders, in the interests of the state, encouraged people in Japan proper to emigrate to Brazil and Manchuria. He documented how the Ainu in Hokkaidō and aborigines in Taiwan were controlled in similar ways, questioning the distinction between Japan proper and the colonies.

In the section 'War and the Japanese Nation', Moon described the mobilization of Japanese nationals both in Japan proper and in the Japanese colonies, whose differentiated integration into the empire was documented in the previous sections. He displayed posters and booklets about the construction of a Greater East Asia Co-Prosperity Sphere, the ethnic hierarchy in this sphere, the conscription of Koreans and Taiwanese, and the invasion into the South Pacific. He placed many booklets on the topics of '*kokumin no kakugo*' (nationals' preparedness for war) and '*shinmin no michi*' (the way of imperial subjects) to show the hardship of Japanese nationals.

Given his background, Moon was particularly interested in designing the final section, 'The New Constitution and Nationals/Foreigners'. He demonstrated how Nihonjin, or those holding household registries in Japan proper, were granted civil rights under the new Constitution of 1946; and how those holding colonial registries were deprived of Japanese nationality and became gaikokujin. He put up flyers announcing the rights and duties of Japanese nationals. One flyer stated: 'I am Japanese, and What are My Rights?' Juxtaposed with those flyers were documents on the alien registration system and the anti-discrimination movement led by Koreans who wanted access to the national pension. Moon also displayed documents on Japanese repatriation from Manchuria, on the abandonment of Japanese emigrants in Korea, and on the deportation of Koreans from Japan, illuminating the state's border control and its inhumane treatment of both Japanese nationals and formerly colonized foreigners.

Thus, in the exhibit hall, Moon demonstrated how various kinds of people in the Japanese empire were assimilated as national subjects through the processes of colonization and war, and how they were differentiated into Japanese nationals and foreigners at the fall of the empire. In doing so, he tried to show not only the unfair treatment of the colonized and the foreigners but also the predicament of those who had continued to be Japanese nationals. Instead of just stressing how much the former suffered, as other activists and commentators routinely did, Moon emphasized that many Japanese nationals also suffered. He sought not to dichotomize Japanese and foreign nationals.

Other old-comer Korean activists held a dichotomous view. Moon supported their view, highlighting it in the design of the PR flyer, which was used for the cover of the exhibition catalogue. The flyer has three posters from the exhibition. Two of them are placed side by side: one for commemorating the creation of the new Constitution and the other for promoting the spiritual mobilization of Japanese for total war. Placed below these posters is the one that celebrated the start of the conscription of Taiwanese. In this way, Moon wanted to point out that while both Japanese and the colonized were sent to war, the former alone received civil rights under the new order. Many old-comers use this historical account as a basis for accusing the Japanese state of discriminating against the formerly colonized. In the exhibit hall, Moon wanted to go one step further and demonstrate how some Japanese were also deprived of civil rights.

In the exhibition catalogue, Moon criticizes a dichotomous view in light of the demographic change in today's Japan, and challenges the ideology of monoethnicity. He states:

> The number of foreign nationals in Japan has increased since the 1990's due to economic globalization. The number of children born between Japanese and foreign nationals has also increased. Most of those children are Japanese nationals as a result of the 1984 change of the Nationality Law.[21] Such being the case, isn't it impossible to draw a clear line between Japanese nationals and foreign nationals? Yet, there is a tendency in society to conflate the term *Nihon kokumin*, which means membership to the state, and the term *Nihonjin*, which connotes ethnicity. This tendency buttresses the legal system that treats the Japanese nation as consisting of one homogeneous ethnic group.
>
> (Moon 2004: 16)

National boundaries have been shifting to include more and more people of foreign descent, whose number has been increasing through intermarriages, which account for 5 percent of the total number of marriages in Japan, and through naturalization, which has been on the rise since the 1990s. Moon thinks it necessary to change the legal system, switching to birthplace-based nationality, for example, and to open up the category of 'Nihon kokumin' for ethnically different people. Yet he also demands an improved treatment of those who stay as foreign residents, separating his position from the government's inclusive policy, which neglects those who refuse to assimilate. He argues some rights of nationals, such as local voting rights, should be extended to foreigners, and calls for collaboration between Japanese nationals and foreigners in bringing about changes.

Though concerned about the multiethnicity in Japanese society, Moon keeps distant from multiculturalism. He supports the politics of cultural identity practised by minority groups, and in this sense, praises the Multiethnic Japan Exhibition. He is especially pleased that first-generation Koreans had a chance to express themselves publicly. Yet his strategy for dealing with multiethnic Japan is to focus on civil rights. In the current exigencies, as in the past, the possession of Japanese nationality matters, but it does not necessarily guarantee access to civil rights. We have seen how returnees from China have had to fight for civil rights. They are joined by those Japanese whose struggles are shown in Liberty Osaka, such as people with disabilities and the homeless. More and more Japanese nationals may have to fight for the protection of their rights because, as the old-comer Korean scholar Kang Sang-jung (2004: 177) observes, their 'social safety net' has been breaking down in the past decade. He calls this social change the *zainichi-ka* (transformation into the resident Korean status) of Japanese nationals, referring to the lives of old-comer Koreans without much social welfare. In a similar vein, Moon (2004: 14) asks a rhetorical question in the exhibition catalogue: 'Isn't the unhappiness of foreign residents related to the unhappiness of Japanese nationals?' He believes that they need to collaborate. He is afraid that the discourse of multiculturalism may contribute to deepening a divide between them in the name of cultural diversity.

The curators could not assess the impact of the exhibition, but they knew that the exhibition catalogue had sold out. About 10,000 people visited Liberty Osaka while it held the exhibition. One-third of them were school-children, who were there for the regular exhibits. No particular report was made in the media. Moon knows of an informal survey indicating that some visitors agreed with the curators, while others thought they were opinionated. Among the latter was a city assemblyman, who expressed strong disagree-ment. Yet such disagreement was nothing new to Liberty Osaka, which stands at the forefront of social activism for human rights. The exhibition presented a criticism against the move to reconstruct Nihonjin as loyal subjects of the state, and invigorated those who shared the criticism.

NIHONJIN IN MULTIETHNIC JAPAN: PAST AND PRESENT

While both exhibitions were concerned with the plight of foreigners, the curators of the two exhibitions treated different issues in different time frames, pursued different goals, and targeted different audiences. The curators of the Multiethnic Japan Exhibition focused on the cultural rights of foreigners in today's Japan and on the idea of creating a society of co-living in the future. Challenging the ideology of monoethnicity, the curators encouraged foreigners to express their cultural identities and promoted tolerance for cultural diversity among Japanese. The curators of the Japanese

Nation Exhibition, represented by Moon, focused on the issues of nationality and civil rights, and they situated the issues mostly in the history of the Japanese empire. Moon wanted Japanese visitors to realize their privileged access to civil rights as well as the fragile nature of their privilege and to understand the social exclusion of foreigners through that realization.

When compared in this way, the two exhibitions were complementary to each other as educational forms of social activism, resonating with other social actions. The Multiethnic Japan Exhibition was in line with the grassroots movement of multicultural co-living, which dealt with issues directly relevant to the lives of foreigners. The Japanese Nation Exhibition was in tune with critical academic work on nation building, colonialism, and war. The social situation at the beginning of the 2000s called for both kinds of activism: one dealing with concrete problems and empowering foreigners, and the other providing a historical and theoretical framework for tackling those problems and problematizing the rights of Japanese nationals. These two orientations operate in 'two parallel time frames', which Vera Mackie (2002: 181) often finds in discussions on relationships between Japan and other Asian countries. One concerns 'Japan's place in the post-war political economy of East Asia', and the other concerns 'a legacy of the imperial and colonial past'.

Though appreciated by many visitors, the Multiethnic Japan Exhibition was not free from the possibility of co-optation by conservative forces, partly because of its adoption of the discourse of multicultural co-living. This discourse has been used not only by activists and educators, but also by people in positions of power. Local governments, in dealing with foreigners in their jurisdictions, adopted the expression in the late 1990s. The Ministry of Justice discussed the importance of 'co-living' between Japanese and foreigners in the 2000 Basic Plan for Immigration Control. In 2003, the Federation of Economic Organizations, which leads Japanese business, proposed the creation of an 'Agency of Multicultural Co-Living' within the central government, advocating the entry of foreign labourers to Japan. The Ministry of Internal Affairs and Communications started an investigation in 2005 on how to promote 'multicultural co-living' in local contexts, and it completed a report in 2006. What is common in these moves is the proclamation of the inclusion of foreigners, assumed to be Asian foreigners, into a society of harmonious co-living. While benefiting from inclusive policies, however, foreigners are mostly left without civil rights. One can argue that Japanese leaders, like those in other countries, deploy the discourse of multicultural co-living 'to manage diversity by the strategic inclusion of difference' (Chapman 2006: 100).

Such an argument is convincing when the treatment of foreigners is closely examined. To begin with, the government is willing to accept only certain kinds of foreigners. They are hierarchized according to their different nationalities in terms of legal status and access to rights, and differentially deployed in the labour market (Shipper 2002). In 2006, the Ministry of Justice tightened the control of newcomer foreigners, reinstituting the fingerprinting requirement in the alien registration. Inclusive policies are intended only for those disciplined enough to get along with majority Japanese and business corporations.

In the hierarchical categorization of Asian foreigners, one can see an echo of the past Japanese empire. In a pattern similar to that of the creators of colonial assimilationist policy, the government of today's multiethnic Japan is including as second-class nationals those Asians who are culturally assimilated and those who were born from intermarriages between Japanese and other Asians. As in the past, the government implements inclusive policy as it moves toward militarization. It passed the emergency defence legislation in 2003, sending defence military to Iraq and buttressing the move to revise the pacifist Constitution for the legitimate use of military. Noting that a hierarchy, not equality, is actually at work in the assertion of multicultural co-living by a dominant group, Chris Burgess (2004) argues that 'parallels can be made with the colonial period when the ideology was of multiethnic harmony (*minzoku kyōwa*) within a Greater East Asia Co-Prosperity Sphere (*Dai Tōa Kyōei Ken*)'. Indeed, when multiculturalism began to spread in Japan, scholars studying colonialism were quick to problematize this idea. Tomiyama Ichirō (1995: 388), for example, has argued that 'cooperativism' (*kyōdōshugi*) in the Greater East Asia Co-Prosperity Sphere ideology is not just a problem of the past, warning us about 'the academic genealogy of today's multicultural narratives which have appeared in the midst of the unsettling of national polities'.

As in other countries, multiculturalism thus came with its discontents in Japan (see Fish 1997: 385). Arguing against the tendency to see it as passé, Nishikawa Nagao (2006: 24) points out this idea has the potential to debunk the concept of a homogeneous national culture and bring about a change to the nation state system. To be sure, he does not see multiculturalism as the ultimate solution to the problems of the system. Yet, he believes the idea can open up the possibility of generating 'sensibilities and movements that may contribute to the collapse of the nation state system'. What is necessary in seeking this potential, he argues, is a theoretical framework that can help construct a creative relationship in encounters with difference. Tomiyama (1995: 288) does not discard the idea of multiculturalism either. He says: 'what we need now is to find a site of resistance within "cooperativism" and multiculturalism where we can create ways of being that confuse categories or that are unclassifiable'.

We have seen an effort toward such a subversion of rigid classification in the Multiethnic Japan Exhibition, especially in the section on returnees from China. Within the multiculturalism movement in Japan, there are motions to challenge essentialized categories imposed from above, and to construct a relationship – not a harmonious relationship based on 'consensus', but a creative relationship based on 'dissensus' (Readings 1996).[22] It should be noted that many activists understand *kyōsei* (co-living) as a process of rectifying social inequality through collaboration between the majority and the minority, not as 'harmony' (Hanazaki 1993), though they deploy the latter usage in negotiating with authorities. We have also seen in the making of the Japanese Nation Exhibition and in the renewal process of Liberty Osaka an effort to develop a historical and theoretical framework for debunking essentialized categories. In this effort, which is directed at examining national and ethnic classification under the hegemony of the Japanese empire, there is a realization that today's multiethnic Japan should not repeat the past. Thus there are struggles in Japanese social activism to steer the multiculturalism movement toward 'a non-essentialist critical multiculturalism' (May 1999: 31) that seeks to alter hegemonic power relations and to form creative relationships.

Among various categories, the curators of the exhibitions paid particular attention to the category of 'Nihonjin'. Only by dissecting the category of 'Nihonjin', I argue, can we effectively challenge both the old ideology of monoethnicity and the new tide of nationalism. To fight the ideology of monoethnicity effectively, we need not only to make the presence of non-Japanese visible, but also to demystify the concept of 'pure Japanese', which could be strengthened by the politics of difference. In the current tide of nationalism, this concept is defended. Instead of excluding non-Japanese from the nation as it used to do, the government now includes as Japanese nationals people of foreign descent, as long as they look like 'pure Japanese' genealogically and culturally. Thus 'Nihonjin' is now discursively reconstructed not only as exclusive 'pure Japanese' but also as inclusive 'mixed Japanese'. Oguma Eiji (1995: 296) observes that these two conceptualizations, 'monoethnic theory' and 'mixed-ethnic theory' in his terms, have appeared in modern Japanese history, shifting their popularities according to changing political circumstances. The mixed-ethnic theory, he argues, becomes influential when Japan strengthens its power. It is on the rise today as leaders seek to maintain Japan's hegemony in Asia through militarization. As Tomiyama (1997) points out in reference to the colonial period, the two concepts are not mutually exclusive. Today, as in the past, the inclusive concept of 'Nihonjin' is used to make invisible the internal hierarchy of people and their cultural diversity, while the exclusive concept of 'Nihonjin' is used to protect the privilege of certain people among those included. Therefore, social activism should be directed against the inclusive conceptualization of 'Nihonjin' as well as against the concept of pure Japanese.

The curators of the two exhibitions tackled the problem of 'Nihonjin' in various ways. By praising foreigner-ness, Shōji and the project team tried to devalue the concept of pure Japanese and to intervene in the inclusion of people with foreign backgrounds as Nihonjin. Minami presented returnees from China as forming a community heterogeneous in nationality, culture, and genealogy, challenging the discourse that defines them as second-class Japanese in line with the inclusive concept of Nihonjin as well as the discourse that excludes them as non-Japanese in line with the concept of pure Japanese. Moon demonstrated the shifting nature of national boundaries, while at the same time delineating that inclusion as Japanese nationals, whether conceptualized as pure or mixed Japanese, did not guarantee access to full civil rights.

Using museum displays and representing the process of classification, the curators of the exhibitions thus demonstrated the heterogeneity of Japanese nationals in cultural identifications and in access to civil rights on one hand, and the impossibility of defining 'Nihonjin' and classifying certain people as Nihonjin on the other. In doing so, they dispatched the message that people in today's multiethnic Japan need to collaborate across socially-constructed national boundaries in order to protect, retrieve, and gain civil and cultural rights. In the final analysis, this is probably the most important message from the two exhibitions.

Notes

1 The official English title was 'Multiethnic Japan: Life and History of Immigrants'.
2 Minpaku is the abbreviation of Kokuritsu Minzokugaku Hakubutsukan.
3 The education reform bill was passed into law on 15 December 2006.
4 A Japan-born Korean told me in 2004 that she had never in her fifty-year life been so apprehensive as she was about expressing her Korean identity publicly.
5 The team, consisting of a dozen people, included nationals of Peru, South Korea, and China.
6 South Americans in Japan are mostly Brazilians and Peruvians, and the majority of them are of Japanese descent. The curators argued that Europeans and North Americans were much less likely to engage in 3K jobs (the Japanese version of 3D – dirty, dangerous, and difficult – jobs) than were foreigners from Asian countries, and that speaking English or French was marked as cultural capital, not as social stigma as in the case of speaking an Asian foreign language. Europeans and North Americans were included in the exhibition as individual cases.
7 The discussion is based on my interviews with Shōji between 2001 and 2005.
8 Okinawan music was played at the exhibition.
9 This is translated by the author, as are other translations in the article.
10 The term *gaijin*, instead of *gaikokujin*, is often used to refer to European foreigners.

11 Cultural and civil rights are considered to be part of citizenship rights. See Shafir and Brysk (2006).
12 Minami distinguishes those who returned to Japan after 1972 from those who returned before 1958.
13 Much of the discussion here is based on my interviews with Minami and on his papers posted on his homepage, *Minami Laboratory*.
14 The class lawsuits were settled in July 2007, as the plaintiffs accepted the government's new policy that offered more financial support for the returnees.
15 Fukuoka defines the returnees by Japanese lineage and by non-Japanese culture and nationality.
16 I think what she says about Chinese-Japanese war orphans can be applied to the returnees in general.
17 The movement was started by the Levelers' Association (Suiheisha), founded in 1922.
18 Liberty Osaka has an official schedule for renewals.
19 The discussion here is based on my interviews with Moon in June 2006 and on his article in the exhibition catalogue (Moon 2004).
20 Narita, Komori, Makihara, and Muta Kazue all wrote short essays for the exhibition catalogue.
21 Nationality became available through maternal and paternal lines, instead of only the latter.
22 Nishikawa (2006) discusses this concept in relation to multiculturalism.

References

American Association of Museums (1984) *Museums for a New Century*, Washington, DC: American Association of Museums.
Asaji, T. (1999) 'Jinken Hakubutsukan ga Heiwa ni Hatasu Yakuwari' (The Role of Human Rights Museums in Promoting Peace), *War and Peace*, 8: 62–6.
Bennett, T. (1995) *The Birth of the Museum: History, theory, politics*, London: Routledge.
—— (2004) *Past Beyond Memory: Evolution, museums, colonialism*, London: Routledge.
Burgess, C. (2004) 'Maintaining Identities: Discourses of homogeneity in a rapidly globalizing Japan', *Electronic Journal of Contemporary Japanese Studies*, Online. Available online at http://www.japanesestudies.org.uk/articles/Burgess.html (accessed 10 October 2006).
Chapman, D. (2006) 'Discourses of Multicultural Coexistence (*Tabunka Kyōsei*) and the "Old-comer" Korean Residents of Japan', *Asian Ethnicity*, 7, 1: 89–102.
Dubin, S.C. (1999) *Displays of Power*, New York: New York University Press.
Fish, S. (1997) 'Boutique Multiculturalism, or Why Liberals are Incapable of Thinking about Hate Speech', *Critical Inquiry*, 23: 378–95.
Fukuoka, Y. (2000) *Lives of Young Koreans in Japan*, Melbourne: Trans Pacific.
Graburn, N.H.H. (2007) 'Epilogue: Social scientists in action: Sociologist Hiroshi Komai and anthropologist Hiroshi Shoji', in N.H.H. Graburn, J. Ertl, and R.K. Tierney (eds), *Multiculturalism in the New Japan: Crossing the boundaries within*, New York: Berghahn Books.
Hanazaki, K. (1993) *Aidentiti to Kyōsei no Tetsugaku* (Philosophy of Identity and Co-living), Tokyo: Chikuma Shobō.

160   E. Tai

Hatsuse, R. (1985) *Uchinaru Kokusaika* (Internal Internationalization), Tokyo: Mitsumine Shobō.
Iwabuchi, K. (2004) 'Supekutaru-ka sareru "Nashonaru" no Kyōen' (A 'National' Banquet Made as a Spectacle), in T. Morris-Suzuki and Y. Shunya (eds) *Gurōbarizēshon no Bunka-seiji* (Cultural Politics of Globalization), Tokyo: Heibonsha.
Kang, S. (2004) *Zainichi* (Resident Koreans), Tokyo: Kōdansha.
Kojima, N. (2005) *Jinken Gakushū to Hakubutsukan* (Human Rights Studies and Museums), Osaka: Kaihō Shuppan.
Lavine, S.D. and Karp, I. (1991) 'Introduction: Museums and multiculturalism', in I. Karp and S.D. Lavine (eds), *Exhibiting Cultures: The poetics and politics of museum display*, Washington: Smithsonian Institution Press.
Lee, M.A. (2003) 'Multiculturalism as Nationalism: A discussion of nationalism in pluralistic nations', *Canadian Review of Studies in Nationalism*, XXX: 103–23.
Lee, P.Y. (1997) 'In the Name of the Museum', *Museum Anthropology*, 20, 2: 7–14.
Luke, T.W. (2002) *Museum Politics*, Minneapolis: University of Minnesota Press.
Mackie, V. (2002) ' "Asia" in Everyday Life', in B.S.A. Yeoh, P. Teo, and S. Huang (eds), *Gender Politics in the Asia-Pacific Region*, London: Routledge.
Maritano, L. (2002) 'An Obsession with Cultural Difference', in R. Grillo and J. Pratt (eds), *The Politics of Recognizing Difference*, Burlington, VT: Ashgate.
May, S. (1999) 'Critical Multiculturalism and Cultural Difference: Avoiding essentialism', in S. May (ed.), *Critical Multiculturalism*, London: Falmer Press.
Mesa-Bains, A. (2004) 'The Real Multiculturalism', in G. Anderson (ed.), *Reinventing the Museum*, New York: Rowman & Littlefield.
Minami, M. (2006) *Minami Laboratory*. Online. Available at www.geocities.jp/ xuehaim21/ (accessed 10 October 2006).
—— (2004) 'Chūgoku Kikokusha no Aimaisa' (Ambiguity of Returnees from China), in H. Shōji (ed.), *Taminzoku Nihon: Zainichi Gaikokujin no Kurashi* (Multiethnic Japan: Life of Resident Foreigners), Osaka: Senri Bunka Zaidan.
Moon, K.H. (2004) 'Naze "Tsukurareru Kokumin" Nano ka' (Why is it 'a Nation as Constructed'?), in Liberty Osaka (ed.), *Tsukurareru Nihon Kokumin: Kokuseki, sensō, sabetsu* (The Japanese Nation as Constructed: Nationality, War, Discrimination), Osaka: Liberty Osaka.
Nishikawa, N. (2006) 'Kokumin Kokka to Bunka no Genzai' (Nation State and Culture at Present), *Rekihaku*, 111: 20–5.
Oguma, E. (1995) *Tan'itsu Minzoku Shinwa no Kigen: Nihonjin no jigazō no keifu* (The Origin of the Myth of the Homogeneous Nation: The genealogy of Japanese self images), Tokyo: Shinyōsha.
Ōta, Y. (1998) *Toransupojishon no Shisō* (The Thought of Transposition), Tokyo: Sekai-shisōsha.
Readings, B. (1996) *The University in Ruins*, Cambridge, MA: Harvard University Press.
Shafir, G. and Brysk A. (2006) 'The Globalization of Rights', *Citizenship Studies*, 10, 3: 275–87.
Shipper, A.W. (2002) 'The Political Construction of Foreign Workers in Japan', *Critical Asian Studies*, 34, 1: 41–68.
Shōji, H. (2004) 'Izure Otozureru Kyōsei Shakai no Tameni' (For the Sake of a Society of Co-Living), in H. Shōji (ed.), *Taminzoku Nihon: Zainichi gaikokujin no kurashi* (Multiethnic Japan: Life of resident foreigners), Osaka: Senri Bunka Zaidan.

Siddle, R. (2003) 'Return to Uchinā: The politics of identity in contemporary Okinawa', in G.D. Hook and R. Siddle (eds), *Japan and Okinawa: Structure and subjectivity*, London: RoutledgeCurzon.

Stephens, S. (1995) 'Introduction: Children and the politics of culture in "late capitalism"', in S. Stephens (ed.), *Children and the Politics of Culture*, Princeton: Princeton University Press.

Tamanoi, M.A. (2006) 'Overseas Japanese and the Challenges of Repatriation in Post-Colonial East Asia', in N. Adachi (ed.), *Japanese Diasporas*, London: Routledge.

Tomiyama, I. (1995) 'Colonialism and the Sciences of the Tropical Zones', *Positions: East Asia Cultures Critique*, 3, 2: 367–91.

—— (1997) 'Tan'itsu Minzoku Shinwa no Kigen' (The Origin of the Myth of the Homogeneous Nation), *Nihonshi Kenkyū*, 413: 77–83.

Yoshida, K. (1999) *Bunka no 'Hakken'* (A 'Discovery' of Culture), Tokyo: Iwanami Shoten.

Yoshimi, S. (1992) *Hakurankai no Seijigaku* (Politics of Expositions), Tokyo: Chūō Kōron.

8 Zainichi[1] Koreans in history and memory

Michael Weiner and David Chapman

INTRODUCTION

In common with the other contributions to this volume, this chapter contains multiple foci: the historical formation of the present-day Korean community in Japan, with particular reference to settlement in Hiroshima and Nagasaki; historical memory – its commemoration and suppression – in relation to these two cities; and, set against the decades-long struggle for human rights, the efforts to establish a 'Third Way', a zainichi identity congruent with both a Korean cultural past and a Japanese cultural present.

TWICE VICTIMS: THE KOREAN MIGRATION TO HIROSHIMA AND NAGASAKI

The recruitment and mobilization of colonial labour was a common practice among all colonial powers. For workers from the Korean periphery who entered Japan between 1910 and 1945, economic function and social status were determined by their identity as colonial subjects. Although the act of annexation in 1910 conferred the right to travel and take up employment within the empire, Hantōjin (lit. Peninsulars [Koreans]) were also expected to assume their 'proper place', to accept a subordinate identity and to serve the interests of metropolitan Japan. Economic deprivation and political suppression in Korea figured in the decision to migrate, but the more compelling and decisive incentive was the 'pull' factor. Once underway, the demand for flexible, low-cost industrial labour remained constant, and the migration of workers from colonial Korea was a self-perpetuating response to labour-market conditions in Japan.

Active recruitment of colonial labour was initially stimulated by the rapid industrial expansion that accompanied Japan's entry in the First World War, and it continued more or less uninterrupted until 1945. Although wages in Japan were substantially higher than those available in Korea, migrant workers seldom enjoyed the same rates of pay as their Japanese counterparts. For Korean workers, wage rates and conditions of employment varied considerably by industry, but in all cases were determined by both a lack of marketable skills and by racially informed employment practices. On average, Koreans were paid a third less than indigenous workers, and they were regarded as inherently suited for tasks involving physical strength but little else (Osaka-shi 1924: 17–21). Concentration of Korean migrant workers in small subcontracting firms, where health and safety standards were poorly enforced or ignored entirely, reduced social costs but resulted in a disproportionately high rate of work-related injuries, lay-offs, dismissal and unemployment (Kim 1977: 26). Their role as migratory replacement labour, moreover, reduced the likelihood of trades-union affiliation. When they did participate in or organize industrial action against employers, it only reinforced the more generalized perception of Koreans as cultural and political antagonists (Osaka-shi 1924: 3).

Exclusion from the general housing market reduced Koreans to living in tenements and flop houses adjacent to factory sites, or, in the case of day labourers, to living in work camps operated by labour contractors. As a result, sanitation and basic health care were a constant problem in areas of Korean residence, and this in turn meant that migrant workers were particularly susceptible to dysentery and other infectious diseases. Contemporary accounts, however, attributed the prevalence of poverty, violence and disease within Korean communities to culturally or racially embedded characteristics (Sakai 1931: 133–5). Although Koreans were perceived as an adequate source of low-level manpower, it was assumed that their standard of living took for granted a decadent cultural heritage. (Osaka-shi 1933: 32–3).

Throughout the colonial period, Korean labour exhibited characteristics common to other contemporary migrations. Newly arrived workers, be they permanent immigrants or sojourners, formed the most exploited and least protected segment of the working class. The benefits of employing migrant labour were considerable. In the labour-intensive industries where Korean labour was concentrated, their employment facilitated expanded production without investment in mechanization (Sakai 1931: 118). Reliance on migrant labour also consolidated and perpetuated pre-existing social and economic inequalities. The presence of large numbers of Koreans in the mining and construction industries, for example, decreased the likelihood that indigenous workers would seek employment in these dirty, dangerous and low-status occupations, thereby reducing the possibility of improved wages and working conditions. Large-scale employment of migrant labour also had a deflationary impact on the level of wage increases in certain industries, though racially determined wage structures ensured that direct competition with Japanese workers was the exception rather than the rule (Akiyama 1929: 112). This was not, however, recognized by the majority of Japanese workers, who were encouraged by employers, the media and the state itself to regard Koreans as competitors. The high visibility of Koreans, clustered in shantytowns or abandoned work sites, also confirmed Japanese perceptions of immigrants as unwelcome intruders (Sakai 1931: 133–5).

In common with other Korean communities that dotted the industrial landscape of pre-1945 Japan, those in Hiroshima and Nagasaki had developed as a consequence of both colonial economic policies and the demand for temporary, low-cost industrial labour (Weiner 1994: 112–53, 187–208). As set out in Table 8.1, neither Hiroshima nor Nagasaki became primary immigrant destinations until economic recovery, stimulated by increased military expenditure, began in the 1930s. Compared with the astonishing growth in the size of Korean communities elsewhere, particularly in Osaka, the growth of the Hiroshima population was slow, only increasing by about 11,000 between 1930 and 1937. Nonetheless, this represented a more than twofold increase in the size of the local Korean community. The outbreak of the Pacific War and the subsequent mobilization of colonial labour to offset domestic shortages stimulated further expansion of local communities in Hiroshima and Nagasaki, both of which more than doubled in size between 1940 and 1945. Although precise figures are not available, an estimated

Table 8.1 Resident Korean population 1910–1945 (Osaka, Hiroshima, Nagasaki, Fukuoka): prefectural totals

	Osaka	*Hiroshima*	*Nagasaki*	*Fukuoka*
1910	206	24	173	335
1913	338	39	283	549
1916	762	68	381	894
1919	4,502	808	1,844	6,704
1922	13,337	1,681	2,008	8,304
1925	31,860	4,025	2,407	13,357
1928	55,209	5,827	4,324	21,042
1931	85,567	8,156	4,320	25,126
1934	171,160	18,311	8,934	36,115
1937	234,188	19,525	7,625	50,565
1940	312,269	38,221	18,144	116,864
1943	395,380	68,274	47,415	172,199
1945	333,354	84,886	61,773	205,452

Source: Harada, T. and Kang, J., eds, *Sabetsu to Jinken (4) Minzoku*, Tokyo, Yuzankaku, 1985, 46–7.

52,000 to 53,000 Koreans were living in the city of Hiroshima in August 1945, with smaller communities spread throughout the prefecture (Yi 1979: 251–2). Estimates for Nagasaki are even less reliable, but it is likely that about half (30,000) of the prefectural Korean population of 63,000 could be found within the city proper.

As elsewhere, Korean ghettos in Hiroshima and Nagasaki were located in the poorer downtown districts and in the *basue-machi* (fringe towns) that served as halfway zones connecting rural sources of seasonal labour with urban industrial centres (Yi 1979: 254). In both cities, the great majority of Koreans were accommodated in *nagaya* tenements, low-cost wooden structures covered in corrugated iron or, in some instances, in straw. Tenements were normally constructed in clusters at some distance from ordinary housing but with easy access to the factories that employed their residents. In Hiroshima, the largest *Chōsenjin buraku* (Korean ghettos) were concentrated within 4 or 4.5 km of the hypocentre of the atomic bombing. Approximately 3,000 conscripted Koreans employed by Mitsubishi at its shipyard and engine manufacturing facilities at Koi and Eba respectively (both of which were located 3 km from the hypocentre) were housed in a single dormitory (Yi 1979: 252). Further immigrant clusters could be found in Hirose-machi, Yokogawa, Tenma and Kusunoki-cho, located in the western part of the city. Many of the residents of these areas were employed in general construction or demolition work in the city centre. Others were employed as manual labour in factories operated by Mitsubishi Heavy Industries and Toyo Kogyo. Large numbers of Korean women were working in small and medium-sized factories in Nakahiro and Kusunoki-cho, or at the Military Clothing Depot located in Ujina. Similar conditions existed in Nagasaki, where large numbers of Koreans were employed in general construction, at the Kawanami Shipyard and at the Mitsubishi Shipyard and Ironworks (*Kobe Shinbun* July 8, 1990; Harada and Kang 1985: 23; *Chōsenjin no Hibakusha* 1989: 78–82). Though fewer in number than their counterparts in Hiroshima, the proportion of Koreans residing within 1.5 km of the hypocentre in Nagasaki was greater than those in Hiroshima (*Chōsenjin no Hibakusha* 1989: 87).

Reconstructing an accurate picture of Korean settlement in either city, however, remains difficult for several reasons: (1) contemporary documentary evidence was destroyed by the atomic explosions and the subsequent firestorms that swept through both cities; (2) very high labour-turnover rates and general mobility among Korean workers made identification impossible in many cases, particularly during the closing stages of the war; and (3) survivors were often unable to provide addresses or to otherwise identify the precise locality in which they lived in August 1945 (Kosho 1991: 113).

At the time, the decision to use the atomic bomb against Japan was viewed by most within the American political and military establishment as little more than a continuation of the policy of strategic bombing (Lifton and Markusen 1990: 23). The distinction between a military target and a city had already been largely erased by the bombings of Dresden and Hamburg and by the bombing of Tokyo, where the incendiary raids of March 1945 resulted in the deaths of more than 100,000 people. Nonetheless, the consequences for the victims of the atomic bombings of August 1945 were unprecedented. The Hiroshima bomb of August 6 exploded with the force of 20,000 tons of TNT near the centre of a flat city constructed mainly of wood. All buildings within a 2-mile radius were completely destroyed, and flash burns occurred at a distance of up to 2.5 miles from the hypocentre. The number of fatalities, both immediate and as an indirect consequence of the bombings, may never be known. The figure most commonly cited is 78,000, but previous estimates have ranged as high as 240,000, while the city of Hiroshima's estimate of 200,000 is equivalent to between 25 and 50 per cent of the daytime population in 1945. Of approximately 50,000 Koreans residing in Hiroshima, an estimated 30,000 died, either as a direct result of the blast, or soon thereafter. The surviving 20,000 Koreans constituted between 15 and 20 per cent of the total Hiroshima hibakusha (atomic bomb survivors) population.

Three days later, a further 70,000 inhabitants of Nagasaki suffered a similar fate. The corresponding figure for Korean hibakusha in Nagasaki has been estimated at 20,000, including 10,000 fatalities (*Chōsenjin no Hibakusha* 1989: 87; Sato and Yamada 1986: 111). The wide disparity in estimates is at least in part accounted for by the fact that systematic health surveys of hibakusha were not introduced until 1950 – five years after the bombings had taken place. During the American Occupation, the Atomic Bomb Casualty Commission was charged with examining survivors of the Hiroshima bomb, but the resulting data was dispatched to the Pentagon for analysis, and little was done to alleviate the condition of those suffering the effects of radiation. On the contrary, in their attempts to downplay the after-effects of nuclear warfare, the Occupation authorities initially denied the existence of residual radiation.

Korean hibakusha   100,000 affected

Throughout much of the post-1945 period, public education institutions in Japan have represented the Pacific War as a natural disaster that swept all the nations of East Asia. In fact, due to its unique experience of the horrors of atomic warfare, Japan has often been depicted as having suffered pro-portionately greater damage and loss than its neighbours (Dower 1993: 19). Externally, however, this retrospective defence of Japanese imperialism has served to reinforce the perception that Japanese regrets for the war extend only to their own sufferings (Yamamoto 1991: 322). It is as if a moral symmetry exists in which the experience of colonial exploitation in Korea, or atrocities committed by the Japanese military in Nanjing, Singapore and elsewhere in Asia, have somehow been erased by the bombings of Hiroshima and Nagasaki. Although the term 'hibakusha' is normally reserved for Japanese victims of the atomic bombings of Hiroshima and Nagasaki, it applies equally to the tens of thousands of other sufferers, predominantly Koreans (Ryu 1991: 256–7). In 1974, the Korean Association for Assistance to Victims of the Atomic Bomb estimated that the number of Koreans affected by the bombings of Hiroshima and Nagasaki were 70,000 and 30,000 respectively, of whom 50,000 had died immediately after the bomb (So 1989: 23–4).

Due to the effects of censorship, initially under American aegis and thereafter by the Japanese state, the voices of the thousands of Koreans resident in Hiroshima and Nagasaki in August 1945 were stilled for decades (Ryu 1991: 256–7). Indeed, it was only in 1991 that the Japanese government allocated the sum of $25 million to assist Korean hibakusha, virtually all of whom had been transported to Japan as conscripted labour during the Pacific War. This sum is hardly generous compared to the $1.2 billion awarded by the United States government to citizens of Japanese descent who were incarcerated during the war (*Asahi Shinbun* November 29, 1991). It also came too late for thousands of hibakusha repatriated to Korea after the war, who received few of the benefits provided to their Japanese counterparts (*Mainichi Shinbun* February 18, 1992; Won 1986: 144–5).

Under Article 19 of the San Francisco Peace Treaty, the United States was released from any responsibility for the care and treatment of hibakusha (*Chōsenjin no Hibakusha* 1989: 244). Thereafter, the matter of compensation was left entirely to the Japanese state, as was the negotiation of appropriate levels of subsidized medical treatment for victims. At the national level, two pieces of legislation determined the extent of care provided for hibakusha: the 1957 Genshi Bakudan Hibakusha no Iryō nado ni kansuru Hōritsu (Law for the Treatment of Hibakusha) and the 1968 Genshi Bakudan Hibakusha ni taisuru Tokubetsu Sochi ni Kansuru Hōritsu (Special Measures Law for Hibakusha) (Won 1986: 145). Under the 1968 legislation, hibakusha entitlements (social and medical) became dependent upon possession of a valid *techō* (hibakusha allowance book), issued by the appropriate prefectural authorities (*Chōsenjin no Hibakusha* 1989: 245). Neither the 1957 law nor the 1968 law contains a *kokuseki jōkō* (nationality requirement), which might otherwise restrict the laws' application to holders of Japanese nationality (Won 1986: 145–6). Moreover, although financial responsibility largely rests with the national government, the municipal authorities in Hiroshima and Nagasaki administer the *techō* system (Harada and Kang 1985: 108).

In theory, this should have ensured equal treatment for Japanese and non-Japanese hibakusha, since both municipalities have declared their intent to provide treatment for Korean hibakusha under the *techō* system. For many Korean claimants, however, the acquisition of this essential document remains a lengthy and often fruitless journey through the Japanese bureaucracy.

A literal interpretation of the law suggests that the issuance of a *techō* would immediately follow the submission of written testimony or a contemporary record attesting to the applicant's whereabouts in August 1945. This in itself presented particular difficulties for Koreans who may well have been unaware of where they actually were, who were known only by their Japanese names, or whose identity cards and other forms of identification were destroyed at the time. The cross-referencing of claims has been further complicated by the failure of the Japanese government to undertake a systematic survey of resident Korean hibakusha at any time since 1945 (Kosho 1991: 108–15; *Nagasaki Shinbun* May 9, 1991; Yi 1979: 262; Won 1986: 146).

Confronted by legal actions brought by Korean hibakusha throughout the post-war period, both the Japanese state and the corporate employers of conscripted labour have resisted the payment of compensation. In their view, Japan was relieved of any responsibility for the payment of compensation to Korean nationals by virtue of the 1965 Treaty of Normalization. This is particularly relevant in the case of hibakusha resident in Korea, where, until relatively recently, little effort had been made to either identify or provide treatment for sufferers. During the immediate post-war period of repatriation, 23,000 Korean hibakusha would have been lost among the nearly two million Koreans who returned to the peninsula. Similarly, there is no way of knowing how many hibakusha were numbered among the nearly three million Koreans who died during the Korean War, or how many have died of radiation-related illnesses since that time. These factors, coupled with the absence of specialist medical facilities in rural parts of South Korea, where the largest concentrations of hibakusha can be found, have made identification extremely difficult (*Chōsenjin no Hibakusha* 1989: 253; *Yomiuri Shinbun* August 2, 1986). In 1971, under pressure from local government officers in Oka City, the Mayor of Nagasaki conceded that the existing system discriminated against Korean claimants, and undertook to ensure greater flexibility in the issuance of *techō* in future. It was not, however, until 1983 that Koreans began to enjoy the results of this commitment to greater flex-ibility (*Chōsenjin no Hibakusha* 1989: 248). In 1972 there were an estimated 2,000 Korean hibakusha living in Nagasaki, yet as late as 1978 only 110 had been issued with an allowance book (So 1989: 24; Ito 1987: 228; *Chōsenjin no Hibakusha* 1989: 253).

It was not until August 1990, at a commemorative ceremony marking the forty-fifth anniversary of the Nagasaki bombing, that the obligation to compensate Korean hibakusha was publicly acknowledged (*Asahi Shinbun* August 9, 1990; *Yomiuri Shinbun* August 9, 1990). An official apology to Korean hibakusha was included in the annual peace declaration, and Korean women were invited to appear at the ceremony in traditional dress (*chima chogori*). In October 1992, Nagasaki's mayor, Motoshima Hitoshi, became the first mayor of either city to visit South Korea for the purpose of meeting atomic bomb survivors. This was followed by an announcement that the Nagasaki municipal government would allocate part of its budget to assisting Korean survivors of the atomic bombings. For the fiscal year of 1993, the sum of 2 million yen was set aside to fund projects designed to facilitate Korean access to Japanese-government-sponsored programmes. Under this project, Nagasaki city officials would visit South Korea to provide information about medical treatment available in Japan and to explain to survivors the process by which *techō* could be obtained (*Mainichi Shinbun* February 24, 1993). In August 1993, a peace conference in Hiroshima issued an appeal for a revision of hibakusha assistance legislation to ease access for Korean survivors (*Asahi Shinbun* August 3, 1993). A similar appeal to delete all nationality requirements from existing legislation was made by the mayor of Hiroshima during the annual commemorative ceremony. (*Asahi Shinbun* August 3, 1993).

Numerous factors accounted for the failure of Korean hibakusha, whether resident in Korea or Japan, to obtain adequate and consistent treatment. The governments of the United States and of Japan were undoubtedly responsible for the suppression of information concerning Korean hibakusha. But this in itself does not account for the virtual disappearance of Korean hibakusha from post-war memory. As with many other events in their century-long presence in Japan, the marginalization of the Korean atomic bomb experience within a dominant image of the past is but one aspect of a broader revisionist historical project. In contesting the official narratives of Hiroshima and Nagasaki, Korean hibakusha have sought not only to restore this episode in the history of their community but also to challenge the ways in which minority issues are presented to the public.

In the face of denials of both government and corporate liability, Korean hibakusha and other victims of forced-labour programmes implemented during the Pacific War have, on numerous occasions, been compelled to initiate legal action in Japanese, United States and Korean courts. Assisted by human rights law groups in Japan and encouraged by the South Korean Truth Commission on Forced Mobilization under Japanese Imperialism, Korean hibakusha continue to seek legal redress. In February 1995, forty-six plaintiffs filed suit in the Hiroshima District Court seeking compensation from both the Japanese government and from their former employer, Mitsubishi Heavy Industries (MHI). This legal action was composed of two distinct strands. The first sought compensation from the state based on the denial of hibakusha medical benefits, while the second focused on compensation from MHI for unpaid wartime wages and pension benefits. In contrast to previously unsuccessful legal actions against the government, and after a decade of appeals, the Hiroshima High Court ruled in favour of the plaintiffs on January 19, 2005. As subsequently upheld by the Japanese Supreme Court on November 1, 2007, the denial of health-care benefits to Korean hibakusha who had been employed at the Mitsubishi Hiroshima Shipyard, was deemed illegal. In its ruling, the Supreme Court ordered the state to pay 1.2 million yen to each plaintiff in lieu of lost medical benefits. On the other hand, the Supreme Court denied the plaintiffs' demands for compensation for lost wages from MHI. The court's ruling was at best a partial victory for the twenty-eight surviving plaintiffs, whose status as hibakusha had come about as a direct consequence of their conscription as forced labour.

For much of the post-1945 period, the attention of human rights organizations and other Korean organizations in Japan has focused upon broader concerns with civil liberties, particularly those pertaining to alien registration, immigration and nationality, employment and education, and welfare provision. The struggle for hibakusha recognition has therefore been but one aspect of a multi-layered agenda, which has been affected not only by institutional and legal processes within Japan but also by the continued division of the Korean peninsula and by the political fragmentation of the Korean community in Japan. Even the Hiroshima Peace Park has not been entirely free of controversy, as competing interest groups have attempted to mobilize this most potent symbol of anti-nuclearism for parochial interests. While the Peace Park and the cenotaph around which the park was constructed reflect a long-standing commitment to the three anti-nuclear principles, the appeal of this shrine also extends to spokesmen for the pro-nuclear lobby. The multi-dimensional politicization of hibakusha iconography has also been apparent in the decades-long battle to commemorate Korean victims of the Hiroshima bomb. It is a conflict that also illustrates the continued marginalization of a dissonant Korean history within the master narrative of post-war Hiroshima as a city of peace and modernity.

To circumvent city ordinances that prohibited the construction of additional cenotaphs within the borders of the Peace Park, the Hiroshima branch of Mindan (the Korean Residents' Union in Japan – the principal South-Korean-affiliated Korean support group) erected a separate memorial to Korean victims on the opposite bank of the Ota River in 1970. While the positioning of the Kankokujin Genbaku Giseisha Irei Hi (Memorial for the South Korean Victims of the Atomic Bomb) outside the park's boundary was itself suggestive of continued alienation, the use of the term 'Kankokujin', which usually denotes citizens of the then Republic of Korea, was also criticized by the North-Korean-affiliated Chōngryun (General Federation of Korean Residents in Japan). It was not until the summer of 1999 that a memorial to all Korean victims of atomic warfare was erected within the administrative boundaries of the Hiroshima Peace Park.

POST-WAR INTELLECTUAL DEVELOPMENTS

There have been a number of definable stages in the intellectual history of Koreans in Japan over the sixty years since the end of the Second World War in 1945. These changes have been influenced by various social events, as well as by debates and discussions that have continually attempted to define zainichi Korean identity. Isogai Jirō (2004: 9–19) has divided post-war zainichi literature into three stages. The first stage, from the end of the Second World War until 1960, he calls the 'season of politics'; the second stage ends in the mid-1980s when the zainichi began considering permanency in Japan; and the third stage starts in the mid-1980s with increasing numbers in the zainichi community naturalizing as Japanese and marriages between zainichi and Japanese nationals also increasing. Isogai's description of this history also closely aligns with zainichi social discourse and commentary and follows a similar trajectory.

The overarching theme of zainichi intellectual history, whether discussed through literature or through the discourse of social critics and commentators, is one dominated by the tension between the preservation and the loss of zainichi identity. In protecting Korean identity, the zainichi community has targeted notions of homogeneous Japanese national identity and culture. As with many diaspora communities, the zainichi community's presence has for a long time subverted and transgressed the notion of the Japanese nation-state as home to only a single national identity. However, the fight for preserving Korean identity has also been waged on the inside of the zainichi community. Although appeals to diasporic solidarity have been powerful in critiquing notions of a unified Japanese national identity, such an approach often carries its own set of inevitable boundaries and expectations of conformity. As Anthias (1998: 577) has argued, we need to exercise caution, for 'diaspora may indeed have a tendency to reinforce absolutist notions of "origin" and "true belonging"'. This was certainly the case in earlier post-war zainichi intellectual history, when strong Korean nationalism saturated discourse and debate on zainichi existence. However, as Isogai's description above reveals, the second and third stages from the mid-1960s through the early 1970s and beyond have led to more complex debates on zainichi ontology.

What has in fact happened over time is that, for most zainichi, identity has hybridized, becoming increasingly complex, diverse and fluid. Considering the zainichi condition through the notion of hybridity helps us to go beyond the framework of identity and to avoid the pitfalls of identity politics and essentialism that often plague such situations. As Ien Ang (2003: 141) argues, 'unlike other key concepts in the contemporary politics of difference – such as diaspora and multiculturalism – it [hybridity] foregrounds complicated entanglement rather than identity'. Through tracing the intellectual history of Koreans in Japan, we can see how zainichi hybridity has destabilized beliefs of homogeneous Japanese identity and contested the limited notions of Korean ethnicity and diaspora.

Prejudice and politics

At the end of the Second World War, approximately two million Koreans lived in Japan, and within seven months of Japan's surrender, around 1,400,000 had returned to the Korean peninsula. For the remaining 600,000, the period from 1945 until the mid-1970s can be described, for the most part, as one in which the zainichi population considered themselves temporary residents in Japan. Although technically still Japanese nationals until 1952, Koreans, Taiwanese and Chinese in Japan were not treated as such; instead they were registered under the 1947 Alien Registration Ordinance (Gaikokujin Tōroku Rei) and differentiated from the majority Japanese population. Strict naturalization processes based on the *jus sanguinis* (nationality according to bloodline) system also prevented many from adopting Japanese nationality. Most Koreans believed that they would inevitably return to the Korean homeland, and that their life in Japan would be only transitory. As argued elsewhere (Chapman 2008), during this period (1945–1970) the relationship between the Japanese state and the zainichi population was dominated 'not only by exclusivist notions of Japanese homogeneity but also by powerful and influential Korean homeland affinity and the internal politics of the zainichi population'. Powerful affinity for the Korean homeland and a determined belief of an eventual return to the united Korean peninsula helped to entrench feelings of temporary residence in Japan.

This period can also be characterized as a time in which Korean nationalism and Korean identity prevailed in the struggle against the legacy of colonial dominance. Partha Chatterjee has pointed out that 'anticolonial nationalism creates its own domain of sovereignty within colonial society well before it begins its political battle with the imperial power'. One way suggested by Chatterjee for this to materialize is through the 'spiritual domain' where cultural identity is preserved (1993: 6). The spiritual domain, Chatterjee continues, contains 'aspects of culture, such as language or religion or the elements of personal and family life ... premised upon a difference between the cultures of the colonizer and the colonized' (1993: 26). Early zainichi resistance reflects

Chatterjee's description of the spiritual domain above, in which anti-colonial strategies underscored the difference between Japanese and Korean culture and were heavily based on maintaining a strong Korean national identity as a core focus in resisting the Japanese state and fighting for liberation.

Such anti-colonial nationalism was further complicated by the Korean War (1950–1953), which resulted in the division of the Korean peninsula into the capitalist South and communist North. This split was reflected in political division within the zainichi population from the early 1950s in which a number of organizations emerged that were affiliated to either North or South Korea. Reflecting Isogai's description of this period as the 'season of politics', numerous organizations were created and disbanded, with two dominant zainichi political groups eventually emerging: the League of Koreans (Zai-Nippon Chōsenjin Renmei or 'Chōren'), which was affiliated with North Korea, and the Korean Resident's Union in Japan (Zai-Nippon Daikan Kyōryū Mindan or 'Mindan'), which was affiliated with South Korea. In contemporary Japan, there are now only two organizations remaining that reflect a North and South divide. These are the General Association of Korean Residents (Zai-Nippon Chōsenjin Sōrengō Kai or 'Sōren'), which was formed in 1955 and is also known in Korean as Chongryun, and Mindan.

The already acrimonious division of Mindan and Sōren intensified when residency rights for the zainichi population were discussed as part of the 1965 normalization of ties between South Korea and Japan. The 1965 Republic of Korea-Japan Normalization Treaty reviewed residency rights, and it facilitated equal access to some welfare benefits and unrestricted access to public education and the public health system for zainichi holding South Korean nationality. This was achieved through a 'special permanent resident' (*tokubetsu eijū*) category for all South Korean residents in Japan.[2] Sōren strongly opposed the Treaty and the special residency category because of the belief that they did not recognize the sovereignty rights of North Korea. Sōren also believed the Treaty was an impediment to the reunification of the peninsula and that it would result in the elimination of ethnic rights for the zainichi (Yang Yong-hu 1994: 209–15). Conversely, Mindan saw these developments as an opportunity to establish the legal position of Koreans in Japan as permanent residents (Pak Kyŏng-sik 1989: 447). Although there were some members in Mindan opposed to the Treaty (Pak 1999: 35), most were in favour. This event divided the zainichi community into those who supported permanent residency and those who opposed it and was one of a number of events that acted as a catalyst for major change.

In 1970, five years after the creation of a special permanent residency status, another significant event occurred that further deepened the divide within the zainichi community. This event involved a zainichi high school graduate from Aichi Prefecture, Pak Chŏng-sŏk, who passed the employment exam for the Japanese electronics company Hitachi. He decided to sit the examination under his Japanese name, Arai Shōji, which he considered to be his 'real' name at the time (Pak Kun o Kakomu Kai 1974: 252).[3] During the process of employment, Hitachi discovered that Pak did not actually have Japanese nationality. The offer of employment was consequently revoked, and Hitachi stated that it did not employ foreigners (Pak Kun o Kakomu Kai 1974: 255).[4] This led to Pak appealing the decision and making complaints against Hitachi. At one stage, Pak and his followers engaged in a sit-in at the company and a public 'denunciation' (*kyūdan*) of Hitachi. In 1974, Pak won his case on all counts in a landmark decision through the Yokohama district court. The victory saw Hitachi conceding racial prejudice in its recruitment practices. Consequently, Pak was accepted for employment with Hitachi as a software systems developer in September 1974.

The majority of support that Pak received was from the second- and third-generation zainichi community. In contrast, many of the older generation zainichi and the political organizations they controlled considered the actions of Pak and his supporters to be inappropriate. Demanding equal employment rights, they believed, was supporting assimilation into Japanese society (Pak Kun o Kakomu Kai 1974: 4–5), and therefore supporting the eventual loss of Korean identity.

Permanence and belonging

As Ang (2003: 142) argues, it is important to recognize the 'double-edgedness of diasporic identity' as a site in which 'support and oppression, emancipation and confinement, solidarity and division' exist side by side. It is this double-edged nature of diaspora identity that led to significant change within the zainichi community from the 1970s through to the end of the 1980s. Although zainichi solidarity provided support and liberation from oppression in Japanese society, it was also a mechanism of suppression and control within the community. Authority and power were mostly in the hands of the first generation and the political organizations they dominated. The effects of such oppression therefore were particularly felt by the younger generation. Often referred to as the period of generational change (*sedai kotai*), the 1970s and early 1980s was a time when the first generation's dominance began to be questioned and resisted. First-generation leadership was being replaced by an emerging second and third generation wishing to express their thoughts and feelings on the future of the zainichi community. The ideology of a displaced diaspora began to be replaced by a discourse of belonging and permanence.

Perhaps the best-known public comment on this change was Kim Tong-myung's articulation of a 'Third Way' (1988).[5] The Third Way was a hybrid stance located in the interstices between a homogeneous national Japanese identity and a closely protected diasporic Korean national identity. Many second- and third-generation Japan-born zainichi believed the Third Way symbolized both liberation from being either Korean or Japanese and an alternative and independent path that would allow for other possibilities. In particular, the younger generation felt frustrated by first-generation control and domination. The Third Way discussion made the feelings of many of the younger generation zainichi public for the first time.

Subsequent to the emergence of the Third Way were numerous debates and discussions for and against such change. Naturally many of the first generation, with concerns about assimilation and the dilution of Korean identity, were opposed to such new directions. Opposition also came from some second-generation individuals who felt that the severing of ties with the homeland of Korea and a distancing from Korean-ness would adversely affect the struggle against Japanese oppression (Kang Sang-jung, 1988). Kang Sang-jung saw the situation in the 1980s as 'zainichi as method' (*'hōhō toshite no zainichi'*), in which resistance to Japanese authority was facilitated by emphasizing difference and maintaining a strong link with Korea. Contrary to this was the approach adopted by Yang Tae-ho, who saw the zainichi as members of Japanese society and belonging in Japan. He referred to this approach as 'zainichi as reality' (*'jijitsu toshite no zainichi'*) (Yang 1988). Yang adopted an approach that was critical of links to the Korean homeland and was in favor of a closer alignment with Japanese society, somewhat similar to Kim's Third Way.

Reflecting an in-Japan-ness (Ryang 1998: 5) that Yang and many of the younger generation were adopting, the 1980s became a period where an increasingly bottom-up approach to activism surfaced. This was in contrast to the hitherto top-down dominance of zainichi political organizations (Pak 1999: 69–70). The feeling of in-Japan-ness for the second and third generation was perhaps at the core of the drive for generational change and a movement away from the confines of homeland attachment. Breaking away from first-generation dominance and the emergence of feelings of belonging and permanency in Japan eventually changed the relationship between the zainichi and the Japanese state. As active members of a community in which they felt they belonged, the zainichi began to focus on civil rights, addressing issues of inequity and marginalization that affected them as rightful residents of Japan.

Rights and wrongs

In 1952, the San Francisco Peace Treaty (San Furansushiko Kōwa Jōyaku) established Korea's independence from any claim of title by Japan. However, far from being a positive outcome for the zainichi, the Treaty led to Japanese nationality being revoked for all former colonial subjects living in Japan. Instead, they fell under the legislative control of the Alien Registration Law (Gaikokujin Tōroku Hō) and the Immigration Control Law (Shutsunyūkoku Kanri Hō). This meant that those who could not naturalize, by far the majority, had little rights as citizens and a very insecure residency status that could see them deported as 'undesirables' at any time. Registration was enforced by law, with severe penalties for those who did not undergo the process. In 1955, as part of the procedure in alien registration, a system of fingerprinting (*shimon ōnatsu seido*) was introduced.

Throughout the 1980s, the fight of the younger generation against the wrongs of legislative exclusion and for the right to access these benefits was thus focused mostly on the legal status (*hōteki chii*) of zainichi. In particular, the areas of concern were inequities associated with political representation (*sanseiken*), limited access to welfare, restrictions in public service employment (*kōmu shūnin ken*) and the fingerprinting of 'non-Japanese' residents in the processes of 'alien' registration. A number of factors influenced these struggles, for example, the involvement of significant numbers of Japanese nationals who were also opposed to such social marginalisation, as well as the pressure from the international community monitoring how Japan treated Indo-Chinese refugees arriving on Japanese shores from Vietnam, Cambodia and Laos around the late 1970s and early 1980s. As a result of this outside pressure, Japan ratified the International Covenant on Economic, Social and Cultural Rights and the International Covenant on Civil and Political Rights in 1979. In 1982, Japan also ratified the United Nations Refugee Convention. In ratifying this convention, Japan was obligated to remove the nationality clause (*kokuseki jōkō*) from the national pension law and from three child allowance laws (Takao 2003: 527, 538). The removal of the nationality clause in this legislation essentially provided access to these welfare benefits for the zainichi community.

The struggle that began in the late 1970s and early 1980s was fundamentally a fight for rights as contributing citizens (*shiminken*) of Japan rather than simply as temporary foreign residents. Access to welfare options through the removal of the nationality clause was the first step in gaining rights as permanent members of Japanese society. It was also a step forward in broadening the definition of what constitutes a Japanese citizen. The struggle thus changed from one against Japanese society to one from within Japanese society, reflecting the growing emergence of zainichi hybrid subjectivity. This approach began to interrogate notions of Japanese citizenship and its close nexus with nationality and ethnicity. The distance between the zainichi and Japanese communities and the feelings of displacement of the first generation were slowly being replaced by closer alliances with the majority Japanese community and feelings of permanency and belonging.

The Japanese Constitution has been particularly targeted by the zainichi community as a conduit in legislatively ensuring an inextricable nexus between nationality and citizenship. In the past, the link between nationality and ethnicity was also protected by strict conditions on naturalization. Nowadays, although the process has become much easier, naturalization is still a step that many zainichi are not prepared to take. Instead, many still believe that rather than naturalizing to gain full access to civil rights, the interpretation of the Constitution and what constitutes a Japanese citizen needs to be reassessed so that long-term foreign residents have the same privileges as Japanese nationals. The contention lies with the interpretation of the term '*kokumin*', used to describe 'the people of Japan' in the Japanese Constitution. For many zainichi, this term is limited to interpreting the people of Japan as those holding Japanese nationality, not those who are classed as foreign residents. Even though most zainichi have been born and educated in Japan, speak only Japanese and believe Japan to be their home, their presumed status is that of a foreigner. In fact, according to Koseki Shoichi (1988: 235–6), the term *kokumin* was originally substituted for the English translation of 'all people' (*subete no kokumin*) so as to deprive all non-Japanese citizens, especially former colonial subjects such as the Korean and Chinese, from holding constitutional rights (also refer to Hook and McCormack 2001: 6).

Alien registration and fingerprinting

All long-term residents in Japan are recorded on one of two systems of registration. Japanese nationals and naturalized Japanese are placed on a family register called the *koseki*, and non-nationals are entered in the alien registration system (*gaikokujin tōrokushō*).[6] Through these national registration systems and the accompanying legislation, 'alien' and 'Japanese' residents in Japan are clearly differentiated.

Alien registration was introduced in 1952, and in April 1955 fingerprinting (*shimon ōnatsu seido*) became a requirement for all foreign residents once they turned 16 years of age. All residents holding foreign passports were required to register and be fingerprinted every three years.[7] Zainichi activism in the 1980s and early 1990s tried to address the problems inherent in alien registration and, in particular, in the contentious issue of fingerprinting. The most serious contention was the close association of fingerprinting with criminal activity. In 1980, Han Jong-seok, a first-generation Korean resident, was the first to refuse to be fingerprinted because he believed this to be a form of racial or ethnic prejudice. Soon after this initial protest, others followed suit, and in less than five years more than a hundred zainichi had refused to be fingerprinted (Pak Il 1999: 53–4). Although the zainichi community led these protests, by 1985 more people had joined, and the total number of protesters refusing to be fingerprinted grew to over 10,000.

Refusing to be fingerprinted was not a decision to be made lightly. Those who joined this growing movement faced imprisonment and other harsh penalties. This prospect forced Kang Sang-jung, introduced above, to eventually submit to fingerprinting. When Kang joined the protests in the early 1980s, he was the first zainichi in the prefecture of Saitama to resist being fingerprinted. However, once he discovered that he was soon to become a parent, he became concerned about how his impending imprisonment would affect his family (Kang and Morisu 2002: 131–4). The protest of zainichi and foreign residents against this unfair system eventually led to changes in which fingerprinting was abolished and replaced by a signature. Special permanent residents were the first to benefit in 1993, and eventually in March 1999 the fingerprinting requirement for all foreign residents was amended. Despite these amendments, however, other aspects of the alien registration system remain unchanged. For example, penalties for failing to register remain harsh, with the prospect of criminal charges a possibility. It is also still a requirement that alien registration cards be carried at all times.

The protests in the 1980s and 1990s against the alien registration system were clearly led by the younger second- and third-generation zainichi, reflecting the generational change that began in the 1970s (Jung Yeong-hae 1996: 11). The fact that it took around 30 years for these protests to gain such momentum demonstrates the dominance of the first-generation over the zainichi community and the pervasiveness of the ideology of a displaced diaspora foreseeing an eventual return to the homeland. The younger generation's notions of permanence and belonging in Japanese society also highlighted their membership of and contribution to Japanese society as participating citizens with a stake in its future.

Political representation

From 1925, as Japanese subjects, Korean men residing in Japan had the right to vote and to stand for candidacy in national and local elections. However, according to Suh Yong-dal (2001: 149), soon after Japan's defeat in the Second World War the Speaker of the House of Representatives, Kiyose Ichiro, who wanted to keep the emperor system intact, insisted that Koreans be excluded from political participation.[8] As a result, a ruling was made that only those on the family register (*koseki*) were allowed political representation. Koreans were never allowed to register on the Japanese *koseki*; during annexation they were registered on another *koseki* that contained the names of *gaiichijin* (outsiders). The *koseki* for Japanese nationals retained the names of *naiichijin* (insiders). Thus all Korean males with Korean nationality in Japan lost the right for political representation and any form of suffrage at the war's end (Kim T'ae-gi 1997: 222–3).[9] Although Chōren demanded the reinstatement of suffrage for Koreans in Japan soon after this ruling, it was not until the 1980s that the cause was again taken up by the zainichi. Similar to protests against the alien registration system, rights for political representation (*sanseiken*) became a concern for the younger generation.

The modern movement for political representation (*sanseiken undō*) began when the National Council for Combating Discrimination against Ethnic Peoples (Minzoku Sabetsu Tatakau Renraku Kyō gikai or 'Mintōren') highlighted the necessity of voting rights for Japan's permanent resident community in 1987 (Pak Il 1999: 63). In the same year, Mindan also underscored the basis of further protest: the contradiction between a lack of right to political representation and the obligation to pay taxes as residents in Japan (Pak Il 1999: 64). In other words, the call was for 'no taxation without representation', reminiscent of the American War of Independence and other social movements hence. According to the Committee for the Protection of the Human Rights of Koreans in Japan, at the centre of the *zainichi* enfranchisement argument have been notions of permanency and regional-level belonging, as well as limitations created as a result of restrictive legislation. The committee claims that the debates on legislation have focused on the Japanese Constitution, local government laws and international human rights conventions, whilst notions of belonging in the local community have concentrated on tax obligations (1996: 191).

Despite the Supreme Court stating in February 1995 that under Article 8 in the Japanese Constitution local voting rights for foreigners were not illegal (Kajita 1996: 107; Jung Yeong-hae 1999: 28; Kondo 2001: 23), long-term foreign residents, permanent residents and special permanent residents still do not have the right to suffrage or political representation at a federal level. In some municipalities, however, there have been changes in which foreign residents have been granted the right to plebiscite voting regarding local issues, and according to Kondo (2001: 27), there is strong public support for the granting of electoral rights to foreign residents.

In order to obtain the right for national-level suffrage, however, naturalization is still necessary. Naturalization would allow enfranchisement in line with all other Japanese nationals. Although for special permanent residents the process of naturalization has become much easier, as we explain below, consideration of such a step is not simply limited to the process of administrative procedure. Other far-ranging issues still make the decision to naturalize difficult for many.

Public-service employment

Although the Hitachi case introduced above did much to draw attention to the issue of employment discimination and to expose the discriminatory practices of private companies, the problem of employment discrimination against zainichi still exists in Japanese society today. The problem still lies with the nationality clause, because it precludes non-nationals in Japan from many positions in public-service employment. Some public-service positions, however, have had nationality requirements revised. For example, public-service teaching positions came under revision in 1991 when Prime Minister Kaifu visited South Korea and signed a memorandum of the Japanese–South Korean Agreement (Nikkan Kyōtei Oboegaki). Article 4 of the Agreement stated that Japan would broaden the opportunities for zainichi wanting to be employed as teachers in Japanese public schools so that they were in line with 'Japanese' nationals. Furthermore, in 1996 the Ministry of Home Affairs altered the nationality clause in local government hiring laws, and in April 1997 Kobe and Yokohama removed the nationality clause on employment exams, allowing foreigners to sit these tests (Gurowitz 1999: 440). These advances have created a type of denizenship (refer to Hammar 1990: 1) in which there have been improvements to the legal status of long-term foreign residents (*teijū gaikokujin*) in Japan but which still falls short of true citizenship status.[10]

Naturalization or assimilation

The fear of the loss of zainichi identity mentioned above is perhaps most strongly reflected in the debate on naturalization (*kika*). Naturalization has been a contentious issue that has created division and tension within the zainichi community for most of the post-war period. It is an issue that has generated much debate and discussion. Such discussion has been continually influenced by frequent changes to Japanese legislation and by the ideas of successive generations of zainichi. For example, even though Kim Tong-myung's Third Way discussions emphasized a new perspective on identity in the 1970s, he still believed that zainichi who naturalized were advocating assimilation (*dōka*) into Japanese society. The easing of the process, he also argued, was leading to the loss of Korean ethnicity (*minzokusei*) (1988: 56).

Historical legacy has generated strong feelings about naturalization because of assimilationist campaigns and policies conducted during Japan's wartime occupation of Korea. These involved efforts at linguistic and legal-institutional assimilation as well as cultural assimilation (Kashiwazaki 2000: 17). Perhaps the most determined and intensive periods of the overall Japanese assimilation campaign were instigated in the late 1930s under *kōminka*, which aimed to turn Koreans and Taiwanese into imperial subjects of the emperor, or *kōmin*. The *kōminka* movement was 'aimed at the complete regimentation and Japanization of Japan's colonial races, and justified these goals through endless moral platitudes couched in Confucian phraseology and centered on inculcation of a sense of obligation to the Japanese Emperor' (Peattie 1984: 121). It also aimed to mobilize the population in support for the war Japan was engaged in (Peattie 1984: 121). As part of the *kōminka* campaign, the policy of *sōshi kaimei* was introduced in 1939. This policy forced Koreans to change their names to Japanese names and register in the *koseki*. The changing of Korean names to Japanese names during *sōshi kaimei* was particularly problematic because of the Korean clan-system structure and its intimate nexus with family names.[11]

Although there are now approximately 9,000 zainichi naturalizing each year, there is still strong resistance within some quarters.[12] Demonstrative of the divergence of opinion on naturalization and attempts at reconciliation is the recent formation of the Committee for Establishing the Right for Zainichi Koreans to Hold Japanese Nationality (Zainichi Korean Nippon Kokuseki Shutokuken Kakuritsu Kyōgikai). This group has called for open discussion on the right of zainichi to acquire Japanese nationality free from its taboo status and its association with assimilation.[13] Placing importance on retaining Korean ethnic and cultural roots, this group has also suggested the use of the term 'Koriankei Nihonjin' (Korean-Japanese). Such a direction underscores the impossibility of notions of an essentialized Japanese identity in the face of increased social diversity.

Another advocate of this approach is Ha Byung-uk (also known as Kawa Heigyoku), who underscores the opportunity for the zainichi community to 'adopt Japanese nationality' and maintain their Korean-ness by becoming 'Kankokukei Nihonjin' (Korean-Japanese) (2001: 334).[14] Ha also emphasizes the importance of maintaining one's Korean name. In the past, legislation dictated that naturalization meant giving up one's Korean name and registering on the *koseki* using official Japanese characters and a Japanese name. Despite a change in 1987 allowing the use of non-official characters, many undergoing the process of naturalization were still coerced by Japanese authorities into using a Japanese name. Nowadays, however, this practice seems less prevalent, and zainichi are able to use their Korean name or even a hybrid name with Japanese and Korean elements when registering on the *koseki*.

CONCLUSION

Lee Kyung-jae refers to another generational change (*sedai kotai*) in the zainichi population, this time a change from the second to the third and fourth generations. He argues, similarly to Isogai (introduced above), that the changes are characterized by increases in naturalization, by intermarriage between zainichi and Japanese and by the tendency for children of such intermarriage to be immediately naturalized after birth. Like Ha above, Lee has called for the retention of Korean roots through supporting naturalization and recognizing that this new direction is a way for zainichi to be accepted as 'members' of Japanese society rather than as 'guests' (Lee 2006a: 32–3). In many ways, Lee, Ha and other advocates of this direction are doing as Kim Tong-myung did in the 1970s; they are promoting the recognition of a hybrid identity. In essence, they believe the recognition of the right to naturalize as Japanese will overcome problems associated with the politics of zainichi identity. Lee sees the positive acceptance of naturalization as contributing to the recognition of a society of multicultural or multiethnic coexistence (*taminzoku/tabunka kyōsei shakai*) in Japan (Lee 2006a: 34). As argued earlier in this chapter, the acceptance of numerous imbrications of hybrid identity is a step forward in overcoming the problems of zainichi identity that have plagued this population since the end of World War Two. Whether this latest movement is successful in achieving what it aims to do or whether it becomes another sphere of political wrangling over what constitutes zainichi identity is yet to be determined.

Notes

1 The term *zainichi* (lit. resident, or residing, in Japan) conventionally refers to long-term Chinese and Korean residents, as opposed to newcomer (post-1945) foreign residents.

2 This category was created with the intention that it would stand only for twenty-five years, with the intention to be revisited after this period. In 1991 the category was confirmed, ensuring access to this status for all descendants of special permanent resident zainichi Koreans.

3 Zainichi often have both an assumed Japanese name (*tsūmei*) and a Korean name (*honmyō*). Although names may seem inconsequential, for most of the zainichi population names are extremely important. In part, having two names has helped to hide one's identity and therefore prevent discriminatory treatment. However, counter arguments for using one's Korean name have increased. Usually this stance argues for taking pride in one's background, and it is often a form of agency against discrimination and prejudice.

4 Even though Pak was born and educated in Japan, he was considered a foreigner because of his Korean nationality. At this time there was also a system in place in which examinations for employment in local government positions were limited to Japanese nationals only. (Kim Tae-young 1999: 117).

5 For a more detailed discussion of the Third Way refer to Chapman (2004).

6 Alien registration is a requirement for all non-nationals staying longer than three months.

7 In 1980 the requirement was extended to every five years.

8 As part of the emperor system in Japan, families were registered on the *koseki*

with the father as designated head of the family unit. This is referred to as the '*ie*' system, and it has been critiqued as patriarchal and as a vehicle for reproducing cultural symbols facilitating pre-war nationalism and the notion of the emperor as the father of the nation state, who is genealogically linked to all citizens.

9　Korean women in Japan have never had any right to suffrage at any stage. This is despite Japanese women gaining such rights in 1945.

10　Denizens, according to Hammar (1990), are residents who have legal and permanent residence but do not have the same status as citizens.

11　For more detail on the Korean clan system and the effect of *sōshi kaimei*, refer to Fukuoka (2000: 5–7).

12　The Ministry of Justice provides a figure of 8,531 for 2006, a decline from the 2003 figure of 11,778 (Ministry of Justice 2006).

13　This committee was formed in Tokyo in 2004 by Lee Kyung-jae, the head of the Mukuge Group (Lee 2006b: 53–72).

14　Ha is avoiding the term naturalization (*kika*) here because of its historical legacy and association with assimilation.

References

Akiyama, O. (1929) 'Senjin Rōdōsha to Shitsugyō Mondai', *Shakai Seisaku Jihō*, 111: 96–120.

Ang, I. (2003) 'Together-in-Difference: Beyond diaspora, into hybridity', *Asian Studies Review*, 27, 2: 141–54.

Anthias, F. (1998) 'Evaluating "Diaspora": Beyond ethnicity?', *Sociology*, 32: 557–80.

Breuilly, J. (1993) *Nationalism and the State*, second edition, Manchester: Manchester University Press.

Chapman, D. (2004) 'The Third Way and Beyond: Zainichi Korean identity and the politics of belonging', *Japanese Studies*, 24, 1: 29–44.

—— (2008) *Zainichi Korean Identity and Ethnicity*, London: Routledge.

Chatterjee, P. (1993) *Nationalist Thought and the Colonial World: A derivative discourse*, Minnesota: University of Minnesota Press.

Chōsenjin no Hibakusha (1989): see Nagasaki Zainichi Chōsenjin no Jinken wo Mamorukai (ed.).

Committee for the Protection of the Human Rights of Koreans in Japan (1996) *The White Paper on the Human Rights of Koreans in Japan*, Tokyo: Chōsen Seinensha.

Dower, J. (1993) 'Peace and Democracy in Two Systems: External policy and internal conflict', in

Fukuoka, Y. (2000) *Lives of Young Koreans in Japan*, Melbourne: Transpacific Press.

Furedi, S. (ed.) (1991) *Mythical Past Elusive Future, History and Society in an Anxious Age*, London: Pluto Press.

Gluck, C. (1993) 'The Past in the Present', in A. Gordon (ed.) *Postwar Japan as History*, Berkeley and Los Angeles: University of California Press.

Gordon, A. (ed.) *Postwar Japan as History*, Berkeley and Los Angeles: University of California Press.

Gurowitz, A. (1999) 'Mobilizing International Norms: Domestic actors, immigrants and the Japanese state', *World Politics*, 51, 3: 413–45.

Ha, Byung-uk. (2001) *Dai-yon no Sentaku: Kankokukei Nihonjin sekai roppyakuman kanminzoku no ikizama to kokuseki* (The Fourth Choice: Korean-Japanese? The lifestyle and nationality of the six million ethnic Koreans from around the world), Tokyo: Bungeisha.

Hammar, T. (1990) *Democracy and the Nation State: Aliens, denizens and citizens in a world of international migration*, Aldershot: Avebury.

Harada, T. and Kang, J. (eds) (1985) *Sabetsu to Jinken (4) Minzoku*, Tokyo: Yūzankaku.

Harajiri, H. (1989) *Zainichi Chōsenjin no Seikatsu Sekai*, Tokyo: Kōbundo.

Holloway, N. (1989) 'Curriculum Conflict', *Far Eastern Economic Review*, 23 March: 29.

Hook, G. and McCormack, G. (2001) *Japan's Contested Constitution: Documents and analysis*, London: Routledge.

Ikutaro, S. (1980) 'The Nuclear Option: Japan be a state', *Japan Echo*, 7, 3: 33–45.

Isogai, Jirō. (2004) *Zainichi Bungakuron* (Studies in Zainichi Literature), Tokyo: Shinkansha.

Ito, T. (1987) *Genbaku Kimin: Kankoku, Chōsenjin no Shōgen*, Tokyo: Harubu Shuppan.

—— (1988) *Genbaku Hibakusha no Hanseiki*, Iwanami Bukkuretto 116, Tokyo: Iwanami Shōten.

Johnson, C. (1986) 'The Patterns of Japanese Relations with China 1952–1982', *Pacific Affairs*, 59, 3: 402–28.

Jung, Yeong-hae (1996) 'Aidentitii o Koete' (Beyond Identity), in J. Inoue, M. Ozawa, M. Mita and T. Yoshimi (eds), *Sabetsu to Kyōsei no Shakaigaku* (Sociology of Prejudice and Co-Existence), Tokyo: Iwanami Shoten, 1–34.

—— (1999) 'Kokumin Shuken Genri to Teijū Gaikokujin no Sanseiken: Kindai kokka toshite Nihon to zainichi Chōsenjin no shuchō' (The Sovereignty of the People and the Suffrage for Permanent Resident Foreigners: Japan as a modern nation and the claim of the resident Koreans), *Korian Mainoriti Kenkyū*, 2: 25–39.

Kajita, Takamichi (1996) 'Gaikokujin Sanseiken: Seiōno keiken to Nihon ni okeru kanōsei' (The Suffrage of Foreigners: Experience in the West and the possibilities in Japan), in Miyajima Takashi and Kajita Takamichi (eds), *Gaikokujin Rōdōsha kara Shimin e: Chiiki shakai no shiten to kadai kara* (From Foreign Laborer to Citizen: from the viewpoint and theme of the local society), Tokyo: Yūbikaku.

Kang, Sang-jung. (1988) 'Zainichi no Genzai to Mirai no Aida' (Between the Korean Resident's Present and Future), in J. Iinuma (ed.), *Zainichi Kankoku Chōsenjin: Sono Nihon ni okeru sonzaikachi* (Resident Koreans in Japan: The value in their existence in Japan), Tokyo: Kaifūsha, 249–61.

Kang, Sang-jung and Morisu, Hiroshi (2002) *Nashonarizumu no Kokufuku* (The Conquest of Nationalism), Tokyo: Shūeisha Shinsho.

Kashiwazaki, C. (2000) 'The Politics of Legal Status: The equation of nationality with ethnonational identity', in S. Ryang (ed.), *Koreans in Japan: Critical voices from the margin*, London: Routledge, 13–31.

Kim, C.J. (1977) *Kaze no Dōkoku, Zainichi Chōsenjin Jokō no Seikatsu to Rekishi*, Tokyo: Tahata Shōten.

Kim, T'ae-gi (1997) *Sengo Nihon Seiji to Zainichi Chōsenjin Mondai: SCAP no tai zainichi Chōsenjin seisaku 1945–1952 nen* (Post-war Japanese Politics and the Resident Korean Problem: SCAP policies on the resident Koreans 1945–1952), Tokyo: Keiso Shobo.

Kim, Tae-young, (1999) *Aidentitii Poritikkusu o Koete: Zainichi Chōsenjin no esunishiti* (Beyond Identity Politics: The ethnicity of resident Koreans in Japan), Tokyo: Akashi Shoten.

Kim, Tong-myung (1988) 'Zainichi Chōsenjin no "Daisan no Michi"' (The 'Third Way' of Resident Koreans in Japan), in J. Iinuma (ed.), *Chōsenjin: sono Nihon ni okeru sonzaikachi* (Resident Koreans in Japan: the value in their existence in Japan), Tokyo: Kaifūsha, 21–86.

Kondo, A. (2001) 'Citizenship Rights for Aliens in Japan', in A. Kondo (ed.), *Citizenship in a Global World: Comparing citizenship rights for aliens*, New York: Palgrave, 8–30.

Kōseishō (1950) *Hikiage Engo no Kiroku*, Tokyo: Ministry of Welfare.

Koseki, S. (1988) 'Japanizing the Constitution', *Japan Quarterly*, 35, 3: 234–40.

Kosho, T. (1991) 'Chōsenjin Kyōsei Renkō Meibo Chōsa wa Naze Susumanaika', *Sekai*, September: 108–15.

Lee, Kyung-jae, (2006a) 'Zainichi Korian no Nihon Kokuseki Shutokuken Kakuritsu Kyogikai Setsuritsu no Keii' (The Latitude and Longtitude of the Establishment of the Committee for the Protection of the Human Rights of Koreans in Japan), in T. Sasaki (ed.), *Zainichi Korian ni Kenri toshite no Nihon Kokuseki wo* (Japanese Nationality as a Right for Zainichi Koreans), Tokyo: Akashi Shoten, 31–8.

—— (2006b) Zainichi Kankoku Chōsenjin to Kokuseki (Zainichi Koreans and Nationality), in T. Sasaki (ed.), *Zainichi Korian ni Kenri toshite no Nihon Kokuseki wo* (Japanese Nationality as a Right for Zainichi Koreans), Tokyo: Akashi Shoten, 53–72.

Lifton, R.J. and Markusen, E. (1990) *The Genocidal Mentality*, New York: Basic Books.

Ministry of Justice (2006) *Kokuseki Kankei* (In Relation to Nationality). Online. Available online at http:// www.moj.go.jp/TOUKEI/t_minj03.html (accessed July 5, 2007).

Nagasaki Zainichi Chōsenjin no Jinken wo Mamorukai (ed.) (1989) *Chōsenjin no Hibakusha: Nagasaki kara no Shōgen*, Tokyo: Shakai Hyōronsha. Cited as *Chōsenjin no Hibakusha* 1989.

Nakahara, M. (1990) 'Tōnan Ajia no me ni Haetta Nihon', *Sekai*, 544: 125–39.

Osaka-shi, Shakai-bu, Chōsa-ka. (1924) *Chōsenjin Rōdōsha Mondai*, Osaka.

Osaka-shi, Shakai-bu, Rōdō-ka. (1933) 'Shakai-bu Hōkoku Dai 177', *Chōsenjin Rōdōsha no Kinkyō*, Osaka.

Pak, Il. (1999) *Zainichi to iu Ikikata: Sai to byōdō no jirenma* (Life as a Zainichi: The dilemma of difference and equality), Tokyo: Kodansha.

Pak Kun o Kakomu Kai (1974) *Minzoku Sabetsu: Hitachi shushoku sabetsu kyūdan* (Ethnic Prejudice: Denunciation of employment prejudice at Hitachi), Tokyo: Aki Shobō.

Pak, Kyŏng-sik (1989) *Kaihōgo: Zainichi chōsenjin undōshi* (After Liberation: The history of resident Korean movements), Tokyo: Sanichi Shobō.

Peattie, M. (1984) 'Japanese Attitudes Towards Colonialism', in Ramon H. Myers and Mark R. Peattie (eds), *The Japanese Colonial Empire, 1895–1945*, Princeton, NJ: Princeton University Press.

Ryang, S. (1998) 'Inscribed (Men's) Bodies, Silent (Women's) Words: Rethinking colonial displacement of Koreans in Japan', *Bulletin of Concerned Asian Authors*, 30, 4: 3–15.

Ryu, D.O. (1991) 'Zainichi Chōsenjin no Shogu Kaizen to wa Dono yō na Koto ka', *Sekai*, January: 248–60.

Sakai, T. (1931) 'Chōsenjin Rōdōsha Mondai (2)', *Shakai Jigyō Kenkyū*, July: 115–36.
Sato, A. and Yamada T. (1986) *Zainichi Chōsenjin – Rekishi to Genjō*, Tokyo: Akashi, Shōten.
Shimizu, M. (1994) 'Sengo Hoshō no Kokusai Hikaku', *Sekai*, February: 133–43.
So, K.S. (1989) *Kominka Seisaku kara Shimon Onatsu made*, Iwanami Bukkuretto 128, Tokyo: Iwanami Shōten.
Suh Yong-dal. (2001) 'Naze Ima Teijūgaikokujin no Chihō Sanseiken' (Why Permanent Foreign Residents Now?), *Ushio*, 503: 148–53.
Takao, Y. (2003) 'Foreigners' Rights in Japan: Beneficiaries to participants', *Asian Survey*, XLIII, 3, 527–52.
Takasaki, S. (1994) 'Nihon wa Nani wo shita ka, Nani wo Utaerarete iru ka: Kankoku, kita chōsen', *Sekai*, February: 144–49.
Tanaka, H. (1993) *Zainichi Gaikokujin*, Tokyo: Iwanami Shinsho.
—— (1994) 'Nihon wa Sensō Sekinin ni: Dō taishite kita ka', *Sekai*, February: 122–32.
Weiner, M. (1994) *Race and Migration in Imperial Japan*, London and New York: Routledge.
Won, J.G. (1986) *Zainichi Chōsenjin no Seikatsu to Jinken*, Tokyo: Dōseisha.
Yamamoto, T. (1991) 'Shokuminchi Shihai wa Seitō datta no ka', *Sekai*, November: 315–23.
Yang, Tae-ho. (1988) 'Jijitsu Toshite no Zainichi: Kang Sang-jung shi e no gimon' (The Zainichi as Reality: Doubt toward Kang Sang-jung), in J. Iinuma (ed.), *Zainichi Kankoku Chōsenjin: Sono Nihon ni okeru sonzaikachi* (Resident Koreans in Japan: The value in their existence in Japan), Tokyo: Kaifūsha, 263–74.
Yang, Yong-hu. (1994) *Sengo Osaka no Chōsenjin Undō* (The Post-War Korean Movement in Osaka), Tokyo: Miraisha.
Yi, S.K. (1979) *Hibaku Chōsenjin Mondai to (Chōhikyō)*, Tokyo: Rōdō Junposha.

Newspapers

Asahi Shinbun, May 18, 1988.
Asahi Shinbun, May 31, 1988.
Asahi Shinbun, May 18, 1990.
Asahi Shinbun, July 16, 1990.
Asahi Shinbun, August 9, 1990.
Asahi Shinbun, September 25, 1991.
Asahi Shinbun, November 29, 1991.
Asahi Shinbun, August 6, 1992.
Asahi Shinbun, August 13, 1992.
Asahi Shinbun, August 3, 1993.
Asahi Shinbun, August 20, 1993.
Asahi Shinbun, February 5, 1994.
Kobe Shinbun, July 7, 1990.
Kobe Shinbun, July 8, 1990.
Mainichi Shinbun, October 25, 1986.
Mainichi Shinbun, August 6, 1988.
Mainichi Shinbun, February 24, 1989.
Mainichi Shinbun, August 5, 1990.
Mainichi Shinbun, August 15, 1990.

Mainichi Shinbun, December 10, 1991.
Mainichi Shinbun, February 18, 1992.
Mainichi Shinbun, February 24, 1993.
Nagasaki Shinbun, May 9, 1991.
Ryukyu Shinpo, December 7, 1991.
Sankei Shinbun, August 11, 1993.
Yomiuri Shinbun, August 2, 1986.
Yomiuri Shinbun, August 9, 1990.

9 Okinawa, ambivalence, identity, and Japan

Matthew Allen[1]

Okinawa has long been contested territory. Formerly an independent kingdom known since the thirteenth century as the Ryūkyū Ōkoku (Ryūkyū Kingdom), its nationhood status was totally compromised in 1609 when the Satsuma daimyo (feudal lord) of southern Japan invaded the nation. The aim of the daimyo was to secure trading rights for his own southern Japanese fiefdom in an era of encroaching national coherence and isolationism in Japan proper. Although in reality controlled by representatives of Satsuma, the Ryūkyū King formally ruled until 1879, and in keeping with the mandate of Satsuma's demands and Ryūkyū's traditions, the Ryūkyū Kingdom retained its trading, religious, and cultural ties with China. Following Japan's modernization in the late nineteenth century, the Satsuma arrangement was rendered moot when the Meiji state formally annexed the Ryūkyūs and renamed the island chain Okinawa Prefecture. A governor was appointed to administer the islands; Japanese was introduced as the lingua franca; Japanese education, military, and agricultural practices were imposed; and Okinawans were encouraged to improve their sugar cane production through low-cost government loans.

Throughout the early twentieth century, Okinawa remained a Japanese prefecture, albeit the least developed, lagging behind mainland Japanese in standards of living, education, literacy and health. Nominally a prefecture, it was more like a colonial possession. Tragically for Okinawans, it was not until the Battle of Okinawa in May 1945 that they truly understood the nature of their relationship with mainland Japan. Okinawa became a battleground and its citizens largely an impediment to the Imperial Army's confrontation with the US military. The Japanese military's uncompromising stance on civilians and its encouragement of villagers to commit mass suicide rather than fall into enemy hands were responsible for many thousands of Okinawan deaths. In total, between one-quarter and one-third of all Okinawans lost their lives in this most violent conflict. Under the terms of Japan's surrender, Okinawa became a US military territory, a status it retained until its reversion to

Japanese rule in 1972. Subsequently, while Okinawa has once more become a prefecture of Japan, it is perhaps best known today for the proliferation of US military bases and service personnel on the main island and for the conflicts generated by their collective presence.

Although the contemporary rhetoric of resistance to US bases in Okinawa is housed in the language of partnership – that is, Okinawans are a part of Japan, therefore it is unfair that they carry a massively disproportionate burden of the US military presence in Japan – most resistance simultaneously employs ideas of Okinawa's historical difference from Japan and China and the concepts of interrupted cultural evolution, colonization, and exploitation by both Japan and the United States.[2] But, although there are powerful anti-war and anti-American messages employed in the protests, there is little sense of a need for independence from Japan. Rather, protesters demand first that the Japanese state act politically on Okinawans' behalf, and second that further economic support from Tokyo should be forthcoming, as compensation for the bases, the accidents, and the environmental devastation that has taken place since 1945.[3] Such rhetoric illustrates the ambivalence of identity in contemporary Okinawa. Protesters such as Chibana believe that, on one hand, the Japanese state should support and compensate Okinawa for the damage caused to it (as a distinct and separate cultural, if not political, entity), and on the other, it is Japan's duty to bring Okinawa's standards of living into line with all other prefectures in Japan (as part of Japan).[4]

However, although such political actions are conducted within the context of Okinawa–Japan and Okinawa–US relations, the focus on the 'base problem' (*kichi mondai*) elides much of the complexity that underscores the production and reinvention of identity within Okinawa today. The anti-base protests employ popularly shared signifiers. Many Okinawans have experienced fall-out from the bases – airplane accidents, car accidents, violent crimes, noise pollution, chemical spills, and environmental damage – and particularly galling to many Okinawans is the restriction of access to one-fifth of their land, including the richest lands on the main island, as the bases are enclaves of privilege for foreigners.[5] Moreover, the shared perception of their exposure to military actions or reactions from the United States' enemies provokes outrage within Okinawa, which sacrificed so many in a battle between the two powers who have sanctioned the continuation of the bases on their land.[6] In opposing the bilateral exploitation of the prefecture, quite understandably, protesters have placed the concept of Okinawa at the forefront of resistance movements. Yet there is considerable political, cultural, historical, and linguistic diversity within Okinawa; linguistically, the diversity within the Ryūkyūs is, in fact, so substantial that people from one part of the archipelago are unable to understand the speech of people from other parts if they employ their local dialect.[7] It is true, though, that the overwhelming majority of Okinawans also speak a version of hyojungo, or standard Japanese, albeit commonly with an Okinawan accent.

Just as it has been demonstrated that Japan is a multicultural society,[8] so, too, I think it can be argued that Okinawa is literally multicultural in the sense that there are many cultures within the Ryūkyū Islands that interact today. Indeed, even the substantial presence of the US marines and their families contributes to this phenomenon. This is not to suggest that within Okinawa today there are enduring, static cultural forms that remain set in opposition to each other, but rather to recognize that difference within the prefecture is as relevant to the people who live there as the idea that the prefecture en masse represents a single, collective identity of all Okinawans. While it is fair to say that 'Okinawa' as an identity in opposition to the identities of 'Japan' and 'the United States' is a legitimate marker of shared values and political exploitation, there is still a need to go beyond the political manifestation of Japanese and American exigencies and ask questions about where identity is located within Okinawa. In order to situate the multivocality of contemporary Okinawa in context, I believe it is useful to first attempt to locate Okinawa within time and space. This is because the tripartite political relationship – the Okinawan prefectural government, the Japanese government, and the US government and military – has deeply influenced and still influences the nature of emerging Okinawan identities.[9]

As Julia Yonetani has demonstrated, ambivalence of identity was part of the process of being Okinawan in the late nineteenth century.[10] Neither of nor not of the Japanese center, Okinawans struggled to come to terms with a sense of who they were. Unlike Benedict Anderson's (1995) formulation of the imagined community with its elastic but finite boundaries, Okinawa's boundaries have been wrapped in the embrace of empire since the late nineteenth century, its former nationalist incarnation rendered a part of the frontier of Japan, its language, culture, and history relegated to a footnote in the history of Japan before 1945. However, while the political masters may have changed, a sense of a 'communal' of 'Okinawan-ness' has underscored political and social relations within the prefecture since its federation into the Japanese state in 1879. That this identity as Okinawans conflicted with the identity imposed upon them as members of the Japanese empire – albeit on the periphery of empire – is not surprising. Nor is it surprising that ambivalence about identity is one of the more defining aspects of the 'Okinawan issue' (*Okinawa mondai*) today.

Today, Okinawa is a prefecture of Japan, as it has been since the final decades of the nineteenth century and for three-quarters of the twentieth century. However, while Japanese warlords were attempting to unite Japan under one sword in the fifteenth and sixteenth centuries, Okinawa (or as it was known then, the Ryūkyū Kingdom), was conducting peaceful diplomatic and trading relations with China and many South East Asian nations, a situation that had matured in the fifteenth century to include a tributary relationship with China. In fact, since the fourteenth century Okinawa had been incorporated into a single kingdom, eventually under the auspices of the Chinese state. It had an established aristocracy (the *aji*), a long history of education and cultural connections with China, a well-established network of trading relations with China and many East and South East Asian nations, and a complex religious and political network throughout the island chain, which served the interests of the throne. Ruled by a king located in Shuri – today's Naha – the Ryūkyū Kingdom became a tributary state of China. While the king ruled over secular affairs, his sister ruled over religious matters in a system that mimicked the secular rule. That is, the high priestess, located in Shuri, presided over a nationwide structure of religious practitioners (almost exclusively women) named *kaminchu* (literally 'god people'), who had regional control over the religious lives of their constituents. In effect, men ruled the political sphere, while women controlled the religious lives of Ryūkyūans.

After the Satsuma domain invaded the Ryūkyūs in 1609, it allowed the king to retain his title, and encouraged the continuation of the relationship with China. This relationship enabled Satsuma to engage covertly in trade with China and other nations, enjoying the trading privileges of the Ryūkyū Kingdom within the Chinese-controlled trade routes. While the Tokugawa shogunate closed most of Japan's borders from early in the seventeenth century, and restricted much of its trade to the island of Deshima, where Dutch and Chinese traders were based, Satsuma managed to continue to trade with outsiders through the agency of the Ryūkyūs.

Political tensions between Japan and China saw the Satsuma domain decide to keep secret from the Chinese their control of the Ryūkyūs, hence within the kingdom no direct Japanese influence was to be made apparent. Many of the strong Chinese influences that had preceded the seventeenth century were retained – Confucianism, Chinese dress, trading practices, writing, and class and marriage practices, for example. However, the inherent ambivalence of the rulers toward their subjects made their existence an interesting exercise in identity manipulation. This situation was compounded by intermittent dictates from reformers within the governments of the kings, demanding, for example, more commitment to Chinese customs and the elimination of base and primitive practices (such as shamanism and fortune-telling).[11] Throughout this period of Japanese political control, the deception that Ryūkyū was an independent kingdom was maintained for Chinese consumption, and, to a large extent, for consumption among Ryūkyūans – in particular, the elite in Shuri.

The annexation of the kingdom in 1879, and the social and political upheavals that followed, created further waves of ambivalence with respect to Ryūkyūan identity. The name 'Ryūkyū' was replaced with 'Okinawa,' discursively removing the newly formed prefecture from its historical identification, and imposing a new set of identifying standards. No longer even putatively an independent and cosmopolitan society, Ryūkyū was transformed in Japanese consciousness into a relatively backward, linguistically inept, impoverished, resource-poor periphery of the expanding Japanese frontier.[12] From the outset marginalized as the inhabitants of an outlying province of the 'new' imperial Japan, Okinawans struggled to accommodate the social and linguistic changes that were pressed upon them. Throughout the twentieth century, Okinawa lagged behind mainland Japan in education, health care, standards of living, economic development, and political leadership. Japan's 'assimilation' program slowly introduced Okinawans to the artifacts of modernization – electricity, telegraph, steam, and the development of an urban proletariat, reflecting the changes that were taking place in the main islands of Japan. At the same time, the state introduced major changes in the class structure, language, and cultural orientation.[13] As Iha Fuyu noted in 1911, Okinawans were born at a disadvantage, and had to learn to articulate their needs in the language of the masters if they were to achieve recognition.

After introducing a state-controlled and standardized education system,[14] the Japanese state established village political structures that reproduced those of the mainland and a prefectural police system that kept much of the population within its gaze. To a large extent, the state was successful in creating erstwhile citizens of the Japanese nation by employing education as a tool for standardizing knowledge among Okinawans. Through instruction, coercion, and observation, the Japanese state set becoming 'Japanese' as an object of desire for Okinawans. This politics of desire saw Okinawans learn to imitate Japanese, from their use of language, to their dress, to their recitation of the Imperial Rescript on education, and their accommodation of Japanese social mores (Morris-Suzuki 1998). Japanese philosophy was reflected in the media,[15] and people were exhorted to embrace the spirit of the Japanese nation. Although the control of the Japanese state was imperious, many Okinawans strove to improve themselves and to take advantage of better opportunities for education and travel. Other Okinawans, feeling the economic pressures of increased taxation, poor crops, and failing markets as competition from the mainland increased,[16] chose to leave Okinawa to seek better opportunities abroad, either in the mainland of Japan or in other nations.[17]

The belief that Okinawans had become a genuine part of Japan was shattered in the last months of World War Two. Proscriptions against the use of Okinawan dialects were employed on the battlefield, and Okinawans learnt what it meant to be a disposable people. Between one-quarter and one-third of the population is estimated to have died in the fiercest confrontation of the Pacific War.[18] The so-called Typhoon of Steel unleashed by the overwhelmingly superior military power of the US assault fleet devastated the south and southeast of the main island in particular, rendering it a barren and uninhabitable wasteland (Okinawa-ken Kyouiku Iinkai 2000). As Ota Masahide, Okinawa's governor between 1990 and 1998, stated, it was clear that the Japanese army was prepared to sacrifice Okinawans for the sake of delaying an Allied landing on the mainland of Japan (2000: 42). Such actions, compounded by the violence meted out against Okinawan civilians by the Japanese military, were initially perceived as betrayal by Okinawans. A retired Kumejima school teacher asked: if the Japanese wanted Okinawans to be part of Japan, why did they treat them as a different (and implicitly inferior) people during the war? (Motonaga, interview, July 2000). By the end of the Battle of Okinawa, most survivors probably feared the Japanese army more than they did the Americans,[19] but it was still with great trepidation that they waited to see how they would be treated by the US occupation authorities.

Although initially treated with relative kindness by the occupying forces, Okinawa was differentiated from the rest of 'Japan proper' by both Japanese and US officials in the post-surrender discussions. In differentiating Okinawa from mainland Japan, the two parties were able to form an agreement that would satisfy the strategic and security interests of both, without compromising the integrity of the security plans for the region of the Supreme Commander of the Allied Powers (SCAP). In short, a 'marriage of convenience' between Japan and the United States in which both governments saw mutual advantage at the expense of Okinawans was proposed and agreed. Not only had Okinawans been identified by the Japanese in the war as potentially untrustworthy and, at best, marginal Japanese, in the settlement that followed the mass destruction of Okinawan life and property, Okinawans were once more identified as outside of Japan (by both Japanese and US officials), hence able to be 'sacrificed' by Japan to meet US (and Japan's) regional security needs. More precisely, through the separation of Okinawa from Japan under US occupation, the identity of Okinawans as non-Japanese was reinforced as a rationale for transferring the stewardship of the former prefecture to the United States.[20]

Thus the United States set up occupation processes in Japan and in Okinawa on quite different bases, eventually pursuing a policy that encouraged the development of democracy, a vibrant economy, and independence in Japan,[21] while in Okinawa a US military government wielded power with an eye more or less exclusively to pacifying Okinawans in the service of US strategic interests. According to Ota Masahide, this was because, as MacArthur's desire to render Japan militarily impotent was the top priority for US security reasons, Okinawa was increasingly separated from the mainland, as both a potential means for the United States to maintain surveillance over Japan and as a strategically important Cold War possession (2000: 228). Perhaps most importantly, Okinawans were excluded from the terms and conditions of the Japanese Constitution, promulgated in 1947 under the auspices of SCAP. The obligation-free arrangement led the US military to organize the Okinawan installations as one of the keystones to their strategic interests in East Asia.[22] It also made the people of Okinawa quite literally 'stateless.'

The relationship between the US military and the people of Okinawa was a difficult one. While attempting to acknowledge some human rights for Okinawans, the United States confiscated land from them to build bases, initially with no compensation.[23] Riots and protests in the 1950s against the forced appropriation of land[24] led to some financial compensation being offered to land owners stripped of their assets. Disastrous air accidents[25] and other violent incidents between the military and civilians prompted further popular protest against the military and calls for reversion to Japanese control (Ota 2000: 258). Okinawans believed that following the reversion the island would be 'free of nuclear weapons, and that the reversion would be "mainland-level," meaning that military bases in the prefecture would be physically downsized to their relative density in mainland Japan. These hopes were in vain' (Ota 2000: 259).

In the late 1960s, the United States and Japan together announced that Okinawa would become a prefecture of Japan once more. In 1972, the reversion to Japanese rule took place with strong local popular support, fueled in large part by reactions to the heavy-handed US military occupation of the preceding quarter century.

Twenty-seven years of American rule had brought about increasing hybridization of cultures, especially in the vicinity of the military bases. Molasky's (1999) book on the American occupation of Okinawa paints vivid portraits of how life in the base cities revolved around servicing the servicemen. American popular culture, the English language, American media, and American military culture all served to influence the nature of Okinawa under American rule. The period of American political control had also led to the re-emergence of 'traditional' Okinawan activities – folk music, folk dancing, weaving, and the revival of shamanism, for example – and eventually to a backlash against American military rule.[26]

The reversion opened new possibilities for Okinawans to reclaim some control of their history and identity, although once more they would live under the political control of Japan. The specter of war, personified by the American military presence, remained, however, following the agreement between Japan and the United States, distorting economic and cultural development of the prefecture (Ota 2000:159) and provoking intermittent, but passionate, popular protests.

Controversy surrounding the high-profile US military presence escalated after late 1995, when a twelve-year-old schoolgirl was raped by three American service personnel. Five years after the incident, it was still invoked in casual conversation and in politically volatile circumstances. The cause that was awakened with the rape incident continued throughout Ota's governorship, and, in August 2000, more than 30,000 people linked hands to surround the Kadena Airbase as a protest against the presence of the American military in Okinawa. This protest was timed to coincide with the 2000 Okinawa Summit of G8 nations and the presence of the international media.[27]

If one looks behind the headlines, it becomes clear that one of the major issues underscoring the 'American bases problem' is that of how Okinawa is perceived. After all, why does Okinawa bear the brunt of the responsibility for the security pact between United States and Japan? Is it sheer political strategic expediency, based on Okinawa's geographical location? Do Okinawans and Japanese not have tragic, even catastrophic, historical ties, which include the sacrifice of some hundreds of thousands of Okinawans for the Japanese nation during the Pacific War? Within this context, many Okinawans believe they have been systematically exploited and discriminated against by both Japan and foreign powers throughout the post-war era, a perception that is one of the factors behind the long-running anti-base movement. Many ask why Okinawa should continue to house such significant quantities of foreign military hardware and personnel. The Japanese state, the official government of Okinawa since 15 May 1972, seems prepared to continue to use the prefecture as the repository of forces that purportedly aim to 'stabilize the region' (Prime Minister Hashimoto Ryutaro, speech to the Diet, 4 April 1997). Implicit in this is the clear understanding that Okinawans' geographical and cultural distance from the mainland notwithstanding, as part of the 'nation-state' of Japan they are required to play their part in regional security. In fact, Okinawa shoulders the burden for the greater part of the United States' and Japan's security in East Asia.[28]

In return for having the US military bases located within Okinawa, the Japanese state has provided Okinawa Prefecture with special funding and with opportunities for 'development,' particularly in construction.[29] However, as Ota (2000) and others note, the financial compensation offered by Tokyo cannot balance the inordinate distortions in the local economy created by the existence of the American bases. The discourse of the state, then, sends contradictory messages to the people of Okinawa: on one hand it articulates the incorporation of Okinawa into the discourse of the Japanese 'self,' certainly when there are security issues of the nation at stake; on the other, it reinforces Okinawan perceptions that they are different from other Japanese in that they carry a disproportionate responsibility for the region's military security.

In response to such ambivalent discourse, the identity of Okinawa as a singular, inclusive political entity can be iterated in challenging the pervasive nihonjinron-driven rhetoric of the state at a number of historical junctures.[30] Although people from different parts of Okinawa have strong perceptions of self, family, and regional identity, when placed in opposition to the United States, and often to Japan, a unity of purpose informs these perceptions; people redefine themselves as 'Okinawan' – regionalism as a perceptual discourse, or what Bourdieu (1990) would refer to as performative discourse. One could say that for political purposes, the creation (or reconstruction) of Okinawa as an imagined community, to appropriate Benedict Anderson's term, has provided political leaders with a means to challenge the terms of the American military presence. Underscoring such concepts is the idea that Okinawa has historically been a peaceful culture, and that it is entirely inappropriate to have such a strong foreign military presence in an area that has already suffered so greatly in wars not of its own making.

In articulating 'Okinawan identity,' the self/other relationship has been invoked to create a pastiche of images that together form a less-than-coherent picture of a not-Japan. In this sense, the word 'identity' has been appropriated and combined with the adjective 'Okinawan'[31] to form a neologism in (ironically) the Japanese language. As Japanese does not have a word for 'identity' that conveys the European meaning/s of the word,[32] it has been incorporated into Japanese as *aidentitii* and rendered into katakana, thus signified as a foreign word. That a foreign, non-Japanese word (identity) can invoke such depths of feeling when combined with the word 'Okinawan' is not inappropriate, given that the Okinawan people have been subjected to external control for more than four centuries; why not a foreign word to describe something that has been compromised, contradictory, and confusing?[33]

At many sites within Okinawa, the creation, re-creation, maintenance, and development of aspects of identity are carried out at the local level, with a highly specific regional focus. For example, with respect to the cultural milieu, it is apparent that cities, towns, villages, and hamlets produce and then reproduce the mechanisms and contexts for highly specific localized identification among their populations.[34] These perceptions are often based on pride (*hokori/jiman*) in the locale, which in turn is based on attributes (educational, cultural, material, religious, climatic, and so forth) that are idiosyncratic. The self/other dialectic is highly localized and reconstituted to view even those in the next town and village as 'outsiders,' or at least as non-participants in the cultural constructions of the locus/habitus.[35] In the literal sense, then, identity can be located in the local.

However, identity in Okinawa, like all forms of identity, is something that has highly flexible geographical, sociocultural, and political boundaries. It can take the form of an island's singular representation within the outer island chain (rittō), in opposition to the mainland of Okinawa (hontō). It can take the form of specific cultural or religious practice, history, language, or politics, geographically bounded by individual islands or by the islands as a group in contrast to the mainland of Okinawa. It can take the form of the general Okinawan 'nationality,' based largely on the reconstruction of the history of the Ryūkyū Kingdom, which is a position that former governor Ota has taken over the years.[36] At an even more 'local' level, it can become an individual buraku/*aza* (hamlet) identity within a single community or district, distinguished from other hamlets or districts. What all these perceptions have in common is that they exist in a dialectical relationship with others, and are products of the process of naming what is culturally close in the presence of some body/culture/colonial power that is culturally distant.

IMAGINING OKINAWA

Increasingly, the issue of cultural difference emerges at points of social crises, and the questions of identity that it raises are agonistic; identity is claimed either from a position of marginality or in an attempt at gaining the center; in both senses ex-centric.

(Bhabha 1994: 177)

Bhabha provides us with a useful perspective from which to assess how culture and identity can be negotiated.[37] In the process of producing contemporary 'Okinawan identity,' cultural, linguistic, and historical differences are becoming more readily articulated at many sites. Although from the perspective of Japan these attempts at restructuring the present are marginal, from the perspective of those living their own culture and speaking their own dialect few issues are more seminal. It is, in particular, when ideas of representation clash that some of the tensions inherent in the process of identity formation become clear. In the context of Okinawa's historical relations with the mainland, such tensions have emerged as crises of confidence in who Okinawans were, as we have seen above.

Since the beginning of the twenty-first century, within Okinawa fore-grounding of local festivals, language, dance, ritual, music, and so on has taken place as the so-called Okinawa boom (*buumu*) occurs – an ill-defined but substantive resistance to the homogenizing influences of Japan and the

United States. A celebration of difference that has led to the hybridization of some cultural forms within Okinawa,[38] the Okinawa boom continues to ride a wave of populist support. The production of formal and informal counter-narratives to Japanese history has led to the emergence of a number of essentialist representations of 'Okinawan-ness.' Okinawa is represented as peaceful, linguistically unique, a marine paradise, culturally distinct (from mainland Japan), an excellent investment choice, an 'international' community, the home of karate, and so on. Yet the concepts of regionalism and locality remain dominant motifs within Okinawa. Bourdieu's understanding of the performative act of developing regional discourse is helpful in emphasizing how the construction of a regional identity has limitations. In *Language and Symbolic Power* he talks of identity and representation:

> Regionalist discourse is a *performative discourse* which aims to impose as legitimate a new definition of the frontiers and to get people to know and recognize the *region* that is thus delimited in opposition to the dominant definition.
>
> (Bourdieu 1991: 223)

The categorization of a region as a region is, in itself, a powerful means of legitimating identity. In the case of Okinawa, discursive elements were incorporated into the triplet mentioned above: Okinawa Prefecture, the US military, and the Japanese government. Although the Okinawan prefectural government has continued to foreground the identity of Okinawa in opposition to both Japan and the United States, it has been politically confounded by complex economic, social, budgetary, and security issues, and has remained disempowered in its relationship with the two powers. This situation has continued following the election in 1998 of Ota's Liberal Democratic Party successor Inamine Keiichi. Yet the discourse of public performance in resisting state demands to maintain the US military presence calls upon culture, music, history, religion, ritual, language, and other 'shared values' to empower popular opposition. 'Coherent' images of 'Okinawa' have become important symbols in attracting broad popular support for what is, in effect, a radical movement at a critical moment.[39] It is the construction of this imagined community that has captured the imagination of many Okinawans.

However, beneath the level of such meta-discourses, there is a multitude of fragmented cultural, linguistic, ethnic, religious, and social forms that coexist within the prefecture. Together, these may be seen to provide further evidence for a diversified, changing, and multicultural Japan.[40] These factors may also be seen as providing the foundation for a multicultural Okinawa. The very popular and ubiquitous local dish *goya champuruu* could be seen as a metaphor for contemporary Okinawan society.[41] A wok-fried dish consisting of a mixture of Japanese and Okinawan cuisine, it matches the bitter taste of the goya (a spiny cucumber)[42] with plain noodles and whatever happens to be lying around the kitchen when it is being prepared. The ad hoc nature of the dish means that individuals can interpret the 'recipe' as they wish and, apart from the mandatory use of goya, can add whatever ingredients they see fit. Okinawa has had centuries of cosmopolitan influences, and has come to represent a mixture of ethnicities, cultures, and histories. The bitterness that followed the destruction of Okinawa during World War Two and the tensions within Okinawans' inequitable relations with the American military are mixed with ambivalent Japanese influences. The symbols of Okinawans' sacrifice for the Japanese people (such as the Peace Park and the caves where thousands were slaughtered by Japanese soldiers or forced to commit suicide)[43] are intermittently lionized as iconoclastic reminders of Okinawa's history; they are also mixed with events such as the Satsuma invasion of Okinawa (1609), the annexation of the prefecture, the Battle of Okinawa, and contemporary issues that involve crimes against the people of Okinawa committed by US servicemen.[44]

The often random mixing of these ingredients can confuse rather than enhance our understanding of the identity of Okinawa, precisely because there are so many overlapping and contradictory identities in operation at any one time. This is as it should be; fragmented identities have long been part of the Ryūkyūan/Okinawan experience. Okinawa Island, and the former capital, Shuri, engaged in a highly sophisticated network of trade relations with those from inside the Ryūkyū Kingdom and with other nations (Smits, 1999:143). These relations were seldom driven by territorial desires, but were based on the recognition of difference, and the production and purchase of artifacts for commercial gain. In particular, Chinese and South East Asian political, religious, and economic influences on Okinawa have been well documented.[45] Underscoring the relations within the archipelago was the recognition of distinctive regional characteristics, familial traits, rights of heredity, and some freedom in the practice of religion.

After the Japanese annexation of the Ryūkyūs, while Japanese influence was profound, regional and cultural variation within Okinawa remained. The spy edicts are evidence of the continuation of such local identities even under Japanese rule; during the Battle of Okinawa, the Japanese army banned, upon pain of death, the speaking of any Okinawan dialect – people's native dialect, a marker of identity, an important symbol of cultural difference, and potentially a secret language.[46] Today the American and Japanese legacies are highly visible in urban Okinawa, where they coexist with other forms of Okinawan culture. In the rural areas of the main island, and in many of the outlying islands, though, other cultural hybridization has occurred.

Images of Okinawa today incorporate a vast number of icons, historical, cultural, linguistic, social, political, economic, and military. Not simply a convenient 'exotic' sub-tropical part of Japan suitable for domestic tourism, Okinawa is a highly complex, diverse, historically, culturally, and linguistically rich society. Like many other former colonized nations, Okinawa still carries the legacy of its colonizers: Japan's and then the United States' military occupation. Unlike in other former colonized nations, though, there is little evidence of strong political independence movements in Okinawa. Its dependent relations with Japan, and via Japan, with the United States, dominate the political climate. While a diverse and multi-textured culture may help provide a powerful underlying coherence of 'not Japan' and 'not the US', the irony of having to physically protest the presence of an occupying military force to demand 'peace' (amongst other issues) should not be lost on observers.

As Chalmers Johnson so succinctly put it in 1999, Okinawa is a 'Cold War island', and while the Cold War is long gone, Okinawa really does retain its anachronistic character today. From its garrisoning of US military to its dependence on Japan for defense, economic welfare, and political influence, Okinawa in 2007 remains a complex, post-colonial society shrouded in political ambivalence: a society that was compromised for the sake of 'regional security' and that has suffered long-term 'collateral damage' as both Japan and the US lament its 'unfortunate history.' Such hypocrisy notwithstanding, Okinawa has had an unfortunate history, most of its unfortunate nature driven by the two nations still influencing it. However, in today's complex and factionalized world, new fissures are opening particularly between the US and much of the Islamic world. In this context, it seems unavoidable that Okinawa, with its very substantial US military presence, will continue to play a relatively low-profile but very high-impact role in security issues in the region. Ironically, while potentially contributing to the political-military stability of the North East Asian region, Okinawa's history and culture remain exposed to the perpetual destabilizing influences of two of the world's most powerful nations: Japan and the United States.

Notes

1 Parts of this chapter have been previously published in a volume by the author on identity and Okinawa (*Identity and Resistance in Okinawa*, Rowman and Littlefield, 2002).
2 See, in particular, the work of Ota Masahide, the former governor of Okinawa, who has written a number of articles and books on Okinawan history and society.
3 See McCormack (1999) for an excellent discussion of the environmental

devastation taking place in Okinawa today as a result not only of the bases but also of the construction boom, funded by Tokyo.

4   See Chibana (1992) for impassioned accounts of the exploitation of Okinawa by Japanese, and a harrowing account of the 'group suicides' of the Battle of Okinawa (1988).

5   The American bases provide access to cheap food, alcohol, electrical equipment, housing, and education for qualified military personnel and their relatives. With a few exceptions (marriage is a common one, another is the annual rights of Okinawans to visit their land actually contained within the American base perimeters), Okinawans are not entitled to enter the bases.

6   After World War Two, Japan and the United States made a cynical deal to trade Okinawa's Japanese prefectural status for that of US military colony (Dower 1999). This was to ensure geopolitical stability in the region. Okinawa's geographical position near the borders of mainland China, Korea, Japan, Taiwan, and South East Asia made it an excellent strategic choice for the US military in the new post-war world. Its physical distance from Japan, and its linguistic, cultural, and historical distance from the mainland, was sufficient for Japanese leaders to agree to surrender terms to include its transference to American hands.

7   Within Okinawa, linguists have identified 800 distinct dialects, contained within four main language groups; the Amami-Oshima, Okinawa, Miyako, and Yaeyama dialect groups (Kouza Hougengaku, Vol. 10). However, most Okinawans speak a variant of standard Japanese, and the Shuri dialect is commonly used and understood.

8   See Denoon *et al.* (1996) and Weiner (1997) for comprehensive discussions in English on the multicultural nature of Japanese society.

9   Gregory Smit's *Visions of Ryūkyū: Identity and ideology in early-modern thought and politics* (1999) is an excellent account of the relationships between Japan and the post-Satsuma-invasion Ryūkyū Kingdom, and between the Ryūkyūs and China. It emphasizes some of the difficulties in essentializing the nature of the Ryūkyū Kingdom as subordinate to Japan, a position commonly taken by early historians of Japan. Michael Molasky's *The American Occupation of Japan and Okinawa: Literature and memoir* (1999) describes the state of Okinawa in the immediate post-war years, emphasizing through the production of fiction the difficult and sometimes vexatious relations between Okinawans and their US colonial masters. Chalmers Johnson's (ed.) *Okinawa: Cold War island* (1999) is also an excellent source of information on contemporary Okinawa and its relations with both the United States and Japan.

10 Yonetani produced an account of how ambivalence over what constituted 'Okinawan-ness' in the early years of Meiji political control of the islands took place. This was related to the blurring of boundaries 'between colony and nation' and to the situation of Okinawa as neither *gaichi* (outside of Japan) nor *naichi* (inside Japan) (2000: 30–1).

11 See Ohashi (1996) for a comprehensive account of the suppression of religious practitioners in Okinawa from the fifteenth to the twentieth century.

12 See Morris-Suzuki (1998) for a discussion on the expansion of the Japanese empire south through the Ryūkyūs to Taiwan and eventually into South East Asia.

13 It was not until the 1894–5 Sino-Japanese War and the cession of Formosa to Japan that the assimilation policies were pursued with any urgency (Okinawa-ken Kyouiku Iinkai 1999).

14 The educational standard in Okinawa was lower than in mainland Japan. Although

compulsory elementary-school education was introduced to Okinawa in 1880, by 1900 only just over half the eligible children attended school (Sakihara 2000: 18). Moreover, there were no high schools available for more able students.

15 The *Ryūkyū Shimpo* was founded in 1897, which coincided with the period of intensive Japanese assimilation of Okinawans that followed the successful 1894–5 war with China. As part of the territorial gains, Japan was ceded political control over Taiwan, which expanded its colonial boundaries farther south. Japanese politicians came to see Okinawa as forming part of the route to Taiwan and, theoretically, all of South East Asia.

16 After initial grants to enable sugar cane farmers to improve production, the recognition from Japan that Taiwan, which became a Japanese colony in 1895, could also produce sugar cane, and more cheaply than Okinawa, led to the suspension of these subsidies by the mid 1890s.

17 It is worth commenting that Okinawans' emigration rates were higher than those for any other prefecture.

18 The data on the deaths of Okinawans in the Battle of Okinawa appear quite unreliable. The Okinawa-ken Kyouiku Iinkai's *The History and Culture of Okinawa* states that between 130,000 and 140,000 Okinawans died, and between 73,000 and 94,000 Japanese soldiers were killed (2000: 45). Other sources place the figures both higher and lower.

19 In chapter 1 of *Identity and Resistance in Okinawa*, I demonstrate how the attitudes of the Japanese military on Kumejima hardened toward the islanders as the battle drew nearer. The 'tiger at the front gate, the wolf at the rear gate' is today a commonly used expression to describe the situation of Okinawans, caught between two fanatical armies.

20 See Chalmers Johnson's (1999) edited volume of papers on this topic.

21 The 'reverse course' of the late 1940s saw the United States relax its former punitive stance against Japan. Contributing to this change in position was the increasing expense of providing aid to Japan, and the recognition of the 'red threat' in East Asia.

22 Because Okinawa currently is host to the vast majority of US military in Japan – approximately 20 percent of the land is currently occupied by the military, and in 1999 there were approximately 30,000 marines living in the prefecture – the relationship between Japan and the United States reinforces in Okinawans the sense that they remain 'others' within Japan, their present prefectural status notwithstanding.

23 The confiscation of land to build military bases was made less complicated for the occupying army because most of the land-ownership records had been destroyed during the war (Ota 2000: 243).

24 Protests were particularly vociferous after the base expansion program got underway in 1955–6. Land was grabbed from peasants 'at the point of a bayonet' (Ota 2000: 244), and the relocation of former landowners to barracks, such as those that were used in the immediate post-war years, did little to placate the people.

25 In June 1959, for example, a marine jet crashed into a primary school near Kadena Air Base, killing eleven school children and six adults and injuring 120 others. This incident galvanized outrage amongst Okinawans, who protested that children should be protected from such actions and that Okinawans should have better human rights (Okinawa Taimusu-sha 1987: 76).

26 Okinawa-ken Kyouiku Iinkai (2000: 47–8) provides a damning account of the suppression of Okinawans' rights under American rule.

27 The protest, which was completely pacifist, was met with incomprehension and cynicism by the American media, those who the protesters were most trying to impress. The American Broadcasting Commission sent to air an item on the 'radical protesters' of Okinawa, commenting that 'underneath the quiet, polite exterior beats a radical heart' (6 August 2000).

28 In statistical terms, 75 percent of the US military presence in Japan is accommodated within Okinawa. Approximately 20 percent of Okinawa's land mass is occupied by the US military, and there are almost 70,000 Americans on the islands, of whom approximately 30,000 are military personnel. The total number of American service personnel in Japan is about 47,000.

29 See Gavan McCormack's article 'From the Sea That Divides to the Sea That Links: Contradictions of ecological and economic development in Okinawa' in *Capitalism, Nature, Socialism: A journal of socialist ecology* 10 (1), March 1999.

30 Nihonjinron literature is literally 'theories of the Japanese people,' but contained within its loose paradigmatic formulation are many views that have in common the basis of non-conflictual, harmonious, and consensus-based versions of Japanese society and culture. Inevitably teleological, they incorporate idiosyncratic interpretations of history to reify why Japanese are 'unique,' or as I see it, 'uniquely unique.' There are many good critical accounts of nihonjinron, but Dale's (1986) and Mouer and Sugimoto's (1986) are two of the better English-language texts.

31 *Uchinanchu* is used with *aidentitii* to form the term 'Okinawan identity."

32 The nearest approximation to the concept of 'cultural identity' in Japanese is the word *tokusei*, which has a strongly implied meaning of 'special' or 'different from the norm.'

33 This is especially appropriate in the sense that Okinawa is in many ways a cultural hybrid of Japan–US–Okinawa relations.

34 The production of village, town, and city histories, sponsored by local government and made available to the population at a discounted price, is an example of how the local is foregrounded.

35 Pierre Bourdieu discusses the concept of habitus in his 1990 work on language and culture.

36 The latter is to establish a sense of difference in order to distinguish Okinawans (*uchinanchu*) from mainland Japanese (*naichu*).

37 However, he himself inspires 'agonistic' questions – if identities undergo constant change, how can a 'center' or 'margin' be articulated with any degree of certainty?

38 The electric shamisen of the new age Okinawan bands is an example of this hybridization. Employing rock rhythms, Okinawan lyrics, and a blend of traditional Okinawan folk tunes and modern rock melodies, bands such as the Aiyumi Bando deliver high-energy rock-and-roll.

39 There have been many and varied calls for independence from Japan since World War Two, but they have lacked cohesion as movements and were not well supported by the population at large. The reversion movements, on the other hand, were far more widespread and coherent.

40 There is an increasing number of English-language books available on the perceived status of Japan as a multicultural nation. Denoon *et al's Multicultural Japan* (1996), Weiner's *Japan's Minorities: The illusion of homogeneity* (1997), Morris-Suzuki's *Reinventing Japan: Time, space, nation* (1998), and Lie's

Multiethnic Japan (2001) are all examples of approaches that look at diversity and heterogeneity in Japanese society, culture, and history.

41 The concept of *champuruu bunka* was widely used in the 1970s in the Koza region (now known as Okinawa City) to describe the 'hybridization' of Okinawan and American military cultures. For more on this topic, see Michael Molasky's (1999) book on the US occupation of Okinawa and Japan.

42 Goya is popularly regarded as a healthy food, and is also commonly used to make tea or juice. The latter is an idiosyncratic and acquired taste.

43 The prefecture has recently started to market the memorials as a tourism destination. Indeed, since 1998 100 'peace guides' have been trained by the prefectural government with the express intention of guiding visitors from the mainland of Japan and from overseas around World War Two sites.

44 In particular, former governor Ota has written extensively on the topic, but others such as Iha Fuyu (1911, republished 1961), Tomiyama (1990, 1994), Tsuha (1997), and many popular writers such as Chibana (1992) have incorporated selective historical accounts of the Ryūkyū Kingdom's independence with descriptions of the exploitation of the former kingdom's people.

45 See Kerr's (1959) seminal work on Okinawa, for example, for a solid account of the relations between China and Okinawa in the pre- and post-Satsuma eras.

46 See Tomiyama Ichiro's article 'Spy: Mobilization and identity in wartime Okinawa' (2000) for an insightful analysis of Okinawan responses to the Japanese military presence.

References

Allen, Matthew. 2002. *Identity and Resistance in Okinawa*. Maryland: Rowman and Littlefield.

Anderson, Benedict. 1995. *Imagined Communities: Reflections on the origin and spread of nationalism*. New York: Verso.

Bhabha, Homi (ed.). 1993. *Nation and Narration*. London: Routledge.

—— 1994. *The Location of Culture*. London: Routledge.

Bourdieu, Pierre. 1990. *In Other Words: Essays towards a reflexive sociology* (translated by Matthew Adamson). Oxford: Polity Press.

—— 1991. *Language and Symbolic Power* (translated by Gino Raymond and Matthew Adamson). Cambridge, Mass.: Harvard University Press.

Chibana Shoichi. 1988. *Yakisuterareta Hinomaru*. Tokyo: Shinsen-sha.

—— 1992. *Burning the Rising Sun* (translated by South Wind). Kyoto: South Wind.

Dale, Peter. 1986. *The Myth of Japanese Uniqueness*. New York: St. Martin's Press.

Denoon, D., M. Hudson, G. McCormack, and T. Morris-Suzuki (eds). 1996. *Multicultural Japan: Palaeolithic to postmodern*. Melbourne: Cambridge University Press.

Dower, John. 1999. *Embracing Defeat: Japan in the aftermath of World War II*. London: Penguin.

Iha Fuyu. 1911. *Ko-Ryūkyū* (The Old Ryūkyūs). Naha: Okinawa Kouronsha.

Johnson, Chalmers (ed.). 1999. *Okinawa: Cold War island*. Cardiff, Calif.: Japan Policy Research Institute.

Kerr, George. 1959. *Okinawa: The history of an island people*. Tokyo: Tuttle.

Lie, John. 2001. *Multiethnic Japan*. Cambridge, Mass: Harvard University Press.

McCormack, Gavan. 1999. 'From the Sea That Divides to the Sea That Links: Contradictions of ecological and economic development in Okinawa.' *Capitalism, Nature, Socialism: A journal of socialist ecology* 10, no. 1 (March).

Molasky, Michael. 1999. *The American Occupation of Japan and Okinawa: Literature and memory*. London: Routledge.

Morris-Suzuki, Tessa. 1998. *Reinventing Japan: Time, space, nation*. Armonk, NY: M.E. Sharpe.

Mouer, R., and Y. Sugimoto. 1986. *Images of Japanese Society: A study in the structure of social reality*. London: Kegan Paul.

Ohashi Hideshi. 1996. *Okinawa Shaamanizumu no Shakaishinrigakuteki Kenkyuu* (Social Psychological Research on Okinawan Shamanism). Tokyo: Kobunsho.

Okinawa Taimusu-sha. 1987. *Okinawa Sengoshi* (Postwar History of Okinawa). Naha: Okinawa Taimasu.

Okinawa-ken Kyouiku Iinkai. 1997. *Okinawa Kenshi* (History of Okinawa Prefecture): *Tenth Army Operation Iceberg. Shiryoson 4*. Naha: Yugen Kaisha Sun.

—— 2000. *The History and Culture of Okinawa*. Naha: Yugen Kaisha Sun.

Ota Masahide. 1990a. *Okinawa-ken Chiji Shogen* (Okinawa's Prefecture's Governor's Testimony). Tokyo: Shin Nippon Kyoiku Tosho.

—— 1990b. *Showa no Okinawa* (Okinawa of the Showa Period). Naha: Naha Shuppansha.

—— 1992. 'Straggler.' In *Japan at War: An Oral History*, edited by H.T. Cook and T.F. Cook. New York: New Press.

—— 1999. 'Re-examining the History of the Battle of Okinawa.' In *Okinawa: Cold War island*, edited by Chalmers Johnson. Cardiff, Calif.: Japan Policy Research Institute.

—— 2000. *Essays on Okinawa Problems*. Gushikawa City: Yui Shuppan.

Sakihara Mitsugu. 2000. 'Whence Were They? The Twenty-Six Men.' In *Okagesamade 2000: Bridging a century of Uchinanchu Aloha*, edited by the Issei Commemorative Booklet Committee. Honolulu: private publication.

Smits, Gregory. 1999. *Visions of Ryūkyū: Identity and ideology in early-modern thought and politics*. Honolulu: University of Hawaii Press.

Tomiyama Ichiro. 1990. *Kindai Nihon Shakai to Okinawajin: Nihonjin ni naru to iu koto* (Modern Japanese Society and Okinawans: About becoming Japanese). Tokyo: Nihon Keizai Ronbunsha.

—— 1994. 'Kokumin no Tanjō to "jinrui"' (The Birth of the People and 'the Japanese Race'). *Shisou*, 845, no. 11.

—— 2000. '"Spy": Mobilization and identity in wartime Okinawa.' In *Japanese Civilization in the Modern World XVI. Nation State and Empire*, edited by T. Umesao, T. Fujitani, and E. Kurimoto. Osaka: Senri Ethnological Studies, no. 51, National Museum of Ethnology.

Tsuha Hisashi. 1997. 'Tai Yamato no Bunka Jinruigaku' (On the Shared Consciousness of Non-Yamato Identity), *Nihon Jinruigaku Bunkasho* 2, no. 3 (June).

Weiner, Michael (ed.). 1997. *Japan's Minorities: The illusion of homogeneity*. London: Routledge.

Yonetani, Julia. 2000. 'Ambiguous Traces and the Politics of Sameness: Placing Okinawa in Meiji Japan.' *Japanese Studies* 20, no. 1.

10 Japanese-Brazilian ethnic return migration and the making of Japan's newest immigrant minority

Takeyuki (Gaku) Tsuda

INTRODUCTION: JAPAN AS A 'RECENT' COUNTRY OF IMMIGRATION[1]

International migration has been responsible for creating many of the world's ethnic minority groups. When migrants cross national borders and settle in foreign countries, they become immigrant ethnic minorities that are racially and culturally different from the dominant populace, and they frequently become targets of discrimination and socioeconomic marginalization. Although many countries have indigenous minorities, most ethnic minorities in the contemporary world are immigrant minorities.

Until the late 1980s, Japan was one of the few advanced industrial countries in the world that had not imported large numbers of unskilled immigrant laborers since World War II to sustain its economic growth. Although the country experienced labor shortages in the late 1960s and early 1970s, government officials decided against admitting unskilled foreign workers, partly because they wished to maintain Japan's supposed ethnic homogeneity. Instead they embarked on a concerted effort to increase labor productivity and mechanization and the utilization of female and elderly workers (see Mori 1997: 37–42). At the end of the 1980s, however, Japan finally succumbed to the pressures of global migration as it faced various labor-market and demographic pressures that forced it to import large numbers of unskilled foreign workers. The rapid expansion of the Japanese economy in the 1980s created a rising demand for unskilled labor that could not be met by the domestic labor supply. This was because the country had a rapidly shrinking and aging populace (Japan has the world's lowest fertility rate) and a well-educated and affluent populace unwilling to perform unskilled 3D (dirty, dangerous, and difficult) jobs, and also because of inability to further tap previously underutilized sources of labor power (women, elderly, and rural workers) and because of the limits of further mechanization and off-shore production. The result was an acute unskilled-labor shortage, especially among small and medium-sized firms, which threatened to cripple the booming economy.

Despite its economic need for immigrant labor, when it revised the Immigration Control and Refugee Recognition Act (implemented in 1990) the Japanese government maintained the country's long-standing ban on unskilled foreign workers and imposed tough penalties on those employers and labor brokers who knowingly recruited and hired illegal immigrants. However, the government tacitly created or condoned various 'side-door' policy mechanisms that enabled the legal importation of large numbers of unskilled foreign workers under visa categories officially intended for other purposes, such as 'trainees,' 'students,' 'entertainers,' and Japanese-descent ethnic return migrants (nikkeijin). In addition, because Japan has insisted on a closed-door immigration policy despite its strong economic demand for foreign labor, a large number of illegal immigrants have entered the country in response to the plentiful relatively high-paying, unskilled jobs.[2]

Although it may seem that Japan made a transition from a former country of emigration to a country of immigration in this manner (Douglass and Roberts 2000: 7; Watanabe 1994), the notion that Japan was not an immigration country until recent decades is itself a myth. From 1910 to 1945, when significant numbers of Japanese left the country to colonize Asia and then to fight in World War Two, 2.1 million Koreans immigrated to Japan – some as forced laborers – to work in Japanese factories (see Weiner 1994), creating a Korean-Japanese minority group that continues to suffer from ethnic discrimination and economic marginalization. Thus the post-1985 influx of foreign workers is just the latest chapter in Japan's immigration history.

For a country that continues to pride itself on its ethnic and racial homogeneity, Japan has a very diverse immigrant population, who come from various countries in East and South East Asia, Latin America, and even the Middle East. The total number of foreign workers is probably close to 950,000, approximately 850,000 of whom are unskilled or semi-skilled. Although this is still just 0.75 percent of Japan's total population of 127 million, it represents a sharp increase from the pre-1985 period.

THE RISE OF NIKKEIJIN IMMIGRANT COMMUNITIES

The largest and most prominent group of Japan's recent immigrants are the South American nikkeijin (Japanese descendants born and raised outside of Japan), who began 'return' migrating to Japan in the late 1980s and currently number well over 330,000. As part of the revised 1989 Immigration Control and Refugee Recognition Act, the Japanese government decided to implement an ethnic preference immigration policy that grants the nikkeijin renewable visas with no activity restrictions; this was a partial concession to labor-deficient employers who had been clamoring for unskilled foreign workers. Although it was evident that the nikkeijin would be manning Japan's factories, Japanese government officials were able to justify this side-door policy by claiming that the nikkeijin were not unskilled immigrant workers *per se*, but ancestral returnees who were being invited back to their ethnic homeland to explore their Japanese heritage. In addition, because of an essentialized racial ideology in which those of Japanese descent are expected to be culturally Japanese to a certain extent, even if they were born and raised abroad, government policymakers assumed that the nikkeijin would be culturally similar and would assimilate smoothly to Japanese society – in contrast to racially and culturally different foreigners (Roth 2002; Sasaki 1999: 258; Yamanaka and Miyajima 1992: 20). Admitting nikkeijin migrants was viewed as an effective way to deal with the labor shortage without undermining Japan's official ban on unskilled immigrant workers or disrupting Japan's cherished ethnic homogeneity (see Miyajima 1993: 59).

Most of the nikkeijin immigrants have been second- and third-generation Japanese-Brazilians who began migrating to Japan because of an economic crisis in Brazil in the 1980s. Although they are relatively well educated and mostly of middle-class background in Brazil, they still earn five to ten times their Brazilian salaries as unskilled factory workers in Japan. Because most of the Brazilian nikkeijin migrate with the intention of returning to Brazil in a couple of years, they are called *dekasegi*, the Japanese word for temporary migrant workers. However, many have brought their families to Japan, and the process of long-term immigrant settlement has already begun (Tsuda 1999b; Yamanaka 2000). Since the Japanese-Brazilians were born and raised in Brazil, they do not speak Japanese very well and have become culturally Brazilianized to various degrees. As a result, they are treated as foreigners in Japan despite their Japanese descent, and they have become the country's newest immigrant minority.

The expansion of the Japanese-Brazilian immigrant community has been quite remarkable. Whereas the number of Brazilians registered as foreigners in Japan was only 14,528 in 1989, it rose to 254,394 by 2000, despite a prolonged Japanese recession. The population of Brazilian nikkeijin immigrants has continued to steadily increase and currently stands at 286,557 (2004 figures). The initial immigrants were poorer and used their personal connections with relatives in Japan to migrate, but as a large number of successful Japanese-Brazilian migrants began returning to Brazil from Japan with considerable wealth, the tremendous economic benefits of migration became quite clear, enticing others to follow suit. Transnational labor-broker networks were quickly established to recruit nikkeijin in Brazil, obtain visas for them, and finance their travel to Japan, and then to provide them with factory jobs, housing, insurance, and social support in Japan. These labor brokers have greatly expanded the migrant flow by reducing the difficulty and risk of migration and by enabling those who do not have transnational social connections to Japan (or even funds to buy a plane ticket) to migrate. As a result, a 'culture of migration' (see Cornelius 1991: 112) has developed among Japanese-Brazilian communities in Brazil, with migration becoming so prevalent and routine that many depend on it for their economic wellbeing and socioeconomic advancement. Because these sociocultural structures facilitating and sustaining migration have become so firmly entrenched, the volume of migration continues to increase even though its original economic causes have subsided.[3]

The regions with the highest concentrations of Brazilian nikkeijin are the Tomo area of Gunma Prefecture (consisting primarily of Oizumi, Ota, and Tatebayashi cities) and the cities of Hamamatsu, Toyota, and Toyohashi in Aichi Prefecture. Large populations of nikkeijin are also found in the Nagoya city area, Kanagawa Prefecture adjacent to Tokyo city (especially in and near Kawasaki, Tsurumi, and Fujisawa cities), and the coastal areas of Shizuoka Prefecture. Since a majority of Japanese-Brazilian immigrants work in small and medium-sized businesses in the manufacturing sector, they tend to be clustered in satellite industrial towns, and only a minority work in the service sector in Japan's big cities. Although they are not residentially segregated, prominent Brazilian immigrant communities have developed in cities such as Oizumi and Hamamatsu; these areas have an expanding array of ethnic businesses, including Brazilian restaurants, food stores and supermarkets, clothing stores, and even boutiques and discos, as well as nikkeijin churches and other organizations. Large labor brokers are especially active in such communities, providing extensive employment, housing, transportation, and other social services, mainly in Portuguese. Local governments in such cities have generally been receptive to the Japanese-Brazilians, and they offer information handbooks and pamphlets, health insurance and emergency medical coverage, consultation services, language classes and translation services, educational programs in local schools with nikkeijin children, and even limited political representation through foreigner advisory councils.

AN AMBIVALENT HOMECOMING: THE JAPANESE ETHNIC RECEPTION OF THE JAPANESE-BRAZILIANS

Although the daily lives of the Japanese-Brazilians are dominated by long days in the factories, it is the ethnic aspects of their immigrant experiences that are the most interesting. Despite their relatively privileged status in

Japan as 'ethnic Japanese,' they are still subject to notable prejudice and social marginalization as an ethnic minority group. Most of the mainstream Japanese informants I interviewed felt a certain amount of ethno-cultural affinity with the Brazilian nikkeijin because of their Japanese descent, clearly preferring them to foreigners of non-Japanese descent. For example, this type of general sentiment was expressed by a Japanese factory worker in Oizumi:

> Discrimination and disparagement is less toward the Brazilian nikkeijin because they have a Japanese face. This creates a feeling of commonality with them as our brethren. Since we see them as people who were originally Japanese, we feel closer to them than other foreigners. There is much more discrimination toward the Korean-Japanese.

There was general consensus among those Japanese I interviewed that prejudice and discrimination toward Korean-Japanese is higher because they are not of Japanese descent, even though most of them have been born and raised in Japan and are culturally assimilated.

Despite this general sense of racial and cultural affinity, most of my Japanese informants harbored notable ethnic prejudice toward the Japanese-Brazilians. These migrants were often perceived as descendants of poor and uneducated Japanese of low social class background who could not survive economically in Japan and thus had to abandon their homeland and emigrate to Brazil. The current return migration of the Brazilian nikkeijin to Japan as unskilled factory workers therefore subjects them to a double social class stigma – the descendants of those who initially fled to Brazil because they supposedly could not survive in Japan have now returned to Japan because they could not survive economically in Brazil either.[4]

In addition to this type of social class prejudice, there is also considerable cultural prejudice toward the Japanese-Brazilians based on negative evaluations of their 'Brazilian' behavior. Because of the essentialized Japanese ethnic expectation that those who are racially Japanese will also be culturally similar, virtually all of my Japanese informants mentioned that they were disappointed when they realized how culturally foreign the Brazilian nikkeijin have become (see Yamanaka 1997: 84). The Japanese employees on the assembly line at the factory where I conducted participant observation (which I will call Toyama) generally gave their nikkeijin counterparts rather low marks for their work ethic and ability, seeing them as lazy, slow, irresponsible, and careless on the job (Yamanaka 1996: 84), which was sometimes attributed to their 'Brazilianness.' Although Japanese employers generally had favorable impressions of their nikkeijin workers, they sometimes saw them as excessively individualistic and conflictual, and also as lacking in company loyalty because they frequently quit for higher paying jobs. Outside the factory, Japanese residents complain that the Japanese-Brazilians are a disturbance because they make excessive noise in apartments, turn up their stereos too loud, and party until late at night on weekends (see also Japan Institute of Labor 1995; Watanabe *et al.* 1992). Even in cities with relatively high concentrations of immigrants, where local residents have become used to constantly encountering foreigners in the streets, some still do not like to see nikkeijin walking around in groups, dressed in a strange manner, speaking loudly in Portuguese, and otherwise behaving in ways that seem alien.[5]

In addition to ethnic prejudice, Japanese-Brazilian immigrants also experience considerable social marginalization as an ethnic minority in Japan. At Toyama factory, nikkeijin and Japanese workers always remained apart during breaks and lunch hours, sitting in separate rooms or at different tables and conversing only among themselves. Inter-ethnic interaction was limited at most to brief smiles or greetings in the morning and short exchanges of a few words or simple questions. Although the Japanese-Brazilians often worked together with the Japanese on the same factory assembly lines, general conversation between the two groups was kept to a bare minimum and was usually limited to work instructions. Likewise, only a few Brazilian nikkeijin have sustained social relationships with their Japanese co-workers outside the factory, have contact with their Japanese neighbors, or participate in local community activities. As a result, what interaction they have with Japanese outside the factory is generally limited to clerks and workers at local stores, banks, and municipal offices.

The reasons for the social marginalization of the Japanese-Brazilians as an ethnic minority are quite complex. Because of a narrow Japanese ethno-national identity in which Japaneseness is defined not only by racial descent but also by complete linguistic and cultural proficiency, the nikkeijin are ethnically excluded in Japan as foreigners, despite their Japanese descent, because of their cultural differences. The remarks of one local Japanese resident in Oizumi-town were quite representative of this general Japanese reaction:

> There's a lot of *iwakan* (sense of incongruity) towards those who have a Japanese face but are culturally Brazilian. If they have a Japanese face, we interpret this to mean they are Japanese, so we initially approach the nikkeijin this way. But then when we find they are culturally different, we say they are *gaijin* [foreigners].

At Toyama factory, the Brazilian nikkeijin were often addressed as *gaijin-san* (Mr or Mrs Foreigner), although personal names were usually used in more familiar situations. The Japanese-Brazilians are also referred to as *gaijin* outside the workplace, especially when they speak Portuguese in restaurants, stores, and trains, and most Japanese tend to keep their distance from such ethnically unfamiliar foreigners. Although most of the Japanese-Brazilians are not phenotypically distinct from the Japanese, they wore different-colored uniforms at the Toyama factory as temporary workers contracted from outside labor-broker firms, making them 'ethnically visible' and immediately subject to social exclusion. Even outside the factory, many of them remain culturally visible as foreigners because of their distinctively different manner of speaking, dressing, gesturing, and even walking.

In addition, since a majority of the nikkeijin immigrants cannot speak Japanese effectively, language is obviously a significant cultural barrier to social interaction. At Toyama factory, many Japanese workers did not even attempt to speak with their nikkeijin co-workers because they were afraid of their inability to communicate. It was also quite apparent at times that the ethnic marginalization of the Japanese-Brazilians on the basis of cultural difference was also motivated by ethnic prejudice (described above). I was told a number of times at Toyama factory about Japanese workers who did not interact with nikkeijin foreigners because of ethnic dislike.

The social segregation of the Japanese-Brazilians in Japan is not simply a result of their ethno-cultural differences; it is also caused by their socio-economic marginalization as migrant laborers. Most of them are employed in the most peripheral sector of the Japanese labor market, since Japanese companies use them as a casual labor force of temporary contract workers who are borrowed from outside labor-broker firms. As a result, they do not belong to the companies where they work and are excluded as outsiders from Japanese social groups on the factory floor. Because their labor broker constantly transfers them from one company to another as a readily disposable workforce, few Japanese workers bother to associate with such itinerant laborers who constantly circulate in and out. In addition, they often eat in separate lunchrooms, are not invited to company outings and events with Japanese workers, and are sometimes even segregated in nikkeijin-only work sections.

The Brazilian nikkeijin respond to their ethnic and social exclusion in Japan by withdrawing into their own social groups in an act of ethnic self-segregation. Most of them do not actively seek out relationships with the Japanese because the Japanese do not seek out relationships with them. Although the Japanese-Brazilians are beginning to settle long-term or permanently in Japan (Tsuda 1999b), many continue to view themselves strictly as sojourners who intend to return to Brazil in a few years after accumulating sufficient savings. As a result, they have little incentive to integrate themselves into Japanese society and establish long-term, meaningful relationships with the Japanese. However, despite their self-perceived temporary status, they have already created very extensive and cohesive immigrant communities in various parts of Japan (described above), which enable them to conduct their lives exclusively within their own extensive social and institutional networks without interacting with mainstream Japanese.

FEELING BRAZILIAN IN JAPAN: MIGRANT NATIONALISM AMONG THE NIKKEIJIN

The ambivalent reception of Japanese-Brazilian immigrants by their Japanese hosts is quite disconcerting to many of them, and it causes them to strengthen their nationalist affiliation as Brazilians in Japan.[6] The impact of ethnic return migration on the nikkeijin is quite significant, given the relatively strong 'Japanese' ethnic identity they had developed in Brazil. As Brazil's oldest and by far the largest Asian minority (population over 1.2 million), the Japanese-Brazilians are generally well-regarded by mainstream Brazilians for what are perceived to be their positive 'Japanese' cultural attributes, their relatively high socioeconomic and educational status, and their affili-ation with the highly respected First World country of Japan. In turn, the Brazilian nikkeijin take pride in their Japanese descent and cultural heritage, and they identify rather strongly with positive images of Japan and Japanese culture, generally distancing themselves from what they perceive negatively as 'Brazilian.' As a result, when they return migrate to Japan, they expect to be ethnically accepted, if not welcomed, as Japanese descendants and think that they will have congenial relationships with the Japanese.

Therefore, when the Japanese-Brazilians are ethnically marginalized as culturally different 'foreigners' in Japan despite their Japanese descent, they feel quite disoriented, if not shocked, and are forced to reconsider their ethnic identities. When talking about their migrant experiences, they frequently say 'nós somos considerados japoneses no Brasil, mais somos vistos como gaijin aqui no Japão' (we are considered Japanese in Brazil, but are seen as foreigners here in Japan). Their previous assumptions of cultural commonality with the Japanese are seriously questioned as they realize that their supposedly 'Japanese' cultural attributes, which were sufficient to be considered 'Japanese' in Brazil, are woefully insufficient to qualify as Japanese in Japan, or even to be socially accepted. The remarks of one second-generation nikkeijin man was representative of this type of experience:

We think we are Japanese in Brazil, but in Japan, we find out that we were wrong. If you act differently and don't speak Japanese fluently, the Japanese say you are a Brazilian. To be considered Japanese, it is not sufficient to have a Japanese face and eat with chopsticks. You must think, act, and speak just like the Japanese.

The shift in ethnic identity among the nikkeijin from an initially stronger Japanese consciousness in Brazil to an increased awareness of their Brazilian-ness is also based on a self-recognition of their Brazilian cultural differences in Japan. For instance, although they had frequently noted their more quiet and restrained 'Japanese' demeanor in Brazil, they discover in Japan that their manner of walking, dressing, and gesturing is strikingly different from the Japanese. It was quite remarkable that virtually all of my informants claimed that it is extremely easy to tell the Japanese-Brazilians apart from the Japanese on the streets because of such differences. For instance, consider the following statement by Tadashi, a good friend of mine at Toyama:

> I can see a [Japanese] Brazilian coming from a mile away with about 90 percent certainty ... The Brazilians walk casually with a more carefree gait and glance around at their surroundings and they are dressed casually in T-shirts and jeans. The Japanese are more formally dressed and walk in a more rushed manner. The Brazilians also gesture much more than Japanese and walk around in groups, whereas the Japanese are usually alone.

In this manner, the Brazilian nikkeijin realize that even at the most basic level of motoric comportment and mannerisms, prominent cultural differences surface that clearly set them apart from the Japanese, forcing them to redefine themselves as more culturally Brazilian than they had previously acknowledged.

The nationalization of ethnic identity among Japanese-Brazilian return migrants is also a response to their negative social experiences in Japan. Partly because of their ethnic alienation from Japanese society, many of them develop negative attitudes about Japanese culture and behavior. They often complain that the Japanese are cold, unreceptive, and impersonal in social relationships, and that they are unfriendly people lacking *calor humano* (human warmth) and affection. They also note that the Japanese work all the time and do not have active and fulfilling family and social lives. Nonetheless, a number of Japanese-Brazilians have negative evaluations of the actual ability and work ethic of their Japanese counterparts, claiming that the nikkeijin work harder, better, and more conscientiously. Some Japanese-Brazilian women had harsh words for the manner in which women are treated in Japanese society, claiming that they are paid less for the same work and are expected to be submissive at work and subject to male patriarchy at home.

Other aspects of Japanese behavior often singled out for special criticism were group conformity, lack of individuality, and submissiveness to authority.

In addition, a majority of nikkeijin immigrants are quite disappointed by the actual material and living conditions in Japan. Because many of them arrive with rather idealistic images of Japan as the '*primeiro mundo*' (First World) of ultra-modern cities, advanced technology and industrial development, and luxurious living standards, they are quite disappointed when they actually experience the narrow streets, small houses, poorer neighborhoods, and relatively low living standards, finding that Japan is much less developed than they had previously imagined. Some of them were also surprised at the small and dingy factories where they were frequently employed, in which much of the work is still being done manually, in stark contrast to images of highly mechanized and modernized Japanese factories. Other Japanese-Brazilians had an antiquated perception of Japanese society based on nostalgic images of traditional Japanese culture, epitomized by ancient Japanese shrines, samurai, kabuki, and kimono, and they had come to Japan with the hope that such historical traditions have been properly preserved. Again, they were disillusioned when they fully realized how completely Westernized Japan has become, lacking any semblance of the old Japan that they had savored in Brazil.

As the initially positive images that the Japanese-Brazilians had of Japan suddenly worsen and are replaced by a much less favorable understanding of Japanese society, this causes many of them to distance themselves from their previous ethnic identification as 'Japanese.' At the same time, when viewed in contrast to the perceived negative aspects of Japanese society, the positive value of Brazilian culture and society suddenly emerges to a much greater extent (see Koga 1995: 44; Mori 1992: 148–9). The supposedly unaffectionate and workaholic nature of the Japanese makes them appreciate the warmth, friendliness, openness, and ability to enjoy life of the Brazilians. When confronted by the relatively low living standards of Japan, a number of Brazilian nikkeijin realize that Brazil is not as underdeveloped as they previously thought, and that urban living standards in Third World Brazil are sometimes better than First World Japan. At the same time, they also feel a need to defend their country against what they believe are the negative images that prevail in Japan of Brazil as poor, backward, and crime-ridden.[7] Although the Brazilian nikkeijin were frequently critical of many aspects of Brazilian society back home, I observed a notable tendency among them to praise Brazil in Japan, even to an exaggerated extent. One of my informants spoke about this positive reassessment of Brazil in the clearest terms:

> Brazilians always think other countries are much better. The Japanese-Brazilians saw Japan in this way too. But now, I realize we were wrong.

We didn't know what we had in Brazil. There is no better place than Brazil to live, especially because we were born there and have no cultural problems. The people are better there and so are the conditions of living. I value Brazil much more now.

Therefore, in response to the perceived negative aspects of Japanese society, the Japanese-Brazilians experience a greater identification with the Brazilian nation through an increased realization and affirmation of those positive qualities that make them ethnically Brazilian. Some of them even used affect-laden terms such as nationalism, patriotism, and love to express their renewed identification with and appreciation of Brazil. This greater sense of Brazilian national allegiance and pride is also symbolized by the prominent display of the Brazilian flag and national colors in nikkeijin ethnic stores and restaurants (and even on their clothes), although the flag is hardly ever displayed in Brazil.[8] During the 2002 World Cup (held in Japan and Korea), thousands of Japanese-Brazilians waving the Brazilian flag and dressed in national colors showed up in stadiums all over Japan to cheer on their national team, causing the American TV broadcasters to wonder why so many 'Japanese' were so fervently rooting for the Brazilian team![9]

The negative immigrant experiences that the Japanese-Brazilians have in Japan also include their low social class status. Because most nikkeijin are well-educated, middle-class professionals or business owners in Brazil, they experience considerable declassing in Japan when they become unskilled immigrant factory workers who must perform 3D (dirty, dangerous, and difficult) jobs that most Japanese shun and despise. Although most nikkeijin come to Japan psychologically prepared to take on these blue-collar jobs and are willing to temporarily endure the loss in social status for the tremendous financial gain, a good number of my informants spoke openly about the demeaning nature of their work in Japan and about their feelings of damaged pride and even shame. This is especially hard for those who held high-status professional jobs or positions of authority in Brazil; they suddenly find themselves powerless subordinates forced to obey orders from less-educated Japanese factory workers. Also, since most Brazilian nikkeijin have no prior experience with manual labor, some have trouble adjusting to the physical rigors and strenuous pace of their factory jobs. Complaints about the mechanical and robotic nature of the work were also frequent among my nikkeijin co-workers at Toyama factory.

Such negative work experiences are compounded by what the Japanese-Brazilians claim is ethnic discrimination on the job. Although they generally report that they are treated well by the Japanese without any problems, they are quite sensitive to being victims of possible exploitation and discrimination because of their subordinate social status, inability to effectively understand

Japanese, and belief that they are lowly-regarded Brazilian foreigners from a poor Third World country. There was general agreement among my nikkeijin informants that they are given the more difficult and worse jobs and they are forced to work harder than the Japanese. For instance, according to a young nikkei woman:

> There's lots of easy work in the factory, but the Japanese never give us this work. I hear my supervisors saying, 'if the work is hard, give it to the Brazilians.' They figure they can give us the hardest and dirtiest work because we are from a different country and are in their land. I feel exploited working at the factory.

Others mention being yelled at on the job and mistreated by supervisors and claim that they are blamed for product defects and mistakes made on the assembly line, as well as other problems that arise in the factory. Other issues that are frequently brought up as evidence of 'discrimination' against them include being fired before Japanese workers during a recession, receiving lower bonuses and fewer benefits, and not being invited to company outings and trips with Japanese workers.

The extent to which this perceived discrimination is 'real' is an open question. Although there are plenty of Japanese workers with prejudices about nikkeijin foreigners, I never observed any mistreatment at the Toyama factory, where the Japanese-Brazilians were in fact treated courteously (partly because of management pressure).[10] Based on my observations and interviews, it seemed unlikely that Japanese factory supervisors were intentionally giving nikkeijin workers the most difficult and worst jobs. However, because most nikkeijin do not speak Japanese well, they are frequently assigned tasks that can be explained physically through movements and gestures, which tend to be the jobs that are more physically strenuous.[11] Japanese-Brazilian workers are indeed the first to be laid off, and they do not enjoy the same employee benefits as most Japanese workers, but this is because they are employed indirectly through outside labor-brokers firms as *hi-seishain* (informal temporary workers), not as regular, permanent *seishain*.[12] In fact, some Japanese workers are surprised to hear that the nikkeijin feel discriminated against in the factory. One worker who had befriended a number of nikkeijin co-workers spoke about this as follows:

> I noticed early on that the nikkeijin would frequently use the word '*discriminação*.' When I checked it up in the dictionary, I was surprised to find it meant *sabetsu* ['discrimination' in Japanese]. I do not think that we discriminate at all against the nikkeijin but treat them favorably. Of course, they are given bad work by the [supervisor] sometimes,

but the Japanese experience this too. The Japanese-Brazilians call this 'discrimination,' but it is only their point of view. I guess when such experiences accumulate, they perceive it as discriminatory.

Nonetheless, such negative work experiences among Japanese-Brazilian immigrants leave them feeling not only ethnically marginalized in Japan but also socioeconomically marginalized, reinforcing their status as Brazilian foreigners who are excluded from Japanese society. This heightens their sense of antagonism against the Japanese and alienates them from their previous 'Japanese' identification, while creating a sense of ethnic solidarity among themselves as Brazilian nationals who share common experiences of occupational degradation and discrimination.

ACTING BRAZILIAN IN JAPAN: THE PERFORMANCE OF BRAZILIAN NATIONALIST IDENTITIES

Although the Japanese-Brazilians represent a rather unusual case of migration in that they are return migrating to their ancestral homeland, their experiences of ethnic and social marginalization, cultural difference, and discrimination are shared by many other migrants. Such negative experiences frequently cause migrants to react against the host society by reaffirming and strengthening their feelings of affiliation to their country of origin. In this manner, the dislocations of migration can produce a form of deterritorialized nationalism where national loyalties are articulated outside the territorial boundaries of the nation-state (Tsuda 2003: Chapter 3).

Ethnic identity, however, is not simply a matter of internal self-consciousness – it is actively displayed, demonstrated, and enacted in practice. Since the resurgence of Brazilian national sentiment among Japanese-Brazilian immigrants is a response to their negative ethnic and socio-occupational experiences in Japan, the behavioral assertion of their Brazilian cultural differences becomes a form of opposition to Japanese society. However, it is also an attempt to resist assimilationist cultural pressures. By behaving in conspicuously 'Brazilian' ways in Japan, they are able to demonstrate to the Japanese that despite their racial appearance, they are not Japanese and cannot be held to Japanese cultural expectations.

A common way in which the nikkeijin display their Brazilian-ness to the Japanese is through dress, which is among the most frequent emblems used to symbolize ethnic difference and identity. In fact, the effectiveness of clothes as an identifying marker of Brazilian-ness has actually increased the demand for distinctive Brazilian clothes in Japan. Of course, some Japanese-Brazilians wear Brazilian clothes in Japan purely out of physical comfort or habit, but for others, it is a deliberate ethnic display of cultural difference, if not defiance. The manager of a Brazilian clothing store explained that the clothes she sells have distinctive designs, fashions, and colors that cannot be found in Japanese department stores. Jeans have colorful ornamental features and those for women tend to be tighter around the hips (as the buttocks, not the breasts, are the primary locus of female sexual attention in Brazil). Shirts have strong (even loud) colors and may have mosaic patterns, while T-shirts with the Brazilian flag, national colors, or the country's name prominently displayed are also popular.

The display of Brazilian identities in Japan also involves the use of language and greetings. For instance, Martina, a nikkeijin woman, mentioned that although she speaks Japanese well, whenever she walks into a store, she makes a point of speaking Portuguese loud enough so that the Japanese will notice. 'I don't want to be confused as Japanese,' she said. 'So I always show them I am Brazilian.' Likewise, the tendency of some nikkeijin to greet each other loudly and affectionately in public by embracing or kissing is a display of Brazilian behavior that is completely incongruous with Japanese culture and thus serves as another means of ethnic differentiation.

Some individuals take their ethnic resistance further by exaggerating their Brazilian behavior in a rebellious, exhibitionist manner, purposefully acting more Brazilian in Japan than they ever did in Brazil. As one informant observed a bit cynically, 'Some of these Brazilian youth have this attitude toward the Japanese: "Hey, I'm Brazilian and I am going to act Brazilian in Japan. And if you don't like it, screw you" ... However, in Brazil, they would never have acted like this and do it only in Japan.'

Others engage in much more subdued performances of their Brazilian nationalist identity. This is especially true among the more acculturated nikkeijin, who are more accommodating toward Japanese cultural expectations and feel more pressure to act in accordance with Japanese norms. For such individuals, the assertion of their Brazilian-ness is much less ostentatious than that of their peers, and it is usually limited to introducing themselves as Brazilians or foreigners in order to avoid being mistaken for Japanese, thus relieving themselves of the Japanese cultural expectations which would otherwise be imposed on them. Such concerns are most salient among those nikkeijin who speak fluent Japanese and are the most likely to be mistaken as Japanese, especially because of their unwillingness to overtly display Brazilian behavior. Therefore, they sometimes find subtle ways to differentiate themselves as Brazilians. This includes not only introducing themselves as nikkeijin or Brazilians, but also writing out their Japanese last names in *katakana* (a phonetic alphabet used for foreign names) instead of Japanese characters. Those who have both Brazilian and Japanese first names sometimes intentionally use their Brazilian names in Japan, although they may have been called by their Japanese names in Brazil. Others use even more personal ethnic symbols; for instance, Marcos, a Japanese-Brazilian journalist in Japan, wears a goatee as his 'little rebellion against the Japanese,' an idiosyncratic emblem of his ethnic differences from Japanese men, whom he believes do not like facial hair.

The performance of Brazilian nationalist identities in Japan occurs not only in individual behavior, but also in collective ritual performances. The most important example is the samba parades that the Japanese-Brazilians organize in local communities with high nikkeijin concentrations. Although most of them never participated in samba in Brazil and even scorned it as a lowly Brazilian activity, they find themselves dancing samba for the first time in their lives in Japan and actually finding it a lot of fun. However, since they have insufficient cultural knowledge of this national Brazilian ritual, their ethnic performance in Japan does not conform to prescribed samba dance forms. Instead, it is spontaneous and generated in the context of enactment. Indeed, the samba parade I observed in Oizumi town was a somewhat random cultural performance that was improvised, haphazard, and casual. The 'samba costumes' the Japanese-Brazilians wore were randomly chosen and ranged from simple bathing suits, clown outfits, and festival clothes with Brazilian national colors, to T-shirts and shorts. Apparently, few of the nikkeijin knew how to design or construct any real Brazilian samba costumes or had the resources to do so. In addition, most of them did not seem to know how to properly dance samba, and even if some of them were familiar with the dance form, almost no one had the experience or will to execute it properly. Therefore, instead of properly schematized body movements, most of the participants seemed to be moving and shaking their bodies randomly, some in a lackadaisical manner. The general result was simply a potpourri of costumes and individuals moving their bodies randomly without any pattern, definition, or precise rhythm that resembles actual Brazilian samba. The only participants in the parade who required any explicit cultural knowledge were the singer of the samba theme and the *bateria* (the drum section that beats out the samba rhythm), both of which were composed almost exclusively of non-Japanese descent Brazilians.

Because of this lack of proper cultural knowledge about samba and the unstructured nature of the costumes and choreography, the nikkeijin samba performance had little in common with samba as it is practiced in Brazil and would have been barely recognizable back home. However, given the Japanese context in which this 'samba' was being enacted, it was seen as very 'Brazilian' because of its cultural distinctiveness in Japan. In other words, as long as the nikkeijin could find some costume that looked vaguely Brazilian and could shake their body in one way or another, the performance remained effective as a collective assertion of their Brazilian nationalist identity. This process of cultural authentication was unintentionally supported by the presence of attentive Japanese spectators, who showed active interest in the unusual and different festivities of another nation. Since the Japanese have even less knowledge about samba than the Japanese-Brazilians, they are unable to provide any cultural critique of the performance as inauthentic. For them, anything that seems culturally different and novel is accepted and appreciated as bona-fide Brazilian 'samba.' Therefore, the implicit collusion between participant and observer in a foreign context validates and authenticates the spontaneously generated and random performance as a true display and assertion of a distinctive Brazilian nationalist culture.

CONCLUSION: THE FUTURE OF THE JAPANESE-BRAZILIAN COMMUNITY IN JAPAN

Although a good number of the Brazilian nikkeijin migrants remain sojourners and 'target earners' who will return in the near future to Brazil, a sizable portion of the immigrant population is settling long-term or permanently in Japan.[13] Many have prolonged their stays in Japan because they find it difficult to save money due to the country's high cost of living as well as the decade-long economic recession that has reduced their incomes. Despite overall improvement in the Brazilian economy since the late 1980s, economic uncertainty in Brazil has remained, making many Japanese-Brazilians rather pessimistic about their long-term futures back home. In anticipation of a longer stay, an increasing number of them have brought their families to Japan, which further encourages settlement by reducing homesickness for Brazil and the insecurity of living alone in a foreign country. Indeed, many nikkeijin have become quite comfortable and accustomed to living in Japan because of the presence of family and friends as well as the development of extensive immigrant ethnic communities. As a result, many of them now desire to live more fulfilling family and social lives in Japan, thus increasing their cost of living, while they become less willing to endure long working hours and economic austerity, making it even more difficult to save sufficient money to return home. In addition, as their children attend Japanese schools and become increasingly assimilated to Japanese society, their social connections and involvement in the surrounding Japanese community intensifies, and they become increasingly committed to the host country. In addition, a good number of Japanese-Brazilians who do return to Brazil have difficulties economically re-establishing themselves back home, which forces them to return to Japan to earn more money, resulting in an increasing amount of circular migration between Brazil and Japan. Because of such migratory patterns, it is quite apparent that the nikkeijin will remain a permanent ethnic presence in Japan, whether as settlers or repeat sojourners.

As for the future ethnic and socioeconomic status of the nikkeijin immigrant community, it is quite apparent that because of Japan's myth of ethnic homogeneity, minorities that are not racially Japanese and culturally assimilated will continue to suffer from discrimination, which obstructs their socioeconomic mobility. However, even those Japanese-Brazilians who have resolved to reside long-term or permanently in Japan maintain their Brazilian nationalist identities and do not show a significantly greater willingness to culturally assimilate in order to improve their social acceptance and mobility in Japan. Since they remain dependent on the labor-broker system for jobs, they continue to be confined to the informal and marginal sector of the Japanese working class, and very few have been given permanent jobs with the possibility of regular promotion. In fact, even the social mobility of the assimilation-minded, Japanized nikkeijin has been restricted thus far to jobs as mini-supervisors in the factory, ethnic liaisons in local company and governmental offices, and owners of small ethnic businesses. Even assimilated nikkeijin are likely to face greater employment and institutional discrimination if they attempt to enter mainstream Japanese society by competing with native Japanese for jobs, housing, education, and other social services and opportunities.[14]

An equally serious issue is what will happen to the growing number of Japanese-Brazilian children who are currently enrolled in Japanese schools. Will they remain culturally unassimilated and therefore confined to marginalized and degrading factory jobs like their parents? Most nikkeijin children who have come to Japan at a very young age face strong assimilative pressures in Japanese schools. The Japanese teachers I interviewed in Oizumi and Kawasaki were generally quite optimistic about their nikkeijin students and reported that they learn to speak Japanese rather quickly, usually in about one year, and most eventually reach an average academic level. Japanese-Brazilian children also face strong cultural pressure from their peers to conform to Japanese thinking and behavior in order to be socially accepted and to avoid ostracism and rejection. As a result, Japanese teachers report that cultural differences among nikkeijin children in classroom behavior, styles of play, dress, food preferences, and study habits eventually disappear (see also Watanabe 1995: 56), and they end up getting along well with their peers. Reportedly, students at this age who refused to study, attend school, or dropped out were rare.

The result of such pressures on nikkeijin children is rapid Japanese cultural assimilation and loss of their Brazilian identity and cultural background (see Yamashita 2001: 90). In fact, some of the nikkeijin children I spoke to who had been in Japan for several years could not be distinguished from Japanese children either in speech, dress, or mannerisms. Some of them could no longer speak any Portuguese. Since there is no semblance of multicultural education in Japan (Sellek 2001: 203), they are not provided with opportunities to develop bilingual competence and a dual ethnic identity. The ability of Japanese-Brazilian parents to maintain Portuguese at home and to instill a Brazilian consciousness in their children is limited, given their long hours at the factory and the language gap that eventually develops between themselves and their children.[15] In fact, a number of Japanese teachers and Japanese-Brazilian parents note that some nikkeijin children actually hide their Brazilian backgrounds at school and attempt to ethnically 'pass' as if they were Japanese children, undoubtedly to avoid the ostracism and bullying[16] than can result from a different ethnic background.

In contrast, Japanese-Brazilian children who migrate during adolescence have much greater difficulty assimilating to Japanese culture. Since they have already had a lifetime of Brazilian socialization and education, they continue to identify with Brazil to a certain extent despite Japanese cultural pressures at school, and they do not completely assimilate Japanese culture or assume a Japanese identity. They also have more prominent cultural and linguistic differences from Japanese students, which makes it difficult for them to learn Japanese, keep up with school, and be accepted by their Japanese peers. Japanese teachers frequently note problems in learning, academic performance, and sociocultural adaptation among their older nikkeijin students, even labelling a number of them as children 'at risk.'[17] Indeed, some of these older nikkeijin youth are already dropping out of school and are able to get only unskilled factory jobs because of their insufficient language ability and education (see Sellek 1996: 258; Tajima 1995: 180; Yamashita 2001: 92). In fact, a good number of nikkeijin who graduate from junior high school do not go on to high school, and very few enter Japanese universities, because they have very little chance of passing Japan's difficult entrance exams (see Linger 2001: 68, 134–5, 193; Sellek 2001: 204). As a result, they are trapped in the working-class jobs of their immigrant parents and are unable to improve their socioeconomic position.

However, except for these older Japanese-Brazilian adolescents in Japan, it is likely that most second-generation nikkeijin children will eventually assimilate on a cultural level, which will enable them to escape the low-class immigrant occupations of their parents and more fully incorporate themselves into mainstream Japanese society. In this manner, it seems the Japanese-Brazilians in Japan will not come to resemble either of the two other large ethnic minorities in Japan, the Korean-Japanese or the burakumin. Unlike the Korean-Japanese, who are culturally assimilated but continue to suffer from discrimination and disparagement because they are racially different, the Japanese-descent nikkeijin are exclusively cultural minorities whose differences can disappear through assimilation. One local city official in Oizumi expressed a common sentiment among my Japanese informants when he said:

> If the nikkeijin children eventually learn to speak the language fluently and to behave just like the Japanese, they will be accepted as Japanese. I believe the Brazilian nikkeijin are fundamentally different from the Korean-Japanese because they are of Japanese descent. The Japanese believe in *kettoshugi* [the principle of blood]. As we say, 'blood is thicker than water.'

Unlike the Korean-Japanese, the burakumin are an indigenous caste-like minority, which, despite its Japanese descent, is considered 'impure' because of its traditional association with ritually unclean occupations. However, the ethnic 'impurity' of the Japanese-Brazilians probably will not continue to linger into future generations; their foreign cultural differences are temporary and their association with despised, dirty immigrant jobs in Japan is not inherited through descent like the that of the burakumin, so it can be expunged through social mobility. Indeed, many of the assimilated second-generation nikkeijin will probably conceal the Brazilian backgrounds of their parents. However, even if an ethnic background is revealed, it is unlikely to remain a significant source of ethnic discrimination, because they will have met both the racial and cultural criteria for being Japanese.

Notes

1 This chapter is based on over twenty months of intensive fieldwork and participant observation in both Japan and Brazil. Nine months were first spent in Brazil (1993–4) between two separate Japanese-Brazilian communities in the cities of Porto Alegre (Rio Grande do Sul) and Ribeirão Preto (São Paulo). During my one-year stay in Japan (1994–5), I conducted fieldwork in Kawasaki (Kanagawa Prefecture) and Oizumi/Ota cities (in Gunma Prefecture), where I worked for four intensive months as a participant observer in a large electrical appliance factory with about 10,000 workers, of whom 1,000 were Japanese-Brazilians. Close to 100 in-depth interviews (in Portuguese and Japanese) were conducted with Japanese-Brazilians and Japanese workers, residents, and employers, as well as with local and national government officials. See Tsuda 2003 (Introduction) for a detailed analysis of my fieldwork experiences.
2 See Tsuda and Cornelius 2004 for an overview of immigration to Japan and Japanese immigration policymaking.
3 Brazil's economy has improved considerably since the late 1980s, and Japan's economy has been in recession. See Tsuda 1999a for a detailed analysis of the causes of Japanese-Brazilian return migration.

4 Most of my Japanese informants associated migrant workers with poverty and did not know that the Japanese-Brazilians are middle class in Brazil.

5 See Tsuda 2003 (Chapter 2) for a more detailed analysis of Japanese ethnic prejudice toward the nikkeijin.

6 For a more detailed analysis of this subject, see Tsuda 2003 (Chapter 3).

7 The Japanese-Brazilians often claim that Japanese ask them ignorant questions about Brazil, such as whether the country has electricity, cars, and televisions.

8 The only exception is during the World Cup, when the Brazilian flag is sold by the thousands and is plastered on every store, office, home, car, and T-shirt.

9 The explanation they finally came up with is that because of the number of Brazilians playing on Japanese teams, Brazilian soccer has quite a following in Japan.

10 At smaller, less well-managed factories, the treatment of nikkeijin workers can be much worse, and they are at times yelled at for mistakes, etc. However, as Japanese workers (and even some nikkeijin workers) that I interviewed noted, Japanese workers also get yelled at in these factories.

11 More technical (and less heavy) work that required extensive explanation in Japanese was never given to Brazilian nikkeijin workers at Toyama.

12 In fact, *Japanese* seasonal and contract workers who are part of the country's casual labor force (including those at Toyama) are treated the same way – they are the first to be dismissed during a production downturn and do not receive the employment benefits of *seishain*.

13 See Tsuda 1999b for an analysis of the causes of Japanese-Brazilian immigrant settlement in Japan.

14 Rohlen (1981) notes a similar pattern among the Korean-Japanese, in which those who compete for higher-level jobs confront more discrimination from the Japanese.

15 Attempts by nikkeijin parents to provide Portuguese instruction to nikkeijin children in Japan through private or community-organized language schools have had limited success so far.

16 A few Japanese-Brazilian parents, as well as some Japanese teachers, mention instances of bullying (*ijime*) of nikkeijin children by their Japanese peers.

17 Some of the adaptational problems of Japanese-Brazilian youth outlined here are also mentioned by Tajima (1995) and Watanabe (1995).

References

Cornelius, Wayne A. 1991. 'Labor Migration to the United States: Development Outcomes and Alternatives in Mexican Sending Communities.' In Sergio Díaz-Briquets and Sidney Weintraub, eds, *Regional and Sectoral Development in Mexico as Alternatives to Migration*. Boulder: Westview Press, pp. 89–131.

Douglass, Mike and Glenda S. Roberts. 2000. 'Japan in a Global Age of Migration.' In Mike Douglass and Glenda S. Roberts, eds, *Japan and Global Migration: Foreign Workers and the Advent of a Multicultural Society*. London: Routledge, pp. 3–37.

Japan Institute of Labor. 1995. *Nikkeijin Rodosha no Jukyu Shisutemu to Shuro Keiken* (The Demand/Supply System and Employment Experiences of Nikkeiin Workers). Tokyo: Japan Institute of Labor.

Koga, Eunice Ishikawa. 1995. 'Kyojyu no Chokika to Aidenteitei no Naiyo: Nikkei Burajirujin no Baai' (Long-Term Residence and the Content of Identity: The Case of the Brazilian Nikkeijin). In Takashi Miyajima, ed., *Chiiki Shakai ni Okeru*

Gaikokujin Rodosha: Nichi/O ni Okeru Ukeire no Genjyo to Kadai (The Foreign Labor Problem in Local Societies: Issues and Realities of Acceptance in Japan and European Countries). Tokyo: Ochanomizu University, pp. 43–52.

Linger, Daniel T. 2001. *No One Home: Brazilian Selves Remade in Japan*. Stanford: Stanford University Press.

Miyajima, Takashi. 1993. *Gaikokujin Rodosha to Nihon Shakai* (Foreign Workers and Japanese Society). Tokyo: Akaishi Shoten.

Mori, Koichi. 1992. 'Burajiru kara no Nikkeijin "Dekasegi" no Suii' (Changes in the Nikkeijin Dekasegi from Brazil). *Ijyu Kenkyu* (Migration Research) 29: 144–64.

Mori, Hiromi. 1997. *Immigration Policy and Foreign Workers in Japan*. New York: St Martin's Press.

Rohlen, Thomas P. 1981. 'Education: Policies and Prospects.' In Changsoo Lee and George A. De Vos, eds, *Koreans in Japan: Ethnic Conflict and Accommodation*. Berkeley: University of California Press, pp. 182–222.

Roth, Joshua H. 2002. *Brokered Homeland: Japanese Brazilian Migrants in Japan*. Ithaca: Cornell University Press.

Sasaki, Elisa Massae. 1999. 'Movimento *Dekassegui*: A Experiência Migratória e Identitária dos Brasileiros Descendentes de Japoneses no Japão' (The Movement of *Dekasegi*: Migration Experiences and Identity of Japanese Descent Brazilians in Japan). In Rossana Rocha Reis and Teresa Sales, eds, *Cenas do Brasil Migrante* (Scenes of Migrant Brazil). São Paulo, Brazil: Boitempo Editorial, pp. 243–74.

Sellek, Yoko. 1996. 'The U-Turn Phenomenon among South American-Japanese Descendants: From Emigrants to Migrants.' *Immigrants and Minorities* 15(3): 246–69.

—— 2001. *Migrant Labour in Japan*. New York: Palgrave.

Tajima, Hisatoshi. 1995. 'Laten Amerika Nikkeijin no Teijyuka' (The Settlement of Latin American Nikkeijin). In Hiroshi Komai, ed., *Teijyuka suru Gaikokujin* (Foreigners who Settle). Tokyo: Akaishi Shoten, pp. 165–98.

Tsuda, Takeyuki. 1999a. 'The Motivation to Migrate: The Ethnic and Sociocultural Constitution of the Japanese-Brazilian Return Migration System.' *Economic Development and Cultural Change* 48(1): 1–31.

—— 1999b. 'The Permanence of "Temporary" Migration: The "Structural Embeddedness" of Japanese-Brazilian Migrant Workers in Japan.' *Journal of Asian Studies* 58(3): 687–722.

—— 2003. *Strangers in the Ethnic Homeland: Japanese Brazilian Return Migration in Transnational Perspective*. New York: Columbia University Press.

Tsuda, Takeyuki and Wayne A. Cornelius. 2004. 'Japan: Government Policy, Immigrant Reality.' In Wayne A. Cornelius, Takeyuki Tsuda, Philip L. Martin, and James F. Hollifield, eds, *Controlling Immigration: A Global Perspective* (second edition). Stanford: Stanford University Press, pp. 439–76.

Watanabe, Masako. 1992. 'Burajiru kara no Nikkei Dekasegi Rodosha to "Nihon" tono Deai' (The Encounter between Japan and Japanese-Descent Migrant Workers from Brazil). *Shakaigaku Chosa Jittshu Hokokusho* (Sociological Survey Report) 8: 309–47.

—— 1995. 'Nikkei Burajirujin Jido/Seito no Zoka ni taisuru Kyoiku Genba deno Mosaku: Nikkei Burajirujin Shujyuchi no Hamamatsu-shi no Baai' (Attempts in Education to Respond to the Rapid Increase of Brazilian Nikkejin Children and Students: The Case of Hamamatsu City). *Shakaigaku/Shakai Fukushigaku Kenkyu* (Sociology and Social Welfare Review) 96: 43–66.

Watanabe, Masako, Masanori Ishikawa, Tomoko Anada, Harumi Yuge, Hiroyuki Watanabe, and Angelo Ishi. 1992. 'Nikkei Dekasegi no Kyuzo ni Tomonau Nihon Shakai no Taio to Mosaku' (The Rapid Increase in Japanese-Descent Migrant Workers and the Resulting Response and Uncertainty of Japanese Society). *Meiji Gakuin Daigaku Shakaigakubu Fuzoku Kenkyujo Nenpo* (Meiji Gakuin University Sociology Division Affiliated Research Institute Annual Report) 22: 55–85.

Watanabe, Susumu. 1994. 'The Lewisian Turning Point and International Migration: The Case of Japan.' *Asian and Pacific Migration Journal* 3(1): 119–47.

Weiner, Michael. 1994. *Race and Migration in Imperial Japan*. New York: Routledge.

Yamanaka, Keiko. 1996. 'Return Migration of Japanese-Brazilians to Japan: The *Nikkeijin* as Ethnic Minority and Political Construct.' *Diaspora* 5(1): 65–97.

—— 1997. 'Return Migration of Japanese Brazilian Women: Household Strategies and Search for the "Homeland."' In Diane Baxter and Ruth Krulfeld, eds, *Beyond Boundaries: Selected Papers on Refugees and Immigrants*, vol. V. Arlington, VA: American Anthropological Association.

—— 2000. '"I Will Go Home, But When?" Labor Migration and Circular Diaspora Formation by Japanese Brazilians in Japan.' In Mike Douglass and Glenda S. Roberts, eds, *Japan and Global Migration: Foreign Workers and the Advent of a Multicultural Society*. London: Routledge, pp. 123–52.

Yamanaka, Keiko and Takashi Miyajima. 1992. 'A Paradox of Skilled Workers "Only": Japan's New Immigration Policies Regarding Foreign Labor.' Paper presented at the 1992 Annual Meeting of the American Sociological Association, Pittsburgh, August 20–24, 1992.

Yamashita, Karen Tei. 2001. *Circle K Cycles*. Minneapolis, MN: Coffee House Press.

Index

CPSIA information can be obtained
at www.ICGtesting.com
Printed in the USA
FSOW03n1226200616
21723FS